Great Yarmouth to the River Roach

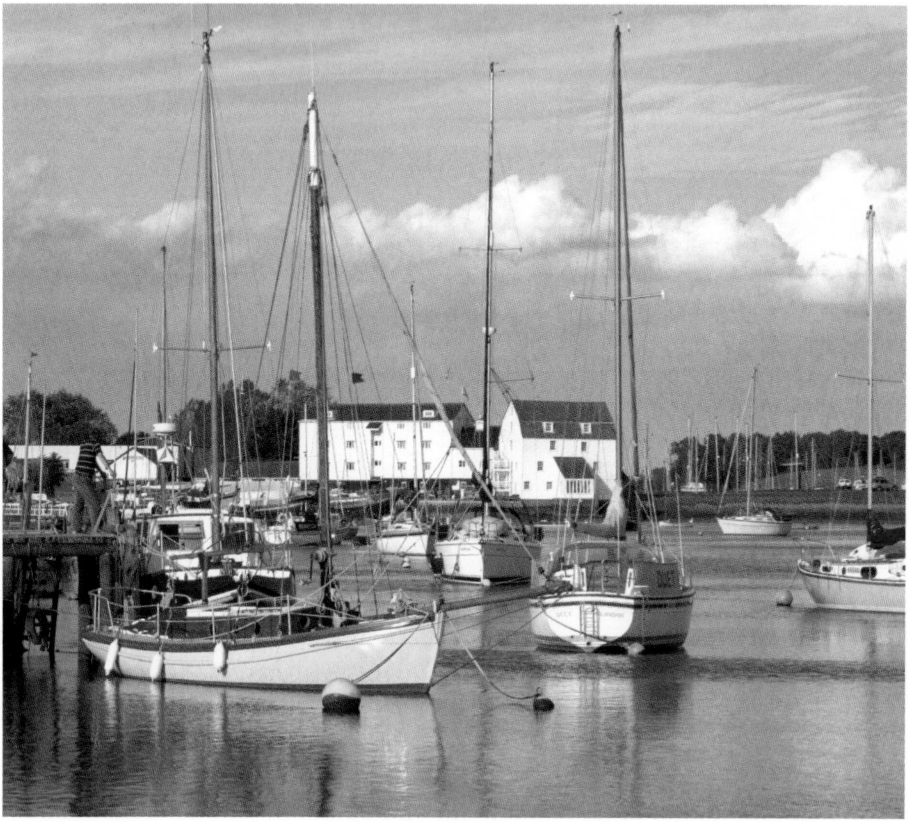

The Local Boating series of companion guide books to the East and South Coasts of England was first published in the mid-1980's and we are delighted to be able to revise this ever popular and invaluable publication.

This, the East Coast edition, covers an area form Great Yarmouth to the River Roach and has been thoroughly researched and completely rewritten, providing up-to-date information, details and contact information. Further editions are being researched to cover the West Country, the South East and the South Coast of England.

Special thanks to the UKHO for permission to reproduce chart extracts used in this edition, with assistance from Trinity House for chart information.

Cover picture: Woodbridge Tide Mill and quay ©Malcolm Farrow

Published in 2007 by Bubbles Publishing Limited
PO Box 111
Kingsnorth
Ashford
Kent TN23 9DX

Tel/Fax: 01233 501107
Email: info@localboating.co.uk
Website: www.localboating.co.uk

ISBN 978 0 9557013 0 6

Editor: Barry Hunter
Design: Carmel Parker
Photographs: Patrick Roach, Claudia Myatt, Chris Blaney, Kevin Rowe, Malcolm Farrow, Barry Hunter, John Hopley
Editorial Director: Dawn Hopley
Commercial Director: John Hopley
Printed & bound by Headley Brothers Limited, Ashford, Kent

Contents

CONTENTS

I have always loved the intricacies of exploring the creeks and rivers of the east coast and having sailed in many places around the UK and Europe, I keep being drawn back to the area. It has so many different faces, from river to river and port to port, that can change dramatically with a shift in the wind or the fall of the tide. You could sail here for a lifetime without seeing every facet of its nature. Where else in tidal waters can you moor up against the quay of a pub or the bank of a river flanked by pasture?

When I first started sailing here a good few years ago now, I found on many occasions that I arrived where I didn't intend to, at a time very different from that planned. Now as a proud holder of a Yachtmaster ticket and a qualified RYA instructor, I still arrive where I didn't intend to, at a time very different from that planned, but now for more sophisticated reasons. Clearly I can now hold myself up as an expert. However, since my first chance encounter with the little yellow Local Boating guide on a charter boat many years back, I have been somewhat cushioned from the inevitable crew criticism, by announcing: "not to worry – I know a good place". No longer the old fool who can't get you where he said on time, I had now become the sage of all that the east coast offers, who leads you into new places and wonderful experiences. As time went on, I discovered that the latest edition of the little book could also give me a good winter read, sat by the fire and a chance to escape into planning next year's cruise whilst rattling into work on an overcrowded commuter train.

Each year I bought updated and further editions, as the reach of these books spread to new areas of the south and south east where I cruised, and the updates allowed me to benefit from new information on familiar areas before I sailed there, rather than just as I was leaving. How often in other parts I have found out things about places, only when reading the pamphlets I have stuffed in my pockets during the visit. It is frustrating to learn that you've missed seeing something of great importance to you, or have made do with a pie and chips and can of grotty lager on a park bench, when two streets away there was a real ale pub with an open fire and a restaurant just to your taste next door.

New publishers have taken on the titles and as you will see, have sharpened up the style whilst maintaining the friendly ethos and feel. I am proud to have accepted the role of editor of these cherished volumes and also look forward to many summers of researching my home turf on the east and south east coasts, and many winters of getting beaten up over looming deadlines. This revised east coast edition is the first of many as we spread our reach around our coasts. Soon to follow will be south east and west country editions – all to be regularly revised and updated.

I hope you get great pleasure from this companion guide and that it will find a sacred place on the bookshelf at home and by the chart table afloat, as mine have always done. May it enhance your boating and fill your winter evenings planning the season to come.

Happy boating
Barry Hunter
EDITOR

Cautions

Pilotage
This publication is not intended to be used in any way as a pilot book. Any pilotage information provided is designed to be used only to support the text and to provide additional information to enhance the description of the rivers and harbours. Persons using this guide should ensure they use up-to-date pilotage information.

Waypoints
The waypoints provided are to support the text and provide an indication of position and should not be relied upon for accuracy. Readers should always ensure that they select their own position from an up-to-date navigational chart for entry into their GPS or other navigational system.

Harbour and River Chartlets
The charts in this guide are designed purely to support the text and are not to be used for navigation. Readers should ensure that up-to-date navigational charts are used at all times.

Charts, pilot books & maps

The following is by no means an exhaustive list, but we hope it will assist readers in purchasing relevant material prior to a visit to the area. Electronic charts are not covered here due to the number and variety.

Charts

ADMIRALTY CHARTS

Leisure Folio SC5607 – East Coast, covers from the Ore and Alde to the River Roach
Leisure Edition SC1536 – Approaches to Great Yarmouth and Lowestoft
Leisure Edition SC1543 – Winterton Ness to Orford Ness
www.admiraltyleisure.co.uk

IMRAY CHARTS

Chart Pack 2000 covers the area from the Ore and Alde to the River Roach
C28 The East Coast – Harwich to Wells-next-the-Sea
www.imray.com

Pilot Books

East Coast Rivers by Janet Harber, covering Lowestoft to the River Swale, published by Yachting Monthly
ISBN: 1904358241
East Coast Pilot by Colin Jarman, Dick Holness and Garth Cooper (2005), published by Imray, Laurie, Norie & Wilson, covering Lowestoft to Ramsgate
ISBN: 0852888341

Dutch visitors may also be interested to know that Anje Valk has produced a Dutch pilot of the area – **Vaarwijzer De Engelse oostkust**, published by Hollandia Boeken
ISBN: 9789064104312

Ordnance Survey Maps

LANDRANGER SERIES
(1:50,000/1¼":1 mile)

134 Great Yarmouth and Lowestoft
156 Southwold, Ore and Alde
169 Deben, Harwich, Orwell, Stour and Walton
168 Colne, Blackwater and Crouch
178 Roach

EXPLORER SERIES
(1:25,000/2½":1 mile)

OL40 Great Yarmouth and Lowestoft
231 Southwold
212 Ore and Alde
197 Deben, Harwich, Orwell and Stour
184 Walton, Colne, Blackwater (West Mersea)
176 Blackwater (West Mersea), Crouch and Roach

www.ordnancesurvey.co.uk

TYHA Gold Anchor Award Scheme ⚓⚓⚓⚓⚓

The Yacht Harbour Association (TYHA) is a group within the British Marine Federation (BMF) and an association of marina and mooring operators and their suppliers of goods and services, both here and abroad. Dedicated as it is to the improvement of yachting and boating facilities, it has successfully run its Gold Anchor Award Scheme for a number of years. This was established to improve the standards of facilities available to all boat owners at marinas. The scheme awards levels from one to five anchors, but any award is a sign of quality, with those achieving three, or more, being of the very highest standard. A five anchor award is a sought after mark of quality and proudly displayed.

The aim of the Local Boating guide, to improve the boating experience of our readers, is shared by the Chairman of TYHA Sam Bourne and the association's Secretary Sue Lambert and they have supported the production of this guide by supplying us with their latest list at the time of publication. This will allow our readers to refer to their anchor symbols as an assurance of the standards they will find on arrival.

For those looking for a berth or mooring they also run a useful online search facility at **www.berthsearch.com**

For further information contact:
The Yacht Harbour Association
Evegate Park Barn
Smeeth
Ashford
Kent
TN25 6SX
Tel: 01303 814434
Fax: 01303 814364
Website:
www.yachtharbourassociation.com
Email: slambert@britishmarine.co.uk

FREE SUPPLEMENTS

The contents of this guide were correct at the time of going to press. This guide will be amended and updated at regular intervals. Readers are asked to register at **www.localboating.co.uk** for email communication of critical amendments and to receive supplements including **FREE** tide tables. If you require a printed 2008 supplement, please send a stamped addressed A4 or A5 envelope to:

East Coast Supplement
Local Boating
Bubbles Publishing Ltd.
PO Box 111
Ashford
Kent TN23 9DX

Travel to/from the area

Air Travel: the main airport in the area is Stansted, Website: www.stanstedairport.com with services to many UK and international destinations. However, although Stansted is on a railway line, this does not directly link to the coast. You will either need to travel into London Liverpool Street and back out again to the coast, or travel to Cambridge, where there are connecting services to Ipswich.

There is also an airport at Norwich, Website: www.norwichairport.co.uk which has both UK and some useful international services plus buses into the town centre for rail connections to Great Yarmouth and Lowestoft, for onward connections down the coast.

Ferries: Stena Line operates the high speed ferry from Harwich to Hook of Holland, Tel: 08705 707070 Website: www.stenaline.com and DFDS Seaways operates a conventional car ferry from Harwich to Esbjerg, Tel: 0871 522 9955 Website: www.dfds.co.uk.

Coach Services: these connect to the area from throughout the UK, although for many destinations you will have to travel via one of the major hubs, some of which are in this area. International coach services generally connect via London. Both Norwich city centre and Stansted airport are served by National Express coach services. For information contact National Express, Tel: 08705 808080 Website: www.nationalexpress.com

Rail Travel: this area is reasonably well served by railways, although you will often need to change trains from local to major services. The train operator in the area is One Railways and for information contact 'One' Customer Services, Tel: 08456 007245 Website: www.onerailway.com or National Rail Enquiries, Tel: 08457 484950 Website: www.nationalrail.co.uk

Local Bus Services: there is an extensive bus network throughout the area operated by a variety of larger and smaller operators. For information contact Traveline East Anglia, Tel: 08706 082608 Website: www.traveline.org.uk

Road Travel: from the south, the southern area is only about 30 miles from the M25 London orbital motorway. The A12 trunk road services this coast from Great Yarmouth to London and almost everywhere in this book is within a short distance of this road. From elsewhere the A14 will now take you quickly to Ipswich and Felixstowe in the heart of the area, from the A1, M1 and M6.

HM Customs & Excise & Immigration

As skipper of your vessel you are responsible for compliance with the customs and immigration regulations and these two aspects will be dealt with separately here. I do not profess to be an expert in these matters and although I hope the following will help, you should ensure that you confirm this guidance for yourself, particularly as regulations change. To check the current position either call the National Advice Service, Tel: 08450 109000, or go to the HM Customs website www.hmce.gov.uk. I recommend that you should carry on board any registration documents, proof that VAT has been paid, passports and any relevant certification.

If you are an EU national, your crew are all EU nationals, your vessel is based in the EU and VAT has been paid, you are free to enter the UK without reporting, or restriction, subject to the following:

- You have come directly from an EU state;

- You are only carrying goods within the Travellers Allowance limits, plus any other goods to £145 in value and have no Prohibited or Restricted goods on board, or you are carrying some goods to be left behind;

- You have no Notifiable Illness on board;

- You have no birds or animals on board (the UK Pet Passport Scheme does not apply to private vessels).

If you need to report (or are in doubt) you may call HM Customs on the National Yachtline, Tel: 08457 231110 and they will advise you and clear you through customs over the phone if possible. If you are carrying birds or animals, you must report even if the animal is staying on board.

If you, or any of your crew need to clear immigration (any non-EU national), it is the skippers responsibility to ensure they do not leave the vessel without obtaining clearance from an immigration official.

Coastguard & Coastwatch

Yarmouth Coastguard, based in Great Yarmouth, covers the northern area of this book down to Southwold, and Thames Coastguard, based in Walton-on-the-Naze, the remainder going south. If calling them by VHF, it is recommended to use MMSI if from a DSC set, otherwise for urgent calls use Ch16, but for routine traffic calls (e.g. radio check), please try calling them first on their working channel Ch67.
www.mcga.gov.uk

Yarmouth Coastguard

Call sign "Yarmouth Coastguard"
MMSI 00230008
Tel: 01493 851338 (use 999 in emergency and ask for "Coastguard")

Thames Coastguard

Call sign "Thames Coastguard"
MMSI 00230009
Tel: 01255 675518 (use 999 in emergency and ask for "Coastguard")

The National Coastwatch Institution is a voluntary organisation aiming to maintain a visual coastal watch service with teams of volunteers, now that the Coastguard has moved largely into the electronic age. They have two stations in this area and there are plans for a further station at Jaywick, just to the north of the entrance to the Blackwater. Great Yarmouth maintains a visual watch (and monitors VHF Ch16) in summer 0800-2200 every day (to 1900 in winter), Tel: 01473 440384. Felixstowe maintains a visual watch 0900-1700 on weekends and bank holidays, Tel: 01394 670808.

Bateman's Tower, Brightlingsea

Weather section

There are many sources of weather information, a number of which are shown here.

Radio

The BBC broadcasts Met Office weather bulletins for shipping on BBC Radio 4 1515m (198kHz) long wave and 92-95 FM as follows (all local time):

0048 Radio 4 on long wave and FM, gale warnings, synopsis, shipping forecast, reports from coastal stations and inshore waters forecast (up to 12 miles from the shore)

0520 Radio 4 on long wave and FM, gale warnings, synopsis, shipping forecast and reports from coastal stations and inshore waters forecast (up to 12 miles from the shore)

1201 Radio 4 long wave only, gale warnings, synopsis and shipping forecast

1754 Radio 4 long wave only and FM at weekends, gale warnings, synopsis and shipping forecast.

Telephone

The Met Office provides Marinecall recorded forecasts at £0.60 per minute, as follows:
Offshore Forecast for Southern North Sea, Tel: 09014 737442
Coastal/Inshore Forecast for The Wash to North Foreland, Tel: 09014 737465.

Text

You can also have Met Office Marinecall forecasts sent to your mobile phone. SMS messages cost £0.25 each and provide current weather and a six hour forecast. To obtain this, send the message MC [coastal location] (e.g. MC SOUTHWOLD) to 83141 and you will receive a text back. If you can receive them, MMS messaging is also possible at £1.00 each which additionally provides the full shipping forecast and inshore waters forecast. To obtain this text MC MMS (coastal location) to 83141. Finally, you can connect via WAP phone at a cost of £0.75 to obtain the equivalent of

VHF Radio

The Coastguard repeats the Met Office weather bulletins for shipping as follows (all local time). They will announce the forecast on VHF Ch16 and you will then need to change to the channel of the aerial from which you get the best signal.

Full: Shipping forecast, gale warnings, inshore forecast, navigational warnings
Inshore: Latest inshore forecast, previous outlook and gale warnings
Repeat: Repetition of previous inshore forecast and gale warnings, plus any new strong winds warnings

YARMOUTH COASTGUARD

0150 Inshore
0450 Repeat
0750 Full
1050 Repeat
1350 Inshore
1650 Repeat
1950 Full
2250 Repeat

THAMES COASTGUARD

0110 Full
0410 Inshore
0710 Full
1010 Repeat
1310 Inshore
1610 Repeat
1910 Full
2210 Repeat

the MMS message by texting MC WAP (coastal location) to 83141.

Coastal Locations in the area (north to south) are:
Great Yarmouth
Lowestoft
Southwold
Orford Ness
Tide Mill Yacht Harbour – for the Deben
Landguard Point – for Harwich
Ipswich Marina, Fox's Marina, Woolverstone Marina or Suffolk Yacht Harbour – for the River Orwell
Titchmarsh Marina – for Walton-on-the-Naze
Brightlingsea, Bradwell Marina, or Tollesbury Marina – for the River Blackwater
Essex Marina – for the River Crouch

Internet
There are also many web weather resources, three of which are:
www.metoffice.gov.uk
www.weatheronline.co.uk
www.bbc.co.uk/weather

Ports of refuge

©PRPA

If coming by sea in your own vessel the only all-weather refuge port is Harwich, but you should not forget that with the offshore winds you will often get in season, many of the others become ports of refuge, however it is very important to think about the effects of wind over tide in these circumstances. If you had been heading for Harwich and you find yourself headed by strong winds, as long as the winds seem settled in direction, instead of turning tail and heading home, you may wish to consider settling for another port slightly off the wind. However, if you find yourself driven even further south by headwinds, you may have no alternative but to aim further afield to Ramsgate or The Medway and then make a short passage back to the area once the winds have died down.

Wind farms

It seems that the growth of wind farms in the area covered by this book is inevitable and to some extent we must accept the need to share the wind with energy production. As yet I am not sure whether I find these monsters of the deep, attractive or an eyesore, but like it or not they are clearly here to stay. No doubt people objected to the grain milling windmills and watermills in days gone by and now we strive to protect and renovate them, so perhaps we'll learn to accept and even grow fond of them, as we also have the old forts in the Thames estuary.

There is a constant battle, largely fought on our behalf by the Royal Yachting Association and the Cruising Association, to protect our rights of navigation and safety. To date, it seems that sense has prevailed and schemes have been amended to avoid small craft routes and as yet navigation exclusion zones have not been granted except during construction, although it would be foolhardy to plan to navigate through the developments if you don't have to, despite a minimum rotor height in any farm of 20 metres above MHWS. So far the only developments in the Thames estuary area have been the Kentish Flats Array off the north Kent coast and Scroby Sands off Great Yarmouth, but the Gunfleet Sands development off Clacton was due to start construction in 2007.

There are also plans to soon extend the Gunfleet development with the Deltiac wind farm and to build new farms off North Foreland (Warwick Energy) and smack bang in the middle of the Thames estuary (London Array). It is this last wind farm that causes most concern due to its sheer scale and the possible threats to a number of small craft cross estuary routes. Despite its planned size (271 turbines) it will surprisingly still only produce 1% of the UK's electricity requirements, but I suppose every little helps.

Had a SEA check?

If you're a boat owner, why not take advantage of the RNLI's free Safety Equipment Advisory (SEA) Check? SEA Check is a completely free, friendly and confidential service that looks at safety aspects involved with your boat, whether you're a sailor or motorboater. It's neither a test nor an inspection and there is no pass or fail. Conducted by one of our highly trained volunteers, SEA Check is a personal face-to-face safety advice service that takes place on board your own craft. You set the time and we tailor our visit to your vessel, the type of boating that you do and your experience.

Like the RNLI's crews, the SEA Checkers are volunteers that give up their time to help prevent tragedy at sea. Some are active or retired lifeboat crew themselves, but most are simply experienced boat users who are willing to share their knowledge. All have taken RNLI sea safety training.

SEA Checks help prevent incidents from happening at sea in the first place, so let us step aboard your boat – before you need to step aboard one of ours. To request a SEA Check, Tel: 0800 328 0600 or visit **www.rnli.org.uk/seasafety**

Comments from people that have received the check have included:

'Their knowledge and experience was excellent.'

'Well worthwhile. Highlighted a couple of items we hadn't thought of.'

'A useful opportunity to review and discuss my safety equipment and procedures. Some fire training will result. Thank you.'

'The SEA Check was carried out in a thoroughly competent and professional manner. I would recommend it to all sections of the boating fraternity.'

'I am recommending your service to my sailing friends without hesitation or reservation. I will purchase extra equipment after the SEA Check.'

'This must make a significant contribution to reducing calls for sea assistance. Thanking you for your help and your time.'

The RNLI Today

The Royal National Lifeboat Institution is a charity that rescues thousands of people at sea each year. To do this it continues to rely on the voluntary spirit of its crew members and voluntary contributions from the public which pay for lifeboats, equipment and training.

For more information on how to support the charity, Tel: 0845 122 6999 or visit **www.rnli.org.uk**

GREAT YARMOUTH

Yarmouth Haven ©PRPA

⊕ **52°34.3N 01°44.7E** *(Entrance)*
Tides Haven Bridge -02:50
(difference from Harwich)

Built on a sand spit, Great Yarmouth's former prosperity was based around the port and the herring fishing industry, although little of the old town survives today. The town's prosperity now rests with a combination of carnival-style tourism and the active commercial port servicing the offshore gas industry, resulting in a mixed and somewhat unappealing vista from the harbour. Despite the best efforts of the Port Authority, due to the competing commercial interest, facilities for the yachtsman are poor. Therefore, disappointingly, Great Yarmouth can currently be viewed as little more than a stopping off point whilst waiting to transit through the bridges into Breydon Water or sail on elsewhere.

But all is not negative, as things are changing. There are plans for a new Ro-Ro port (called East Port) to be built to the north of the current harbour entrance and due to open in 2008 and although this is unlikely to reduce commercial port traffic in the main port, it will provide transport connections to Ijmuiden. Current proposals are that this would be operated by the Greek owned Superfast Ferries, taking just five hours for the crossing. An urban regeneration company has also been formed and there are already signs of improvement in the wharf-side area with plans for a new arts centre. Most interesting of all for the yachtsman are the plans for leisure boating, which include a new marina that I understand may be carved out of the dockside between the bridges and alongside Bure Marine. There is also a study currently being undertaken which will report in April 2007, which should include proposals for facilities for visiting yachtsmen. It is hoped that this will not cost us the convenience of the current length of wharf at Town Hall Quay reserved for small craft and visiting pleasure craft and that both facilities and surroundings will also improve as the regeneration scheme progresses. It would be nice to think that instead of swiftly moving on, visitors in future will be minded to dally a while and see what the town has to offer, particularly as the developments may well widen the town's appeal to a broader audience than before.

APPROACH AND ENTRANCE

As with many east coast ports it is essential to obtain up-to-date charts and pilotage information due to the shifting nature of the sands. In fact, in the 14th century things got so bad that all navigable entrances to Great Yarmouth silted up and they had to dig themselves out again with a new channel. However, as this is now a heavily used commercial port, depths in the entrance and harbour should not unduly concern the average yachtsman.

Although technically entrance can be made at any time with sufficient power, it is preferable to enter or leave on high, or low, slack water, which also avoids the worst of the strong cross tides that can run off the entrance at up to 3 or 4 knots at springs. The entrance itself is difficult to identify, although the wind farm development a mile and a half offshore to the north of harbour on the Scroby Sands provides a general clue, but once close in towards the entrance, the old white and red brick Brush lighthouse at the landward end of the south pier will become evident. Entrance against the ebb, which can run at up to 6 knots, is not recommended and particularly so in strong onshore winds, when heavy seas and broken water can be found in the entrance. Entry at any state of tide in onshore winds in excess of Force 5 would be unwise and small craft should be even more cautious still.

By night the Brush light is Fl R 3s, with occulting white leading lights (rear 6s, front 3s) on a bearing of 264°T on the

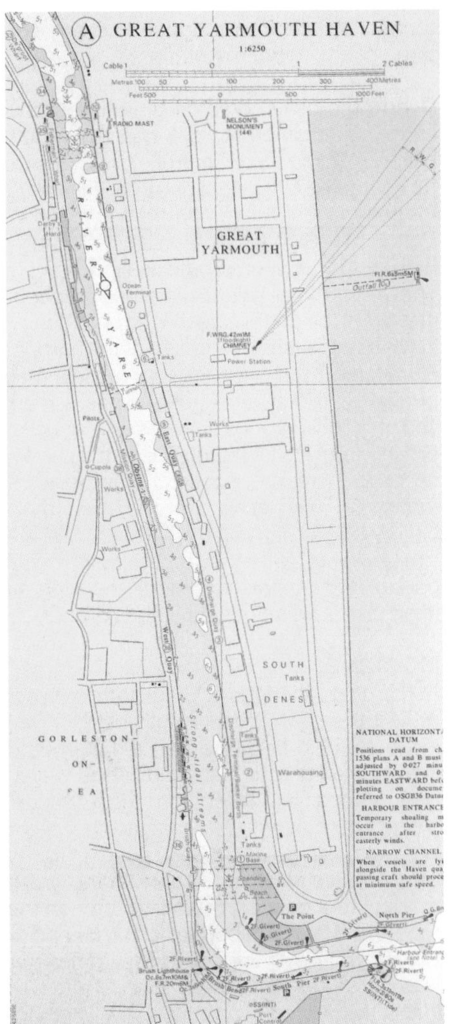

Not to be used for navigation

south pier. The north pier carries a quick flashing Green light (Q G 8m 6M) at the extreme outer end, with five sets of two vertical fixed greens along the inner flank of the wall and the south pier carries two vertical fixed reds at the outer end with further pairs up to and around Brush Bend. Don't be confused if you see an amber flashing light on the south pier, this purely indicates the tide is flooding. In fog there is an electronic signal device giving three blasts every minute.

Due to the busy commercial nature of this narrow and strongly tidal port, Yarmouth Harbour Radio/Port Control should always be contacted (and monitored) on VHF Ch12 for entry or departure and the International Port Traffic Signals on the seaward end of the South Pier should be closely observed. These are three reds for "do not proceed" (flashing if the port is closed in an emergency) in which case, keep well clear of the harbour entrance, or three greens for "vessels may proceed". If you see green, white, green, you may "only proceed on receipt of specific orders" from Port Control. Due to the narrow harbour there are no lights for two-way traffic or navigating outside the main channel. When leaving the harbour there are similar lights facing into the river which control movements south of the lifeboat shed on the western side of the harbour.

MOORINGS

At this time moorings at Great Yarmouth are limited to a 50 metres length of dock set aside at Town Hall Quay on the starboard side of the harbour just short of the Haven Bridge about two miles from the entrance, where you may well be charged, but there are currently no facilities. The only other moorings are at Burgh Castle Marina, which is about four or five miles away, through the Haven and Breydon bridges at the far end of Breydon Water. If traversing Breydon water keep strictly to the marked channel and well inside the posts.

CREW CHANGES AND TRAVEL

There are regular train services from Great Yarmouth to Norwich (30 minutes) for onward train (London Liverpool Street two hours) and coach travel. For train information contact 'One' Customer Services, Tel: 08456 007245 Website: www.onerailway.com, or National Rail Enquiries, Tel: 08457 484950 Website: www.nationalrail.co.uk. There are also scheduled coach services direct from Great Yarmouth to London operated by National Express, Tel: 08705 808080, Website: www.nationalexpress.com. For local bus travel information contact Traveline East Anglia, Tel: 08706 082608 Website: www.traveline.org.uk

EATING AND DRINKING

There are an abundance of eating and drinking establishments to suit all tastes in Great Yarmouth, so I shall purely provide a few suggestions, although even a short walk will provide many more options.

The Star Hotel on the quay has been mentioned to me for its good restaurant, open for breakfast 0700-0900, lunch 1200-1400 and dinner 1900-2100, Tel: 01493 842294. For something special you could try the rather more expensive Rambouillet Restaurant at the Imperial Hotel on North Drive, the other side of the town centre, Tel 01493 842000.

GREAT YARMOUTH SKIPPERS INFORMATION	
Harbour Radio/Port Control	Call on VHF Ch12 Call-sign "Yarmouth Radio"
Harbour Master	Pat McNamara, or his team, whose office is at 20/21 South Quay (by Town Hall Quay). Tel: 01493 335500 during office hours (01493 335511 out of hours – 24 hours), or Email: info@gypa.co.uk
Water	None
Fuel	None
Facilities	None
Boatyard	Bure Marine Ltd. (between the bridges). Tel: 01493 656996 Email: enquiry@buremarine.co.uk
Chandlery	None
Slip	The largest in Norfolk at up to 150 tons and 90 feet at Bure Marine

There is a Wetherspoons pub, the Troll Cart in Regent Street, just back from the quay, offering the usual good value food and refreshment and late opening, Tel: 01493 332932 and if you follow the quay upstream past the bridge, you will find the St. John's Head pub on North Quay, Tel: 01493 843443.

TO SEE AND DO

The Time and Tide museum of Great Yarmouth life is in Blackfriars Road 10 minutes walk from Town Hall Quay and is open every day during the season from 1000–1700, Tel: 01493 743930. The English Heritage properties of Row 111 and The Old Merchants House are closer still in the Historic Quay area and are examples of the 17th century row houses unique to the town, whose exteriors reflect their Dutch links. They are open March to September from 1200–1700. Also close to these is the Nelson Museum open from April to the end of October, Mon–Fri, 1000–1700 (last admission 1630) and Sat–Sun, 1300–1600 (last admission 1530).

For those younger of heart there are the miles of beach and two piers, with the Pleasure Beach funfair on the seafront (South Beach) open March to October. Opening times vary, so ring 01493 844585 for confirmation. For wet days, there is the Sea Life Centre on Marine parade which is open all year round from 1000–1700, Tel: 01493 330631 and the Marina Leisure Centre with pool on Marine Parade open day and evening, all year round, Tel: 01493 851521. There is also a tenpin bowling alley, Regent Bowl, in Regent Road five minutes walk from the quay, open all year round and every day, 1000–2400, Tel: 01493 856830.

GREAT YARMOUTH SHORESIDE INFORMATION	
Stores	Nearby in town plus Market Gates shopping centre in the centre of town
Bank	All major banks either nearby on Hall Quay or near Market Gates shopping centre
PO	In Market Place in the centre of town
Public Tel.	In town centre
Club	None
Taxis	Swift Taxis, Tel: 01493 300300; Albies Taxis, Tel: 01493 331111
Accommodation	A wide selection of accommodation is available in the town, contact Tourist Information
Tourist Info.	25 Marine Parade. Tel: 01493 846345
Police	Howard Street North. Tel: 0845 4564567
Doctor	Eastaugh, Castle, Stammers & Harland, Wenhaston, Halesworth. Tel: 01502 740203
Hospital	(A&E) James Paget Hospital, Lowestoft Road. Tel: 01493 452452
Dentist	John G. Plummer & Assocs., Greyfriars Chambers. Tel: 01493 842559
Pharmacy	A number in town centre
USEFUL NUMBERS	
Marine Engineers	STM Engineering Limited. Tel: 01493 440110 East Coast Diesel Limited. Tel: 01493 332332
Upholsterers	Haven Upholstery. Tel: 01493 843974

GREAT YARMOUTH

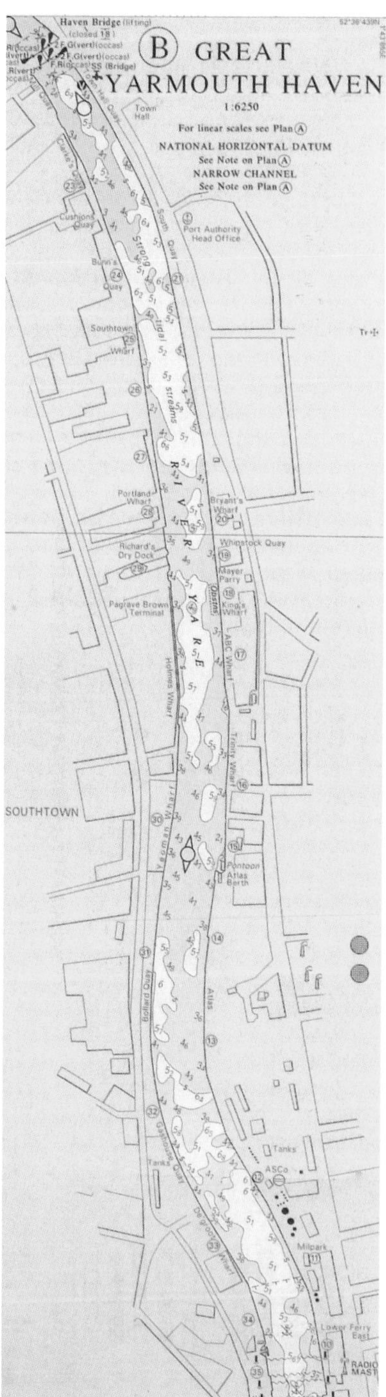

THE HAVEN AND BREYDON BRIDGES

During normal working hours and outside the morning and evening rush hours, the bridges should generally open when required, although pre-booking at weekends is necessary. The Harbour Master's team now man the bridges amongst their other duties, so some patience may be required. Contact the Harbour Office, Tel: 01493 335500, for opening times and bookings. Breydon Bridge can also be contacted VHF Ch12, but is only manned about 15 minutes before lifting. Beware of strong tides near Haven Bridge and adhere to the signal lights on the bridges, details of which can be obtained from the Harbour Office. For those without masts, it may be possible to pass the Breydon Bridge without waiting for an opening as the northern span has a clearance of approaching 4 metres at MHW; check tide times and clearances with the Harbour Office.

BURGH CASTLE

Although this guide does not provide detailed information for The Broads (as an inland waterway), in view of the current limited facilities at Great Yarmouth and the close proximity of Burgh Castle, many coastal travellers use the facilities there and it is therefore treated as a secondary port to Great Yarmouth. A short visit toll or passage toll will have to be paid to traverse Breydon Water and the Great Yarmouth Harbour Master or Burgh Castle Marina, will be able to advise on this.

Burgh Castle Marina is situated in a pleasant rural location and offers 100 fully serviced pontoon berths for up to 1.5 metres draught (or more on the river quay berths), with plans for 40 more in the pipeline with full use of the adjacent leisure park facilities. Tel: 01493 780331 Email: info@burghcastlemarina.co.uk

CREW CHANGES AND TRAVEL

There are regular buses every day (less on Sundays) to Great Yarmouth for onward connections. For local bus travel information

Not to be used for navigation

BURGH CASTLE SKIPPERS INFORMATION	
Harbour Master	Tel: 01493 780331 Email: info@burghcastlemarina.co.uk
Water	On berths
Electricity	On berths
Fuel	Fuel berth
Facilities	WC, showers, launderette (and holding tank pump out)
Boatyard	Goodchild Marine Services. Tel: 01493 782301
Chandlery	On-site at boatyard
Slips	50 ton travel hoist at boatyard
Website	www.burghcastlemarina.co.uk

contact Traveline East Anglia, Tel: 08706 082608 Website: www.traveline.org.uk

EATING AND DRINKING

By the marina there is The Fishermans bar and restaurant, which recently came under new management, therefore services and hours may change, but a range of food has always been available, Tel: 01493 780729. There is also a barbecue area at the marina.

In Burgh Castle, a few minutes walk away, there is the Church Farm Hotel near the church in Church Road back towards Breydon Water, which offers a bar and restaurant open all day, every day to 2300, Tel: 01493 780251. In the High Street, the Queens Head serves real ales and food in its extensive restaurant and is again open all day, every day, to 2300 (2230 Sundays), Tel: 01493 780363.

TO SEE AND DO

There is a Roman fort originally called Gariannonum at Burgh Castle close by the marina, where extensive ruins remain and there are plans for a visitor centre. This was one of the Roman Saxon Shore Forts designed to protect the area from raids from across the water and would have been at the landward end of a large shallow estuary at that time. Open every day for visits.

BURGH CASTLE SHORESIDE INFORMATION	
Stores	Good stores in Belton including a Tesco Express about one mile away open 0700-1000, seven days a week
Banks	Nearest banks in Gorleston
PO	In Tesco Express
Public Tel.	In The Fishermans bar
Club	None
Taxis	Gorleston Travel Cars, Tel: 01493 665022; Yaxley Taxis, Tel: 01493 444810
Accommodation	The Queens Head and the Church Farm Hotel in Burgh Castle have accommodation (see Eating and Drinking), plus the holiday park at the marina may be able to assist
Tourist Info.	nearest Gt. Yarmouth
Police	Howard Street North, Gt. Yarmouth. Tel: 0845 4564567
Doctor	Dr. Dooldeniya & Ptnrs., St. John's Road, Belton. Tel: 01493 780111
Hospital	(A&E) James Paget Hospital, Lowestoft Road, Gt. Yarmouth. Tel: 01493 452452
Dentist	John G. Plummer & Assocs., Bradwell Medical Centre. Tel: 01493 662717
Pharmacy	Lloyds Pharmacy, St. John's Road, Belton. Tel: 01493 781745

Yarmouth Town Hall Quay ©Kevin Rowe

There are a number of good walks in the area, most of which at least in part, feature the Angles Way. The marina keeps a selection of route plans in reception for visitors' use. One pleasant example of about three miles is to follow the Angles Way past The Fishermans to the Roman fort. After passing through the fort you follow the sea wall path past the church and out onto the southern shore of Breydon Water, taking a lane back into Burgh Castle and from there by lanes back to the marina.

THE BROADS

There are two points of access to the Norfolk Broads; Great Yarmouth and Lowestoft via Mutford Lock into Oulton Broad. The main cruising ground for sea-going craft is the area south of Great Yarmouth and Breydon Water due to fixed bridge heights on the northern rivers. Power craft and sailing yachts with less than 9.3 metres/35 feet air draft can cruise right up to Norwich on the River Yare. Yachts entering the Broads at Oulton Broad, Lowestoft, should be aware they are confined by fixed bridges (clearance of 7.3 metres/24 feet) to the River Waveney. You will need temporary licences to navigate the broads.

For more information about the Norfolk Broads, contact the Broads Authority, 18 Colegate, Norwich NR3 1BQ, Tel: 01603 610734
Email: broads@broads-authority.gov.uk Website: www: broads-authority.gov.uk

RN&SYC Marina

LOWESTOFT

52°28.3N 01°45.9E
(half mile off entrance)
Tides -02:15 *(differences from Harwich)*

Lowestoft feels a little like two towns, with a thriving town centre across the road bridge to the north of the harbour and the seaside town to the south. The two are separated by the harbour area, which until recently, was a most unappealing place. But now Lowestoft has got its act together and is a little ahead of its neighbour Great Yarmouth in the regeneration scheme for the inner harbour and dockside area. Although there is still much to be done, the area has already been transformed and the separation of the two ends of town is diminishing. Of interest to our readers is the clear intention to improve yachting facilities, much of which has already been completed.

Lowestoft, on Britain's most easterly point, still has a commercial harbour for fishing, rig support and various other craft as well as facilities for the leisure boating community. The town owes its existence to the fishing industry, having started with the landing of huge quantities of herring that not only provided an income for the local fishermen, but also attracted many others to move into the town. Battles ensued during the 14th century with neighbouring Yarmouth, which tried to stake a claim to all the herring fishing rights. However, Lowestoft harbour thrived with smoking and shipping consignments of fish to other parts of the country, followed by the development of its own North Sea and Icelandic cod fishing fleet. It was only during the 19th century that Lowestoft really developed as a port, partly due to the digging of Oulton Dyke and the New Cut to gain access to Norwich. Shipbuilding began here in earnest around this time and the harbour as we know it was built in 1831. The subsequent arrival of the railway helped speed the distribution of cargoes throughout the country and also brought in holiday-makers.

Today's harbour consists of several docks with different functions. To the north of the entrance Hamilton Dock is used mostly by the inshore fleet, with Waveney Dock housing the fish market. The near waters trawlers occupy the Trawl Dock north of the channel, whilst the yacht basin and yacht club are to the south of this. Hamilton Yard on the outer north pier builds gas platform modules and related structures. On completion, the structures are off-loaded onto barges. A lifting bridge carries the A12 across the channel that leads to the inner harbour and Lake Lothing, where there are quays along both shores for commercial craft and further extensive yachting facilities.

APPROACH AND ENTRANCE

As with all east coast harbours, it is essential to have up-to-date charts and pilotage information, as the banks around here are prone to shifting. If in doubt, contact Lowestoft Harbour Control, which will provide on request the latest waypoints for the local marks. Other than the sand banks there are no other hazards except the number of commercial vessels using the harbour, but it is worth remembering that across the entrance piers, the cross tide runs at a substantial rate. In strong winds from the east or northeast, a heavy and potentially dangerous sea can build up in the entrance and particularly so on the ebb when you should be wary of anything above Force 4.

The harbour entrance is recognised by its two lighthouses. From the south the recommended Stanford Channel is marked on up-to-date charts. From the north or east, you need to avoid the Holm Sand and in the case of the latter, you may be best served to skirt to the south and again use the Stanford Channel. Lowestoft Harbour Control operates 24 hours a day and must be contacted before entry or departure. International Port Traffic Signals are shown on the South Pier close to the harbour entrance and must be observed. The entrance to the yacht harbour is blind, so proceed with caution. The speed limit in the whole of the harbour is 4 knots.

Before leaving your berth contact Lowestoft Harbour Control and you should also observe the signals when coming out of the harbour.

MOORINGS

There are four places where you can find moorings in Lowestoft. The best known and most convenient is the marina in front of the Royal Norfolk and Suffolk Yacht Club in the yacht basin to the south of the main channel. Over the last few years a number of improvements have been made, including new pontoons allowing for over 50 visitors berths and the installation of controlling lights (International Port Traffic Signals) for the entrance to the basin, making this now a safe, comfortable yacht harbour. Added to the hospitality offered at the Royal Norfolk and Suffolk Yacht Club (berthing fees include temporary membership to the club), it is a very convenient place for a stopover, both in terms of access and proximity to town. It is advisable to pre-book your berth in peak season as the yacht harbour can get very full. Please note you need to ask permission of Port Control to leave the yacht basin.

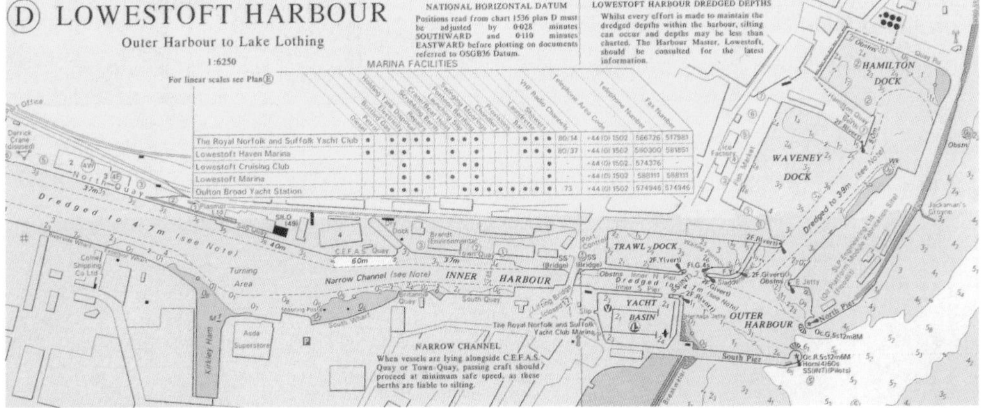

	Diesel	Petrol	Bottled Gas	Electricity	Holding Tank Disposal	Repairs	Scrubbing Berth	Crane/Boat Hoist	Launching Slip	Pontoon Berthing	Swinging Moorings	Chandlery	Provisions	Bar	Laundrette	Showers	VHF Radio Channels	Telephone Area Code	Telephone Number	Fax Number
The Royal Norfolk and Suffolk Yacht Club	•		•	•	•	•		•	•	•				•	•	•	80/14	+44 (0) 1502	566726	517981
Lowestoft Haven Marina	•		•	•		•		•		•				•	•	•	80/37	+44 (0) 1502	580300	581851
Lowestoft Cruising Club				•					•	•						•	-	+44 (0) 1502	574376	-
Lowestoft Marina				•		•		•		•						•	-	+44 (0) 1502	588111	588111
Oulton Broad Yacht Station			•	•	•				•	•	•	•	•	•	•	•	73	+44 (0) 1502	574946	574946

Not to be used for navigation

The other moorings are the other side of the lifting bridge a mile and a half up Lake Lothing past the commercial quays. To starboard is the Lowestoft Cruising Club where you will find vacant moorings marked by a green triangle. In the phone box you will find an information pack and details of how to pay your fees. To port, opposite Lowestoft Cruising Club, is the new ABP owned Lowestoft Haven Marina and further on still, in the south-western corner, the small Lowestoft Marina.

HARBOUR ROAD BRIDGE

The road bridge connecting the inner and outer harbours is not only the main connection between the two ends of Lowestoft, but also carries the A12, so necessarily openings are restricted, but not unreasonably. The bridge does not open during the morning and evening peak travel periods and for a short period at lunchtime. Otherwise the bridge will open at set times 10, or more, times a day (including some at night), details of which can be obtained from Port control. You will need to book transit prior with Port Control.

In addition, the bridge may open for commercial traffic, but you may not slip through with this traffic unless you have agreed this with Port Control prior. Whilst waiting for a bridge opening you can wait on the waiting pontoon to starboard in the Trawl Dock, opposite the yacht basin. Small boats may also pass under the bridge (2.2 metres at MHWS, 4.2 metres at MLWS), but should still ask permission of Port Control.

ROYAL NORFOLK & SUFFOLK YACHT CLUB MARINA SKIPPERS INFORMATION	
Port Control	Lowestoft Port Control (AB Ports) VHF Ch14/80 (and listening Ch16) call-sign "Lowestoft Port", Tel: 01502 572286
Harbour Master	Alfie Plitsch or Tim Gower, VHF Ch80 call-sign "Royal Norfolk Marina", Tel: 01502 566726 Email: marina@rnsyc.org.uk (manned 0730-1930 in season, enquire in yacht club outside these hours)
Water	On pontoons
Electricity	On pontoons
Fuel	Fuel berth
Facilities	WC, showers, launderette (and waste pump out at fuel berth)
Boatyard	The marina can assist with arranging a full range of services
Chandlery	None
Slips	Slip for trailers, plus 2.5 ton crane
Website	www.rnsyc.org.uk

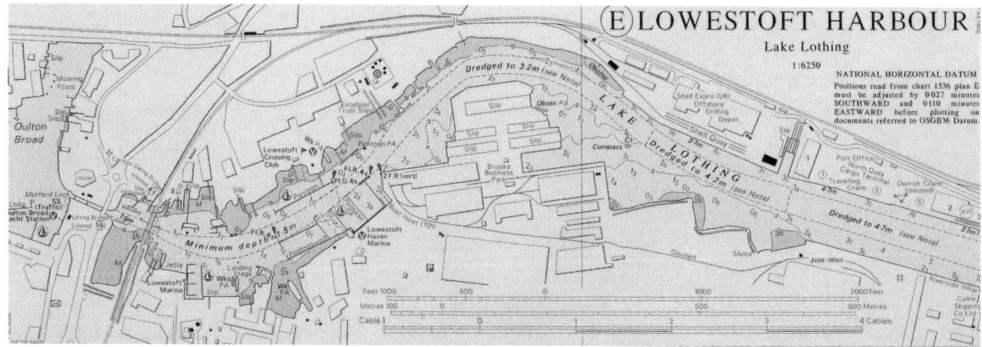

Not to be used for navigation

RN&SYC SHORESIDE INFORMATION

Stores	Nearest, ALDI supermarket just across bridge open every day, 0800-2000 (Sun 1000-1600) and ASDA supermarket five minutes walk along southern shore of inner harbour open every day, 0700-2200 (Sun 1000-1600). A good range of other stores in town centre.
Banks	All major banks in town centre (five minutes walk)
PO	In High Street (five minutes walk)
Public Tel.	In club and just across road bridge
Club	Royal Norfolk & Suffolk Yacht Club. Tel: 01502 566726 Email: admin@rnsyc.org.uk Website: www.rnsyc.org.uk
Taxis	Bluebird Taxis, Tel: 01502 565656; 51 Taxis, Tel: 01502 515151
Accommodation	Reasonably priced rooms available at RN&SYC and a range of accommodation in town (enquire at Tourist Information)
Tourist Info.	East Point Pavilion (next to yacht basin). Tel: 01502 533600
Police	Old Nelson Street. Tel: 01473 613500
Doctor	Cox & Ptnrs., 1 Marine Parade. Tel: 01502 574072
Hospital	(A&E) James Paget Hospital, Lowestoft Road, Great Yarmouth. Tel: 01493 452452
Dentist	Mr. Williams, 7 Regent Road. Tel: 01502 572467
Pharmacy	Three in London Road South (one road back from the front on the south side of bridge)

USEFUL NUMBERS

Boatbuilders & Repairers	Brooke Marine Yachts. Tel: 01502 561479
Boatyard (Oulton Broad)	Pegasus Yachts. Tel: 01502 585631
Marine Electricians	North Sea Marine Electrical. Tel: 01502 562010
Marine Electronics	Charity & Taylor, Tel: 01502 581529; KM Electronics, Tel: 01502 569079
Marine Engineers	Lothing Marine, Tel: 01502 501017; Small and Co., Tel: 01502 585709; JPC, Tel: 01502 500712
Marine Safety Equipment	The Marine Safety Centre. Tel: 01502 500940
Riggers	Lowestoft Yacht Services. Tel: 01502 585535
Safety & Rescue Boats	Seacor Marine. Tel: 01502 573366
Solar Technology	Solar Energy Alliance. Tel: 01502 515532
Surveyors	Anglia Marine Surveys. Tel: 01502 574704
Yacht Brokers & Sales	Fox's Yacht Sales (Lowestoft Haven Marina). Tel: 01473 695010

CREW CHANGES AND TRAVEL

Although it may involve fairly lengthy journeys, Lowestoft does provide access to all the major transport routes and is directly on the main A12 road link. Lowestoft Railway Station is north east of the outer harbour, just over the lifting bridge from the RN&SYC and has frequent daily connections to Norwich, for the airport and onward rail travel to the Midlands and North and to Ipswich, for connections to Harwich for ferries and to London Liverpool Street. From the other end of Lake Lothing, the two lines have stations at both North Oulton Broad and South Oulton Broad. For information contact 'One' Customer Services, Tel: 08456 007245 Website: www.onerailway.com, or National Rail Enquiries, Tel: 08457 484950 Website: www.nationalrail.co.uk. Scheduled coach services are operated from Lowestoft direct to London Victoria by National Express, Tel: 08705 808080 Website: www.nationalexpress.com. For local bus information contact Traveline East Anglia, Tel: 08706 082608 Website: www.traveline.org.uk

EATING AND DRINKING

The RN&SYC's Grade II listed club-house which was built in 1903, has a restaurant, bars and sun lounge, as well as meeting and conference facilities. The bar is open 1200-1430 and 1800-2300 (all day Saturdays and all day Sundays to 2230) and serves bar meals, 1200-1400 and 1830-2130. The restaurant is open every day 1230-1330 (1400 at weekends) and 1900-2100. Breakfast is available 0745-0900 daily, but does need to be booked a day in advance and all these times are reduced out of season. Tel: 01502 566726.

Lowestoft's large shopping centre is just over the lifting bridge where there are some cafés, restaurants and fast food establishments. Alternatively, along the Esplanade, some of the hotels and guesthouses have restaurants open to non-residents. If you wish to cater on board there are some fresh fish stalls over the bridge on the seafront.

LOWESTOFT CRUISING CLUB MARINA SKIPPERS INFORMATION

Harbour Master	(Moorings Officer) John Cooper, Tel: 07913 391950 Email: mooringsofficer@lowestoftcruisingclub.co.uk
Water	On pontoons
Electricity	On pontoons
Facilities	WC and showers
Slips	Up to 10 tons
Website	www.lowestoftcruisingclub.co.uk

If visiting Lowestoft Haven Marina, the on-site restaurant and bar has recently changed hands and is now operated by June Mummery who has local fishing industry interests. It will be re-opening in April 2007 as Go-Fish, still a restaurant and bar, but specialising in (surprise, surprise!) fish and seafood. It will be open daily in season from 0900 onwards.

TO SEE AND DO

There is plenty to see and do for most tastes in and around Lowestoft. It is renowned for the quality of its beaches, especially the award-winning sandy South Beach and there is easy access to the town and shops and all the fun of a seaside town. The attractions are too numerous to cover properly here, but I shall name a few suggestions.

The Lowestoft Maritime Museum is to the north of the town at Sparrow's Nest Park near the Lighthouse and is open May to October, 1000-1700 daily, admission £0.75, children £0.25, Tel: 01502 561963. The Lifeboat Station, at the inner end of the South Pier is open 1100-1630 daily for visitors, Tel: 01502 531507. The Pleasurewood Hills Family Theme Park is to the north of the town centre and a family day ticket costs around £50. For opening days and times, Tel: 01502 586000. The Hollywood Cinema is a couple of minutes walk from the RN&SYC in London Road South, one road back from the front, Tel: 01502 564567 and the Marina Theatre across the bridge

LCC SHORESIDE INFORMATION

Public Tel.	On gate pontoon
Club	Lowestoft Cruising Club, Tel: 01502 574376 Website: www.lowestoftcruisingclub.co.uk

For other Shoreside and Emergency Information see Royal Norfolk & Suffolk Yacht Club Marina

LOWESTOFT HAVEN MARINA SKIPPERS INFORMATION ⚓⚓⚓⚓⚓	
Harbour Master	VHF Ch80 call-sign "Lowestoft Haven Marina", Tel: 01502 580300 Email: lowestofthaven @abports.co.uk
Water	On pontoons
Electricity	On pontoons
Fuel	Fuel berth
Facilities	WC, showers and launderette
Internet	Planned for 2007
Boatyard	A range of services available at marina and on-site workshop
Slips	Travelhoist
Water Taxi	New ferry service planned for 2007 connecting the marina with Mutford Lock, the ASDA supermarket and the town centre (enquire at marina or restaurant)

offers an unusually wide variety of entertainment including performances by the Royal Philharmonic Orchestra, Tel: 01502 533200.

For the walker there are interesting linear walks from Oulton Broad on the Angles Way, both to the north and south of Oulton Broad itself and along the River Waveney, using the railways for the return journey.

MUTFORD LOCK

Access to Oulton Broad and the River Waveney is via Mutford Lock and the Mutford Road and Carlton Railway Bridges. These can open to allow transit in season, 0800-1800 (out of season 0800-1100) at a cost of £8 per vessel each way. For enquiries and booking (sometimes requiring up to 24 hours) contact the lock and bridge control on VHF Ch14 or 73 call-sign "Mutford control" or Tel: 01502 531778. The yacht station on the other side of the lock and bridges, may also be able to assist, Tel: 01502 574946. Broads tolls will be payable for vessels passing through the lock. For information on The Broads, see Great Yarmouth chapter.

LOWESTOFT HAVEN MARINA SHORESIDE INFORMATION	
Stores	Nearest quarter of a mile walk up road from marina, Londis convenience store open every day 0730-2200
Public Tel.	In marina
Club	None

For other Shoreside and Emergency Information see Royal Norfolk & Suffolk Yacht Club Marina

LOWESTOFT MARINA SKIPPERS INFORMATION	
Harbour Master	Tel: 01502 588111
Water	On pontoons
Electricity	On pontoons
Facilities	WC and showers
Boatyard	Some repair facilities

LOWESTOFT MARINA SHORESIDE INFORMATION	
Stores	A range of stores in Oulton Broad (five minutes walk) including a Tesco Express in Beccles Road, open every day 0600-2400
Banks	All major banks in Oulton Broad
PO	In Spar Store in Bridge Road
Public Tel.	In Bridge Road
Club	None

For other Shoreside and Emergency Information see Royal Norfolk & Suffolk Yacht Club Marina

Southwold Harbour from the Walberswick Shore ©Claudia Myatt

SOUTHWOLD

⌖ **52°18'.7N, 01°40'.9E** *(off entrance)*
Tides -1:40 *(difference from Harwich)*

This harbour, in the entrance to the River Blyth, offers a peaceful refuge to yachtsmen and is a popular cruising destination for local and overseas sailors alike. Although the harbour itself sits amongst the salt marshes, the nearby small sedate seaside town of Southwold with its colourful beach huts and the village of Walberswick on the opposite bank, are within easy walking distance of the moorings. To reach Southwold you can either walk up the lane from the moorings through the golf course, or take the road up from the harbour mouth and caravan site; either way, I would suggest you take a torch at night. Things here have a simple charm, but in recent years facilities have been improved and the place has been smartened up, but not so much as to change its character. It is a pleasant place for a stopover and is the ideal destination for those seeking some countryside to walk in, some history to discover and time to relax and reflect in relative peace. The town has many craft shops and galleries to browse and the town's Adnams Brewery still delivers locally by horse-drawn dray – apparently the beer travels better this way!

SOUTHWOLD SKIPPERS INFORMATION	
Harbour Master	VHF Ch12/9 call-sign "Southwold Harbour Master", Tel: 01502 724712
Water	On quay
Electricity	On quay
Fuel	Available from boatyard
Facilities	WC and showers available in sailing club when open or at caravan site by the quay at entrance (mooring receipt required from Harbour Master)
Boatyard	Harbour Marine Services, Tel: 01502 724721
Chandlery	At Harbour Marine Services
Slips	Travelhoists up to 30 tons, contact boatyard

APPROACH AND ENTRANCE

The entrance to Southwold Harbour lies just under 10 miles south of Lowestoft, six miles north of Sizewell nuclear power station and therefore about 20 miles from Orford Haven. The only clear landmarks are the town of Southwold itself and the lighthouse by the town, about a mile to the north of the harbour entrance and there are no off-lying buoys to help. Entry can often be made with up to 1.5 metres draught from one hour after low water, but this must depend on weather conditions and the sands here are hard and unforgiving, so a call to the Harbour Master should be made if in doubt when close to, who will assist both with entrance and moorings. The Harbour Master is only present during normal working hours, outside of this time you should contact Great Yarmouth coastguard for advice.

The River Blyth, on which the harbour lies, can ebb at about 4 knots, so it is generally advisable to plan to enter Southwold harbour on the early (if you have enough depth), or late, flood. There are entry signals at the end of the north pier, three fixed greens means you are okay to proceed, whilst entry must not take place if there are three fixed red lights or two red flags shown in daylight.

You should keep in reasonable depth until you have identified the entrance and then head straight in centrally between the piers. Once in the harbour you will see the small pier at the landward end of

SOUTHWOLD SHORESIDE INFORMATION

Stores	Good shops in town one mile, including Co-op, open every day 0830-1900 (0900-1700 Sun)
Banks	Barclays and Lloyds in town
PO	In High Street
Public Tel.	By caravan site
Club	Southwold Sailing Club, Website: www.southwoldsailing.co.uk
Taxis	Southwold Taxis. Tel: 01502 723400
Accommodation	A good range of hotels and guesthouses in town, enquire at Tourist Information Centre
Tourist Info.	In High Street. Tel: 01502 724729
Police	Station Road. Tel: 01473 613500
Doctor	Eastaugh, Castle, Stammers & Harland, York Road. Tel: 01502 722326
Hospital	There are some services at Southwold Hospital in St. Edmunds Green, Tel: 01502 723333, but the nearest full A&E is at the James Paget Hospital, Lowestoft Road, Great Yarmouth, Tel: 01493 452452
Dentist	The Dental Surgery, St Clements, Reydon. Tel: 01502 722373
Pharmacy	Queen Street Pharmacy, Queen Street, Tel: 01502 722362; or Howells and Brooks, High Street, Tel: 01502 722370

USEFUL NUMBERS

Boatyard & Slipway (10 tons)	Justin Ladd. Tel: 07899 913642
Marine Engineers & Brokerage	Harbour Marine Services. Tel: 01502 724721
Shipwright/ Boatbuilder	G. Brown & Son. Tel: 01502 725050

the north pier known as The Knuckle and you need to turn sharply to starboard as you pass this. From then stick close to the quay on the northern shore past the lifeboat house, before returning to the centre of the river as you approach and pass the stagings. Watch out for the small foot ferry around here and if turning round to moor, do not go too far up towards the bridge on the flood or you will join the unfortunates who have found themselves pinned on the bridge by the tide. At night the entrance piers are both lit (FIG15s and QR) and The Knuckle carries two fixed greens.

MOORINGS

Most of the first stagings to starboard are used by fishing boats, then you will see the shoreside Harbour Master's office (in the old lifeboat shed, although the building of a new office is being planned), followed by the sailing club and soon after you will see the stagings of the visitors moorings by The Harbour Inn. You should, if possible, call ahead to the Harbour Master to make arrangements, as they can become very busy in season, but there are plans to extend these as part of the continued harbour improvements.

CREW CHANGES AND TRAVEL

By road, Southwold is about eight miles from the main A12. It is not the most convenient place for transfers by public transport, but there is a very regular bus service daily (less on Sundays) to Halesworth where you can get trains to Lowestoft and Ipswich for onward rail and coach connections. For train information contact 'One' Customer Services, Tel: 08456 007245 Website: www.onerailway.com, or National Rail Enquiries, Tel: 08457 484950 Website: www.nationalrail.co.uk. For coach services contact National Express, Tel: 08705 808080 Website: www.nationalexpress.com. For local bus information contact Traveline East Anglia, Tel: 08706 082608 Website: www.traveline.org.uk

EATING AND DRINKING

The nearby Harbour Inn is just across the quay from the visitors moorings. This historic pub has recently been extended with new toilets and cellar, as well as a restaurant in the converted net sheds with fine views over the river and marshes and they still do their famous fish and chips. The bar serves a good range of Adnams Ales 1100-2300 every day, with food served 1200-1430 and 1800-2100, Tel: 01502 722381. Next door, Southwold Sailing Club is open at weekends, when visitors may use the bar and other facilities there.

Next to Harbour Marine Services is a tea room, which is usually open from Easter to November during the daytime, Tel: 01502 722593. On the road from the caravan site to town is the Casa Mia Italian Restaurant and Piano Bar open for drinks, dining and live music from the resident pianist, Thursdays to Sundays only, from 1700 onwards (Sundays 1200-1600), Tel: 01502 724416. In Southwold town there are also a number of pubs, tearooms, hotels and restaurants to choose from. If it is fish and seafood you are looking for, there are a couple of sheds selling fresh fish down the riverside towards the harbour mouth.

If you wish to take the foot ferry across to Walberswick or walk across the bailey bridge, you will find the Parish Lantern tea rooms on the village green and the Bell Inn and Anchor Inn pubs. The latter has a particular reputation for its food and is open in summer 1100-1600 and 1800-2300 (Sundays 1100-2230), Tel: 01502 722112.

TO SEE AND DO

Near the harbour entrance is the Alfred Corry Museum. The 44ft 'sailing and pulling' lifeboat 'Alfred Corry' was Southwold's first, dedicated in 1893. She is being restored to her original form in the old Cromer lifeboat shed, which was brought here by sea a few years back. Tel: 01502 723200.

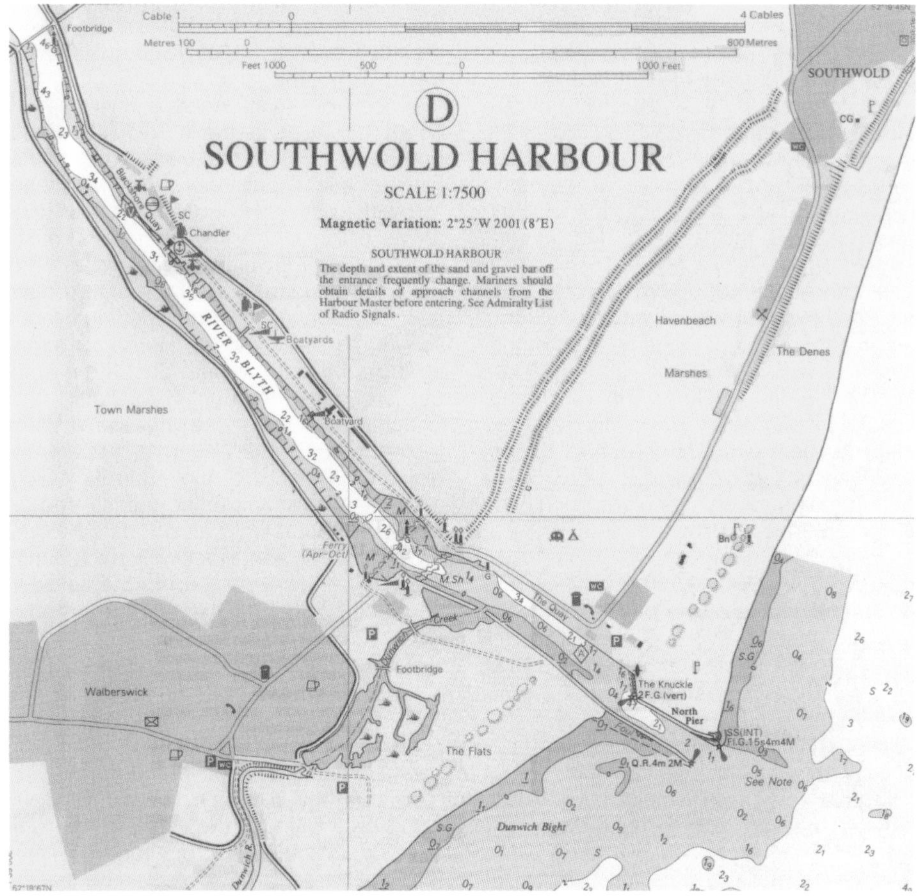

Not to be used for navigation

'Coastal Voyager' is a high-speed RIB that can take passengers on fast sea trips, or again river cruises and will even offer a one-way water taxi service for walkers who wish to cover some of the coastal path, Tel: 07887 525082.

There is a small museum in Victoria Street, near Bartholomew Green behind the High Street, but this will be closed during 2007 for a major refurbishment funded by the Heritage Lottery Fund and Adnams Charity. Due to re-open Easter 2008, you should telephone for opening times, Tel: 01502 726097. It is also worth visiting the Sailor's Reading Room above the promenade, where there are maritime exhibits. The Amber Shop and Museum in Market Place, makes an interesting diversion and is open seven days a week, 0900-1700 (1100-1600 Sundays), Tel: 01502 723394. Southwold Lighthouse in the town is open for tours at weekends and some other days in season, 1100-1300 and 1400-1600, admission is £3, children £2, family £8, Tel: 01502 575989, call to check opening times.

The small 66-seat Electric Palace cinema opened in 2002 and you should call for details of film performances. Tel: 07815 769565.

Southwold Pier has been beautifully restored and stretches 623 feet out into the North Sea from the promenade (it was once longer, in the days of paddle steamers). It is open every day and has the usual range of amusements, an unusual water clock and a number of places of refreshment, with a function room at the end of the pier. Tel: 01502 722105.

You can navigate upriver through the marshes by dinghy if you have a powerful and reliable engine, as far as Blythburgh. Here there is the large and splendid 14/15th century Holy Trinity church, which is open every day. This is felt by some to be the finest church in Suffolk and dwarfs today's village, which is all that remains of this ancient and once important port and town.

It is about a mile and half's walk up and down both sides of the river, crossing at the footbridge, into Walberswick, which provides a change of scenery. If your energy is not that great you could take the foot ferry one way. Another fine walk of about four miles for the sturdy legged and booted, is to follow the road alongside the harbour inland past the bridge and then follow the path north alongside the wildlife haven of Buss Creek. Crossing the main road into Southwold at the road bridge, continue along the south bank of the creek past the boating lake on your right until you reach the car park. Here you strike right on the cliff top path past the pier to the six guns on Gun Hill. During the Second World War these guns were buried following a German air raid, apparently brought about by the German high command misinterpreting aerial photographs of Southwold as a fortified town. From here you can either walk back down the lane or the Ferry Path to the harbour and then back along the river bank road.

HISTORY

The history of the four ports of Dunwich, Blythburgh, Walberswick and Southwold are closely linked by the course of the River Blyth and its estuary and the various disputes caused by their rivalry. In Roman times, Dunwich began to develop as a port, with a boat building industry, a fleet of warships and later a fishing fleet. The town became the largest port in Suffolk, until the recurrent storms and flooding caused much of the town to be washed away and such silting of the estuary that the marine trade diverted to Blythburgh. Blythburgh has evidence of occupation from Neolithic times and although it was an important place from then on, had its heyday in medieval times, when its port thrived. Both Southwold and Walberswick then took advantage of Dunwich's demise by improving their harbours and in the 16th century they cut through the sea wall to provide direct access to the sea. However, a struggle with silting and shifting of the estuary then ensued, not helped by the reclamation of land upriver that greatly reduced the scouring on the ebb tide and the three remaining ports subsequently declined.

In 1659 a devastating fire destroyed much of Southwold, but resulted in the greens that are so much of a feature of Southwold today. The inconclusive "Battle of Solebay" was fought off Southwold in 1672 by the combined English and French fleets (well almost combined – they went in different directions at one point, after which the French fleet appears to have been AWOL!), against the Dutch fleet and involved some 130 ships and 50,000 men. After the battle both sides claimed victory, the Dutch claiming that they had stopped the French fleet linking up with their armies in the Netherlands, but despite this, the Anglo-French fleet had secured their dominance at sea.

THE RIVERS ORE & ALDE

Havergate Island and Butley River ©PRPA

52°01.'6N 01°28.'0E
Orford Haven Buoy *(approximate and liable to be moved, see Approach and Entrance)*
Tides Orford Haven -0:20;
Orford Quay +0:20
Slaughden Quay +1:10; Snape +2.10
(differences from Harwich)

The Ore and the Alde are dual names for different stretches of the same river which combine to provide 16 miles of tidal water, from bleak marsh and shingle to the gently rolling countryside of the upper reaches. Along the way you will have the opportunity to visit the small historic town of Orford, with the possibility of a trip to Orford Ness (one of the National Trust's more remarkable properties), to meander in the pleasant seaside town of Aldeburgh and for the ambitious, to moor up in the middle of the arts complex at Snape Maltings. Less commercialised cruising grounds than many on the east coast, the Ore offers a challenging entrance and the winding upper reaches of the Alde, a test in shoal waters pilotage, with all connected by several miles in which the more self-sufficient can relax and enjoy the natural world.

From the river's mouth at North Weir Point to Pigtail Point, at the top end of Pigtail Reach just upstream of Orford, the river is known as the Ore, and the Orford Town Trust (which also manages Orford Town Quay) seems to have assumed responsibility for it. Upstream of Pigtail Point the river becomes the Alde and although Upsons Boatyard manages the quay at Slaughden and yacht club members mark the upper reaches, authority over the navigation seems unclear.

The two names for the river are as a result of the ever changing courses of the rivers over the centuries. As can be seen from

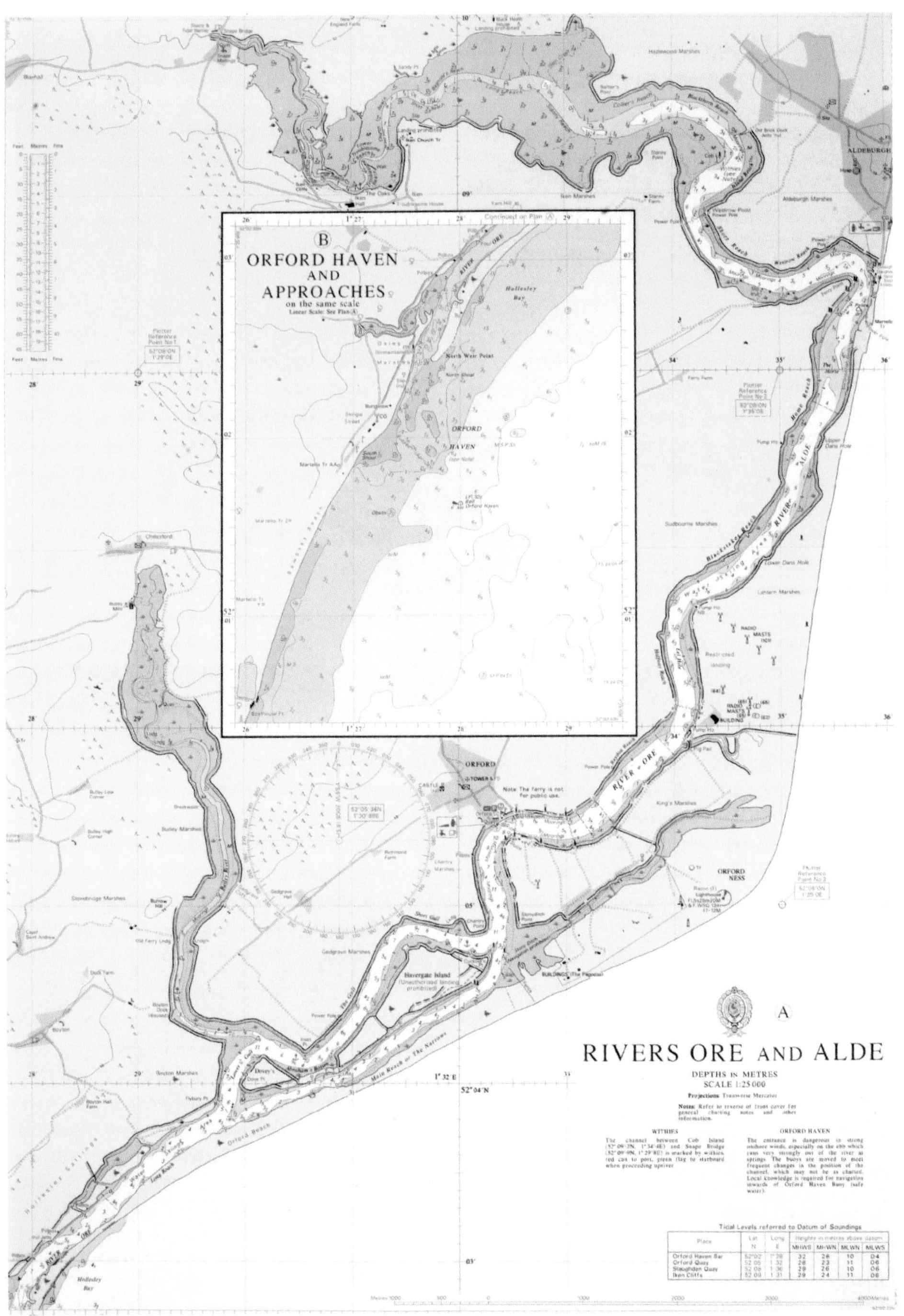

Place	Lat N	Long E	Heights in metres above datum MHWS	MHWN	MLWN	MLWS
Orford Haven Bar	52°02	1°28	3·2	2·6	1·0	0·4
Orford Quay	52 05	1 32	2·8	2·3	1·1	0·6
Slaughden Quay	52 08	1 36	2·9	2·6	1·0	0·6
Iken Cliffs	52 09	1 31	2·9	2·4	1·1	0·8

the chart, the river runs parallel to the coast for much of its length, separated from the sea by only a narrow shingle beach called Orford Ness. The shingle spit is for ever moving and over the years has caused previous river openings to be silted over and the mouth of the Ore to no longer enter the sea separately. Shingle Street at the entrance is a community that has been affected by the whims of the river. Until the spit moved, the village had a flourishing trade around its quay on the mouth of the river (ruins of which can still be seen to port shortly after entry) and even had its own private lifeboat in the 19th century. The effects of the sea on the changing landscape have also caused the loss of much of the community at Slaughden Quay, including its pub The Three Mariners, as recently as early last century. There is much local concern that the sea may again break through the thin strip of land and extensive work has been undertaken in recent times to reinforce the sea wall.

APPROACH AND ENTRANCE

As with the Deben, the entrance to the Ore should not be attempted without up-to-date pilotage information as the sandbanks and buoyage marking them shift often, particularly over winter, or after storms. In settled conditions, with up-to-date pilotage information and careful preparation and timing, it is not as difficult as it may look and well worth the trouble. There is no Harbour Master at the entrance so you will be very much on your own, therefore for the newcomer you are advised to do your homework and have your plans clear.

Approaching from either direction it is vital to stand well off until the red and white Orford Haven safe water buoy (LFl.10s) is found. This buoy is moored off Shingle Street, a hamlet with a Martello tower at its south end, and a few houses with the old Coastguard cottages to the north. You should not attempt to enter the river in strong east or southeast winds and frankly in any severe weather, particularly onshore. I would also not recommend night-time entry, as the only local lit mark is the Orford Haven buoy and even those who know the entrance reasonably well, will often wait for daylight to appear before entering. I've tried entering myself at night and found it a challenging and somewhat hair-raising experience.

Trinity House surveys the entrance and each spring puts down the red PH Oxley and green SH Weir buoys to guide you in and if necessary moves the Orford Haven buoy. These lateral buoys have often not been laid until late April, but I understand more frequent surveys are being discussed, which may allow for an earlier laying. The Oxley and Weir buoys are removed late in the year (usually in November or December), when due to the winter storms, the track they indicate starts to become unreliable. I cannot stress too strongly the need to consult up-to-date pilotage information and not to purely treat the buoys as 'join the dots' for entry. For example, in 2006 rounding up on Weir could have set you on the shoals in a frightening location.

The streams within the river entrance have a maximum rate at springs of 6 knots and continue to run for one hour after the time of local high, or low, water. Therefore, entry should be made on the flood tide as soon as there is sufficient height of tide to suit the draught of the vessel (at the time of writing the entrance carried about a metre at LWS). The latest advice in 2006, is to steer from Orford Haven buoy to Oxley PH buoy leaving it close to port, then to Weir SH buoy leaving it close to starboard, but not turning into the river until at least half way between Weir buoy and the shore. From there the advice is to keep close to western shore up past Shingle Street, the ruined dock and disused orange beacon, until the small Barthorp's Creek starts to open away to port. At this point you will have passed the mid-stream horse and can proceed more towards the middle of the river.

The latest information and a downloadable chart of the entrance can be found on the website: www.orfordentrance.com, (which actually shares its website with www.debenentrance.com), where updates and information are also regularly posted. This is also available in printed form from local chandlers, Harbour Masters, clubs and marinas. Although there is no official pilot for the entrance, if in doubt, or you have to enter in winter, I would suggest you seek local advice and assistance from the Orford, or Felixstoweferry Harbour Masters.

When leaving the river heading north, it is best to do this around HW to HW+1, when the tide will sweep you north. If heading south, it would clearly be best to leave against the flood if you have an engine powerful enough to beat the tidal stream in the entrance, but otherwise you will have no option but to leave as late on the ebb as you safely can for your draft (and don't take any chances) and slog against the last of the ebb tide for a few hours.

ORFORD HAVEN TO ORFORD QUAY

Once past the mid-stream horse described in Approach and Entrance, although a mid-stream course can generally be followed, there is a spit to avoid to port off Hollesley Saltings just after a ruined jetty, where an old ramp can be seen on the shore. It is suggested that for safety, a course to east of the centre be followed for a few hundred metres. Two miles upstream of the entrance at the end of Long Reach you come to Havergate Island, where you have a choice of two channels to follow around the island, separated by a shallow spit which extends from Dove Point at the southern extremity of the island. This spit is marked by an unlit south cardinal buoy.

Sunset on the Ore ©C. Blaney

To the east of the island is Main Reach, sometimes aptly referred to as the narrows which follows a straight and direct course past the island. To the west is The Gull, wider, deeper, but more twisting and therefore a more interesting channel, which after a short northwards reach called Lower Gull, turns sharply to starboard passing the entrance to the Butley River to port, and into the reach known as Abraham's Bosum, where a sheltered anchorage can be found with good holding and splendid isolation. The river then turns north-eastwards for the long reach of The Gull before turning eastwards into Short Gull. Here again is a fine sheltered and isolated anchorage, where you may find the Lady Florence (see Orford section) moored when not working. Off Cuckold's Point (the northern extremity of Havergate Island) the channels meet and the river turns northward towards Orford Quay half a mile away.

Anchoring anywhere on the Ore is possible out of the main channel, although holding in the shingle is variable. The section of Orford Ness from North Weir Point at the entrance to Stony Ditch, opposite the upstream end of Havergate Island, is managed by English Nature and landing is permitted. Clean landing on the shingle makes the first couple of miles of the ness a popular destination for picnics and barbecues, but please take care of the birds and do not go too far from your boat if anchored, due to some poor holding. Landing above Stony Ditch is prohibited.

On the western side of the river there are some points in the entrance where landing is possible, but from the island off Hollesley Saltings to the Butley River the area is designated nature reserves and landing is not permitted. Until the 1953 floods, Havergate Island was still farmed but it is now an RSPB reserve with several lagoons that provide a sanctuary to many migrating shore birds. Landing is not permitted on the island without prior arrangement. Landing on the mainland shore is not easy in The Gull and although a landing at a ruined pier is marked on charts in Short Gull, I have not found this a very practical, or clean, proposition. Upstream of here there is no clean landing short of Orford and landing on the ness opposite here is prohibited.

BUTLEY RIVER

For those seeking peace and tranquillity, the Butley River is navigable by shallow draught boats for just over a mile upstream, after which dinghy exploration would be more sensible. If you can clear the slight bar in the entrance, which carries about one and a half metres at LWS, even moderate draft vessels can stay afloat in a few places for a couple of hundred metres upstream. To enter the river you have to sail upstream in the Ore and double back along the northern shore between the two withies marking the entrance. Then the main channel favours the port hand side for about three quarters of a mile before becoming more central.

There are no facilities ashore on the Butley River, but landings can be made at the disused Boyton Dock to port after quarter of a mile, where it is possible to land at any state of tide (but please note there is no longer a pub in Boyton) and at the ferry landings both sides of the river another third of a mile on. From this point onwards there are oyster layings to avoid, usually very clearly marked. From the port landing you can walk two and a half miles into Butley, where you will find the Oyster Inn and a public telephone nearby. Using the lane one way and river wall path the other, you can make this into a six mile circular walk via Butley Mills if you wish, where you will also find a pottery and tearooms. From the starboard landing it is a two mile walk into Orford and again a circular walk of five miles can be constructed using the lane and river wall path.

The Butley ferry service was absent for some years until some gallant volunteers decided to start it again for the service of walkers and cyclists (at £1.50 per person each way, plus £1.50 per cycle). They operate the service on weekends and bank holidays from 1100-1600 and other times may be possible by prior agreement. If intending to use the service you need to advise them prior. Tel: 01394 450843 or Mobile: 07913 672499.

EATING AND DRINKING

The Oyster Inn at Butley serves real ales and food. The bar is open lunchtimes and evenings, seven days a week and serves food 1200-1400 and 1830-2100, Tel: 01394 450790. The Barn Café by the pottery at Butley Mill serves teas, coffees and lunches, and is open 1100-1700, Thursdays to Sundays, April to December and every day in July and August, Tel: 01394 450800.

TO SEE AND DO

The pottery at Butley Mills has a gallery of art and ceramics. Opening times vary so it is recommended you check prior to visiting. Tel: 01394 450785.

ORFORD

The small historic town of Orford is dominated by the 90 feet high keep of the now ruined 12th century castle and St. Bartholomew's Church. Growing up around the castle the town was once an important port as evidenced by the scale of the church, but declined as the shingle spit lengthened south and moved it further from the sea and now only a small fishing fleet remains. Its remote location has protected the town from the advances of recent centuries, resulting in a small town seemingly little affected by modern times. Orford is well worth stopping at for longer than the usual cursory visit and I can recommend it as place to spend a day or two in.

MOORINGS

Most of the moorings at Orford are now managed by the Orford Town Trust, although a few are privately owned. There are currently seven designated visitors moorings to the starboard side of the river on the bend just before the quay. These are marked, but to be clearer it is intended to replace the buoys with large matching

The moorings at Orford

yellow ones. It is also the Trust's intention to increase the number of visitors moorings over the next few years to encourage us to visit. If none of these are available, in the words of the Harbour Master: "treat any vacant mooring as a visitors mooring, we'll tell you if it's not available". Calling up the Harbour Master to enquire, or visiting his office on the quay, will allay any concerns. Moorings are currently charged at £6 per night, but if you wish to anchor, you will need to find a space either above, or below, the moorings.

Clean landing is to be found at the quay, which has steps at intervals around it. It is both possible with sufficient height of tide, and permissible, to go alongside the end of the quay for a short time, although you should not leave your vessel unattended, as you may be required to move to make way for a ferry or tripper boat.

CREW CHANGES AND TRAVEL

There are five buses a day (three on Sundays) from Market Hill to Woodbridge and Ipswich for train and coach connections. For information contact Traveline East Anglia, Tel: 08706 082608 Website: www.traveline.org.uk. See Ipswich section of River Orwell chapter for further information. For train information contact 'One' Customer Services, Tel: 08456 007245 Website: www.onerailway.com

EATING AND DRINKING

Orford is well served with eating and drinking establishments. There is the new

Riverside Tea Rooms among the fishing sheds on the foreshore open daily in season for teas and snacks.

Moving up Quay Street from the quay you will come first to the snug 16th century Jolly Sailor where you will find good beers and good food and they are proud to have achieved 25 years unbroken in The Good Pub Guide. The bar is open 1130-1430 and 1900-2300 (1200-1445 and closing 2230 Sundays) and serving food 1200-1400 and 1915-2045 (Fridays and weekends only in winter). You are advised to arrive early for evening meals as the fresh fare can run out on busy evenings leaving limited choice later. Tel: 01394 450243.

As you turn into Market Hill you will find the 13th century King's Head Inn on your right, which has recently been taken over by the owners of the Crown and Castle Hotel. I understand they intend to specialise here in good beers and "old-fashioned pub grub", so I am looking forward to my next visit. The bar is currently open 1130-1500 and 1800-2300 (1200-1600 and 1700-2230 Sundays), but I understand the hours may change and food is going to be served 1200-1430 and 1800-2030, although weekend and peak season times may be extended. Tel: 01394 450205.

Pinney's of Orford used to run a restaurant in the Old Warehouse near the quay, but have now taken over the Butley Orford Oysterage Restaurant in Market Hill. They have an interesting and extensive menu with a fish and seafood bias. They are open 1200-1415 and 1830-2100 (from 1800 Friday and Saturday) and I would suggest reserving a table at busy times. Tel: 01394 450277.

Further along Market Hill to Castle Hill on the left, is The Crown and Castle Hotel run by cookery writer and broadcaster Ruth Watson and her husband David. There is a small but pleasant bar at the hotel open 1200-1500 and 1900-2300 (2230 Sundays) and food is served lunchtimes and evenings from 1230 onwards in the Trinity Restaurant which has recently been awarded the Michelin Bib Gourmand and features in a number of good food guides. Tel 01394 450205.

ORFORD SKIPPERS INFORMATION	
Harbour Master	Richard Bantoft, Tel: 01394 459950 or VHF Ch8 or Ch16, call-sign "Chantry". Other moorings may be available from Ralph Brinkley, Tel 07745 250632
Water	Standpipe to rear of the quay
Electricity	None
Fuel	The yard may be able to assist, otherwise Friends Garage is a one and half mile walk at the other end of the village
Facilities	Public WC in car park 200 metres, showers available in club when open
Internet	None
Boatyard	Orford Marine Services, Tel: 01394 450169
Chandlery	None
Slips	By the quay, enquire Harbour Master. If launching a boat here with an engine over 8hp you will need to purchase a licence. Personal watercraft are prohibited
Scrubbing Posts	Near the quay, enquire Harbour Master

For the DIY 'foodie', Orford has a range of stores selling superb local produce (see Shoreside Information panel).

TO SEE AND DO

The keep of Orford Castle, or just Orford Castle as it is known locally, was built between 1165-1175 as an East Anglian stronghold for Henry II against the possibility of invasion or an uprising by his troublesome local barons. It is famous for being one of the first keeps in the country to have a rounded construction to improve its

ORFORD SHORESIDE INFORMATION

Stores	Orford Supply Stores in Pump Street, off Market Hill in the centre of the town. Open seven days a week, 0830-1730, closed Wed and Sun afternoons. Orford Butchers Shop is in Front Street. Butley Oysterage for fresh and smoked fish and seafood is in Market Hill and no visit to Orford is complete without a trip to Richardson's Smokehouse behind the Butley Oysterage Shop which is open seven days a week from 1000 to some time in the afternoon. Fresh fish and seafood can also be bought at Ralph Brinkley's Shed on the foreshore on Fri and weekends.
Banks	None
PO	In Orford Supply Stores
Public Tel.	Near car park 200 metres from quay
Club	Orford Sailing Club open at varying times at weekends Tel: 01394 450997, Tel: (Hon. Sec.) 01394 450090 Website: www.orfordsail.org.uk
Taxis	M & R Cars, Woodbridge, Tel: 08001 694269 or 01394 386191; Atlas Cars, Woodbridge, Tel: 08000 747094
Accommodation	The Jolly Sailor and King's Head both have accommodation (see Eating and Drinking). There are two bed and breakfast establishments, The Old Butchers Shop, Tel: 01394 450517 and Ashanwell, Tel: 01394 450882. For those with a bigger budget, there is the refined Crown and Castle Hotel in Castle Hill, Tel: 01394 450205.
Tourist Info.	In the National Trust office on the quayside
Police	Grundisburgh Road, Woodbridge. Tel: 01473 613500
Doctor	Drs. Yates & Ball, Chapman House, Rectory Road. Tel: 01394 450315
Hospital	(A&E) Ipswich Hospital, Heath Road. Tel: 01473 712233
Dentist	NHS Dental Enquiries. Tel: 01473 329135 Out of hours – Tel: 01473 299685
Pharmacy	Nearest Woodbridge town centre

USEFUL NUMBERS

Boat Building & Repairs	Michael Button. Tel: 07729 107196
Marine Engineers	Orford Marine Services. Tel: 01394 450169
Sailing School	Seatrain Sailing is based in Orford. Tel: 01394 388792

defensive qualities. From the top of the keep there are wonderful views of the river and surrounding countryside. Orford Museum is housed in the keep and of particular interest to yachtsmen are the pictures showing how the course of the river has changed over the years. English Heritage opens the castle to the public daily from April to September, 1000-1800 (Thursdays to Mondays, 1000-1600 in winter) and admission costs £4.50, £2.30 for children.

The part of Orford Ness opposite is now owned by the National Trust and is a wild and remote area being on the largest vegetated shingle spit in Europe. It contains a variety of habitats that are home to nationally rare birds, animals and plants. The Ness was previously a secret military testing site from 1913 and many of the buildings used can still be seen, including the famous pagodas, which it is rumoured were used for testing nuclear detonators.

There is a five-mile pedestrian route with information and displays. It opens on Tuesdays to Saturdays from July to September and Saturdays only from Easter Saturday to the end of June and in October. The only access is by ferry from Orford Quay and tickets can be obtained from the office on the quay. Outward journeys from 1000-1400 with the last ferry back from the Ness at 1700. Tel: 01394 450900 or 01394 450057 (information line). Admission (including return ferry ticket) £6.50, £3.25 for children.

Open daily, St. Bartholomew's church which dominates the centre of town and is evidence of its former prosperity and importance, dates from the 14th century, although there are remains of an earlier church to the rear.

Above Orford Crafts, just up from The Kings Head, is an exhibition of the underwater exploration of local marine sites, such as Dunwich. Opening as shop. Tel: 01394 450678.

Visits from Orford to the RSPB Nature Reserve on Havergate can be arranged, but this has to be done through the visitor centre at Minsmere, Tel: 01728 648281. If time doesn't allow for a day on the island, bird watching trips around the island on the launch 'Regardless' are available by calling Orford Marine Services, Tel: 01394 450169.

The 50 feet ex-Admiralty MFV 'LADY FLORENCE' sails all year round from Orford Quay, regardless of weather and tides, offering brunch, lunch, dinner and Champagne high-tea cruises on the Ore and Alde. She can carry 12 passengers in comfort (she even has a coal fire in the saloon), with informative commentary throughout the trip. Tel: 07831 698298.

As mentioned in the Butley River section, there is a pleasant walk of about five miles down the river wall to the Butley River up the eastern bank to the ferry landing and back along the lane.

ORFORD TO ALDEBURGH

A short distance from Orford, the moorings end and you turn into Raydon Reach with Town Marshes to port and Kings Marshes to starboard. At the end of the reach you will pass a creek called Pigtail to starboard and the point to port called Pigtail Point. Take care of the shallows that extend out from the port hand shore as you approach the point. It is here that the river changes its name to the Alde and over to starboard on the east side of the river there is a large grey building and the line of tall lattice masts that transmit the BBC World Service. It is then a fairly straight run of two and a half miles along Blackstakes and Home Reaches to Slaughden Quay. Blackstakes refers to the remains of jetties that can still occasionally be seen, harking back to the days when this was a busy commercial river. Just short of Slaughden there is a horse that extends across the river charted at less than two metres at LAT of which you should be aware, but in recent years this seems to me to have been deepening.

ALDEBURGH

The moorings and quay at Slaughden are the river port for Aldeburgh, once a thriving port with its own Icelandic fishing fleet. The town is only half the size it once was, but in recent years appears to have found its feet again, as a somewhat quiet but fashionable seaside retreat. There is a long main street where most of the restaurants and shops are to be found and several side streets with some interesting old buildings. The seafront has hotels, fishing boats and huts, a very modern lifeboat station and the 16th century Moot Hall. There are two very active yacht clubs, the more upmarket Aldeburgh Yacht Club and the more DIY-styled Slaughden Sailing Club. Both are very friendly, welcoming and helpful to the visitor.

MOORINGS

The moorings at Aldeburgh are administered by the Upsons or Cables yards. Upsons has laid three designated visitors moorings to starboard just short of Aldeburgh Yacht

Club, for which in 2006, a £5 per night charge was made. If none of these is free, contact either of the yards who will almost always find a mooring for you. Visitors also often anchor just downstream of the visitors moorings, again on the starboard side of the river. Clean landing can be made at Aldeburgh Yacht Club, the quay and the slip nearby, or anywhere on the shingle beach.

CREW CHANGES AND TRAVEL

There are regular buses from the High Street, Mondays to Saturdays (less on Sundays) to Saxmundum, Woodbridge and Ipswich for train and coach connections. For information contact Traveline East Anglia, Tel: 08706 082608 Website: www.traveline.org.uk. See Ipswich section of River Orwell chapter for further information. For train information contact 'One' Customer Services, Tel: 08456 007245 Website: www.onerailway.com

ALDEBURGH SKIPPERS INFORMATION	
Harbour Master	Mr. Brian Upson, Tel: 01728 453047/452896 or when in his launch on VHF Ch80
Water	Standpipes at the quay and Aldeburgh Yacht Club
Fuel	Available from the boatyards
Facilities	Both clubs offer WC and showers to visitors. SSC when open and AYC at all times
Internet	None
Boatyards	R F Upson & Co., Tel: 01728 453047/452896; D M & P Cable, Tel: 01728 452569; Aldeburgh Boatyard, Tel: 01728 452019
Chandlery	At Aldeburgh Boatyard
Slips	Both the yacht club slips are private, so for use of the slip by the quay contact the Harbour Master

The Moot Hall ©Claudia Myatt

EATING AND DRINKING

Not very long ago there was little more than limited pub menus and fish and chips to choose from in Aldeburgh, but these days the town is very well served with a variety of eating and drinking establishments. There are still two fish and chip shops in the High Street and The Aldeburgh Fish and Chip Shop on the right has a fine reputation up and down the east coast. There is also a Chinese takeaway in the High Street. There are a number of bars and pubs in Aldeburgh, some in the centre, such as the small and traditional White Hart Inn on the High Street and others which you will need to search out. The Mill Inn in Market Cross Place by The Moot Hall, which is a favourite of the local fishermen and lifeboat crew, is worth a visit and specialises in fresh fish dishes. Tel: 01728 452563.

The bar at Aldeburgh Yacht Club opens 1200-1430 and 1630-1900 at weekends and on Wednesday evenings 1800-2300 in peak season. It also has a smart restaurant called Bowman's offering lunches and afternoon teas when the club is open. The Slaughden Sailing Club has a galley, serving teas and snacks when the club is open.

There are a number of places to eat in the town, but I shall name a few in the High Street. '152 aldeburgh' restaurant serves lunch and dinner every day 1200-1500 and 1800-2200, Tel: 01728 454594. Aldeburgh Spice Indian restaurant serves lunch and dinner every day, 1200-1400 and 1730-2300, (Saturday 2330). The Lighthouse restaurant is open for lunch and dinner every day, 1200-1400 and 1830-late, Tel: 01728 453377. There is also a smart and pleasant Prezzo Italian restaurant open every day, 1200-2230, Tel: 01728 454452 and the rather up-market Regatta Wine Bar, which is also open for food every day, 1200-1400 and 1800-2200, Tel: 01728 452011.

TO SEE AND DO

The small and delightfully old-fashioned Aldeburgh Cinema in the high street is open for occasional matinees and every evening, showing classic and new films. Tel: 01728 452996.

Aldeburgh Museum is housed in The Moot Hall, and although dating from the 16th century, it is still used for council meetings. Admission is £1.00, children free and it is open every day in summer, 1430-1700 (1200-1700 June, July and August). The modern Lifeboat Station is also well worth a visit and is open daily 1000-1600.

Walkers will enjoy the coast path north from Aldeburgh to the curious houses of Thorpe Ness. There is also the famous and well marked five mile Sailors Path to Snape for the energetic. Officially starting at the beach, the path goes across North Warren, an RSPB reserve, before crossing the route of the old railway, Leiston Road and the golf course and then past The Red House (once the home of Benjamin Britten). From here the path runs parallel to the Alde through heath, marsh, woods and parkland and into a lane to Snape village, providing differing and beautiful views along the way.

ALDEBURGH SHORESIDE INFORMATION	
Stores	Good stores in the High Street, including a Co-op supermarket open 0800-1800 (Sun 1000-1600), butchers, bakers and The Aldeburgh Market which offers a boat provisioning service, Tel: 01728 453600
Banks	All major banks and cash machines in the High Street
PO	In Co-op
Public Tel.	At Aldeburgh Yacht Club and in town centre
Clubs	Aldeburgh Yacht Club, Tel: 01728 452562, Slaughden Sailing Club, Tel: (Sec.) 01508 570142
Taxis	Amber Cars, Tel: 01728 833621; Aldeburgh Cars, Tel: 01728 453063
Accommodation	There is a variety of accommodation available, contact the Tourist Information Centre
Tourist Info.	152 High Street (by the cinema). Tel: 01728 453637
Police	Occasionally open in Leiston Road, otherwise 34 Kings Road, Leiston. Tel: 01473 613500
Doctor	Aldeburgh Surgery, Victoria Road. Tel: 01728 452027
Hospital	(A&E) Ipswich Hospital, Heath Road. Tel: 01473 712233
Dentist	NHS Dental Enquiries. Tel: 01473 329135 Out of hours – Tel: 01473 299685
Pharmacy	Aldeburgh Pharmacy, 125 High Street. Tel: 01728 452763
USEFUL NUMBERS	
Electrics	Contact John Pask at Upsons
Rigger	Contact Aldeburgh Boatyard

ALDEBURGH TO SNAPE

The moorings at Aldeburgh these days extend through Westrow and Short Reaches almost to Westrow Point. Initially the channel keeps slightly to starboard between the moorings and then moves over more towards the port, at which point the first withy will be seen to starboard. The withies are numerous upstream from here and placed close to the drying line. It is important to follow them very carefully, as although at high water the river appears much wider in these reaches, the deep water is confined to quite a narrow channel. Until the 1930's, sailing and motor barges made the journey to Snape and it is still possible today for the adventurous to navigate right up to Snape with a rising tide and enjoy this very rural part of the river along the way.

As you turn the first bend, the outskirts of Aldeburgh can still be seen off to starboard and the moorings off the ruined jetty of the former brickworks come into view. The channel sweeps across to the starboard bank again here to round the tidal Cob Island to port. There is plenty of space to anchor here clear of the moorings and clean landing is possible at all states of the tide on the quay and there is a short footpath leading back into Aldeburgh.

As the river bends to port around Cob Island along Blackthorn Reach, past Stanny Point to port, into Collier's Reach to Barbers Point, Iken Church comes into view in the distance. The bay widens here (but the channel does not) into Stanny Reach and Long Reach and you will see the red brick mansion, Blackheath House, set amongst the trees and rhododendron bushes on the starboard bank. Although the beaches look attractive here and there is a pontoon, landing is not permitted. In fact landing is not permitted either side of the river until past Iken Church. On the south side of the reach here is the distinctive circular shape of Yarn Hill.

As you approach Iken Church the banks close in again and the channel swings to port into Bagnold's Reach and then to starboard again into Short Reach. Parts of Short Reach are very shallow, so you will need to ensure you have sufficient height of tide. To the north of the church the channel turns sharply to the south into Church Reach before the channel starts to become tortuous through Lower Trouble-some and Troublesome Reaches. Great care is now necessary to follow the channel. Sometimes the red and green markers on the withies are missing and it is then difficult to decide on which side to pass, although there tend to be more on the inside of the bends. There is a popular anchorage here known as The Oaks, just downstream of Iken Cliff, with landing on a sandy beach and from here you can access a footpath which leads one way to

Fishing boats at Aldeburgh beach ©Claudia Myatt

Approach to Snape Maltings

the unusually thatched Iken Church dating from 647AD, or the other, after a mile and a half, to Snape Maltings.

The river then winds between several small drying islands, some of which are parts of the old sea wall. The white ventilators of the Maltings and off to starboard up the hill, the village of Snape can now be seen. It is essential that the first time visitor going up to Snape should continue (and leave) only on a rising tide and at slow speed, as the difficulty of the channel will almost certainly result in a grounding at some point. On subsequent visits you should also expect to ground somewhere, but in a far more embarrassing place and with an audience. The bridge at Snape comes into sight round the last bend, as does the quay at the Maltings on the port hand side just before it.

SNAPE

Set on the banks of the River Alde, Snape Maltings is a group of 19th century listed buildings set in a preservation area. When they were originally built they were a hive of activity with the import of coal and export of grain and bricks, the malting of barley and even barge building and repair. Built by Newson Garrett (father of Elizabeth Garrett Anderson, the first woman to become a doctor in England) the maltings ceased production in 1965 and since that time the complex of buildings has steadily been converted into an arts and music centre, with the best known of its features being the concert hall in the old maltings. Snape makes an interesting cruise destination for any time of the year, with the Aldeburgh Festival taking place each year in June. Besides the festival, the hall is used for a month of Proms every August and for a wide variety of musical events all year round. Many of the other buildings have also been put to good use with studios, art galleries, shops, café, pub and restaurant. With less than half the site already developed, there are ambitious plans for the expansion of the centre, including more performance venues which are now in development.

Turning right from the maltings, over the bridge and a few hundred yards up, is the small village of Snape where there is a shop, garage and two pubs.

MOORINGS

There are about 100 metres of good quay where vessels can lie on soft and reasonably level mud, with quayside ladders to assist getting ashore. Mooring fees are payable at the office, just by the quay, but on my last visit they were purely asking for a donation to a charity.

CREW CHANGES AND TRAVEL

There are roughly hourly buses during the day (less on Sundays) to Woodbridge and Ipswich for train and coach connections. For information contact Traveline East Anglia, Tel: 08706 082608 Website: www.traveline.org.uk. See Ipswich section of River Orwell chapter for further information. For train information contact 'One' Customer Services, Tel: 08456 007245 www.onerailway.com

EATING AND DRINKING

At the maltings the Granary tea shop is open 1000-1730 every day for teas, snacks and light meals. The Plough & Sail pub and restaurant is at the front of the complex by the road and serves real ales and food from an extensive menu. The bar is open 1200-1500 and 1800-2300 (2230 Sundays) and the restaurant 1200-1430 and 1900-2130 daily. Tel: 01728 688413.

SNAPE SKIPPERS INFORMATION	
Harbour Master	None, contact Snape Maltings office, Tel: 01728 688303 Email: enquiries@snapemaltings.co.uk
Water	On the quay
Fuel	From garage in Snape village, half a mile
Facilities	WC in the centre of the maltings, during open hours
Boatyard	The garage may be able to assist with emergency repairs
Website	www.snapemaltings.co.uk

The Crown Inn is the first pub you come to in the village and has an unusual bar with a high-backed double settle circling an inglenook fireplace. It serves Adnams Ales and has a large dining area where the food it serves has earned awards and mentions in many guides. The bar is open daily 1200-1500 and 1800-2300, serving food 1200-1400 and 1830-2100, Tel: 01728 688324. Turning right at the crossroads you will find the Golden Key a

SNAPE SHORESIDE INFORMATION	
Stores	Village stores by garage, half a mile. Open 0800-1400 (Sat 0800-1300 and Sun 0830-1200)
Banks	None
PO	In village store
Public Tel.	In the maltings complex and one in village
Taxis	Amber Cars, Tel: 01728 833621; Aldeburgh Cars, Tel: 01728 453063
Accommodation	Snape Maltings has cottages and apartments to let, Tel: 01728 688303. Both The Crown Inn, Tel: 01728 688324 and The Golden Key, Tel: 01728 688510 in the village have en-suite accommodation
Tourist Info.	In Snape Maltings office on the quayside
Police	34 Kings Road, Leiston. Tel: 01473 613500
Doctor	Rendlesham Surgery, 165 Suffolk Drive, Rendlesham, Tel: 01394 420555
Hospital	(A&E) Ipswich Hospital, Heath Road. Tel: 01473 712233
Dentist	NHS Dental Enquiries. Tel: 01473 329135 Out of hours – Tel: 01473 299685
Pharmacy	Co-op, 7 High Street, Saxmundum, Tel: 01728 602051 or Lloyds Chemists, 62 High Street Leiston, Tel: 01728 830545

Snape Quay

few yards down on the left which again has been mentioned in a number of guides for its food. The bar is open lunchtimes and evenings and serves food 1200-1400 (Sundays 1430) and 1800-2300 (closed Sunday evenings).

TO SEE AND DO

The Snape Maltings complex is open every day, all year, from 1000-1730, Tel: 01728 688303 Email: enquiries@snapemaltings.co.uk Website: www.snapemaltings.co.uk

An unusual experience would be to visit the Maltings Concert Hall for an event by boat. Aldeburgh Productions runs the concert hall box office, Tel: 01728 6878110 Email: enquiries@aldeburgh.co.uk, Website: www.aldeburgh.co.uk

The launch 'The Cormorant' runs varying length river trips from the quay and the smaller 'Eel' runs two hour, low tide bird watching trips in the upper reaches and marshes. Tel: 01728 688303.

HISTORY

In Roman Times the Alde was a wide estuary which emptied into the sea near where Aldeburgh now stands and it is believed there was a roman settlement, or port, here on the north bank, which is probably now under the sea. There is evidence to suggest that the Saxons took this settlement over and this is supported by the name of Slaughden, which derives from the Saxon language.

At Barbers Point further up the river, excavations have revealed another settlement dating from Romano British times, which also shows evidence of later Saxon occupation. As you proceed upriver you will see the tree-topped Yarn Hill on the southern side, where the locals claim Queen Boudica is buried! On the bend opposite Iken Church the Romans are said to have built saltpans, and excavations there have discovered Roman pottery. Further up the river still at Snape, evidence of not only Roman and Saxon occupation has been found, including a ship burial, but remains dating from the Bronze Age have also been unearthed.

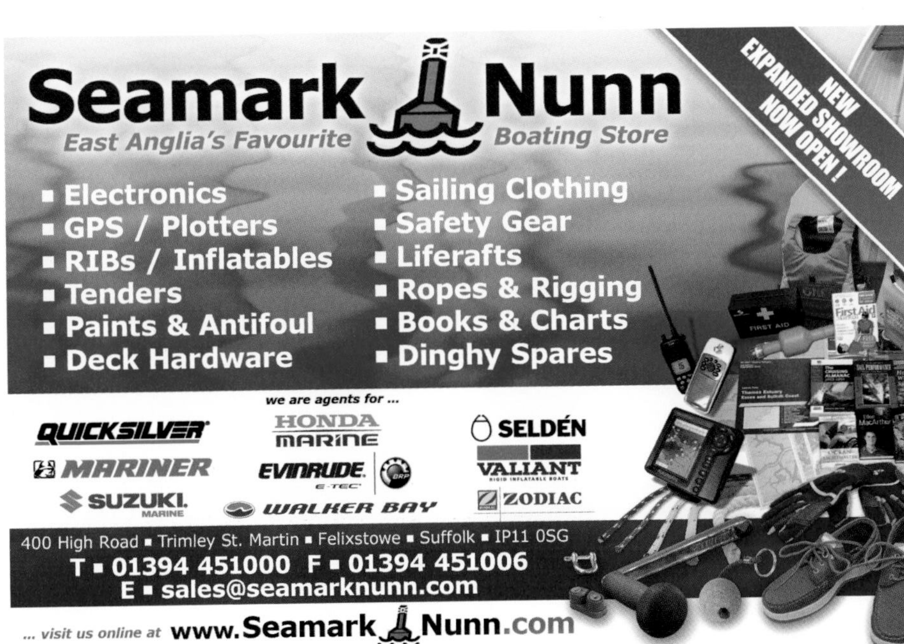
Seamark Nunn
East Anglia's Favourite Boating Store
NEW EXPANDED SHOWROOM NOW OPEN !
Electronics
GPS / Plotters
RIBs / Inflatables
Tenders
Paints & Antifoul
Deck Hardware
Sailing Clothing
Safety Gear
Liferafts
Ropes & Rigging
Books & Charts
Dinghy Spares
we are agents for ...
QUICKSILVER
HONDA MARINE
SELDÉN
MARINER
EVINRUDE E-TEC
VALIANT
SUZUKI MARINE
WALKER BAY
ZODIAC
400 High Road ■ Trimley St. Martin ■ Felixstowe ■ Suffolk ■ IP11 0SG
T ■ 01394 451000 F ■ 01394 451006
E ■ sales@seamarknunn.com
... visit us online at www.Seamark Nunn.com

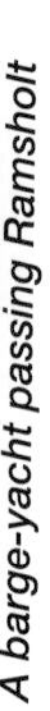
A barge-yacht passing Ramsholt

THE RIVER DEBEN

⌖ **51°58.2N 01°23.85E** Woodbridge Haven Buoy *(approximate and liable to be moved, see Approach and Entrance)*
Tides Woodbridge Haven -0:20
Woodbridge +0:40 *(differences from Harwich)*

The River Deben offers the visitor nine miles of navigation through an attractive and unspoilt part of Suffolk, from the shingle beach entrance and flat marshes behind, through gently rising countryside with woods and low red cliffs flanking the river in places, to the historic town of Woodbridge. In high season this is a busy river, although with no commercial traffic it offers a number of pleasant stopping places along the way, varying from moorings with convenient watering holes nearby, to peaceful anchorages and the marina at Woodbridge. The challenging entrance should not deter visitors from entering this river in which many find themselves spending longer than they intended having been seduced by its varied attractions.

Today the river is managed and the moorings leased from the Crown by the river's Fairways Committees. There are five of these, served by local people with a keen interest in the preservation of their river. There is also an active River Deben Association which aims to reconcile the interests of all concerned with the future of the river and its environs. There is a 10 knot speed limit in force from the entrance of the river up to abreast King's Fleet, with a short unrestricted section above this. From Falkenham Creek, just short of the Ramsholt moorings, the speed limit for the remainder of the river again becomes restricted at 8 knots.

APPROACH AND ENTRANCE

The entrance to the river can be located between two Martello Towers to the south and the conspicuous radar pylon and Bawdsey Manor with its green roofed towers, to the north. The entrance should not be attempted in strong onshore winds and never without up-to-date pilotage information, as the sandbanks and buoyage marking them shift often, particularly over winter or after storms. Don't let the entrance frighten you off though; with up-to-date knowledge and careful preparation it is not as difficult as it first looks.

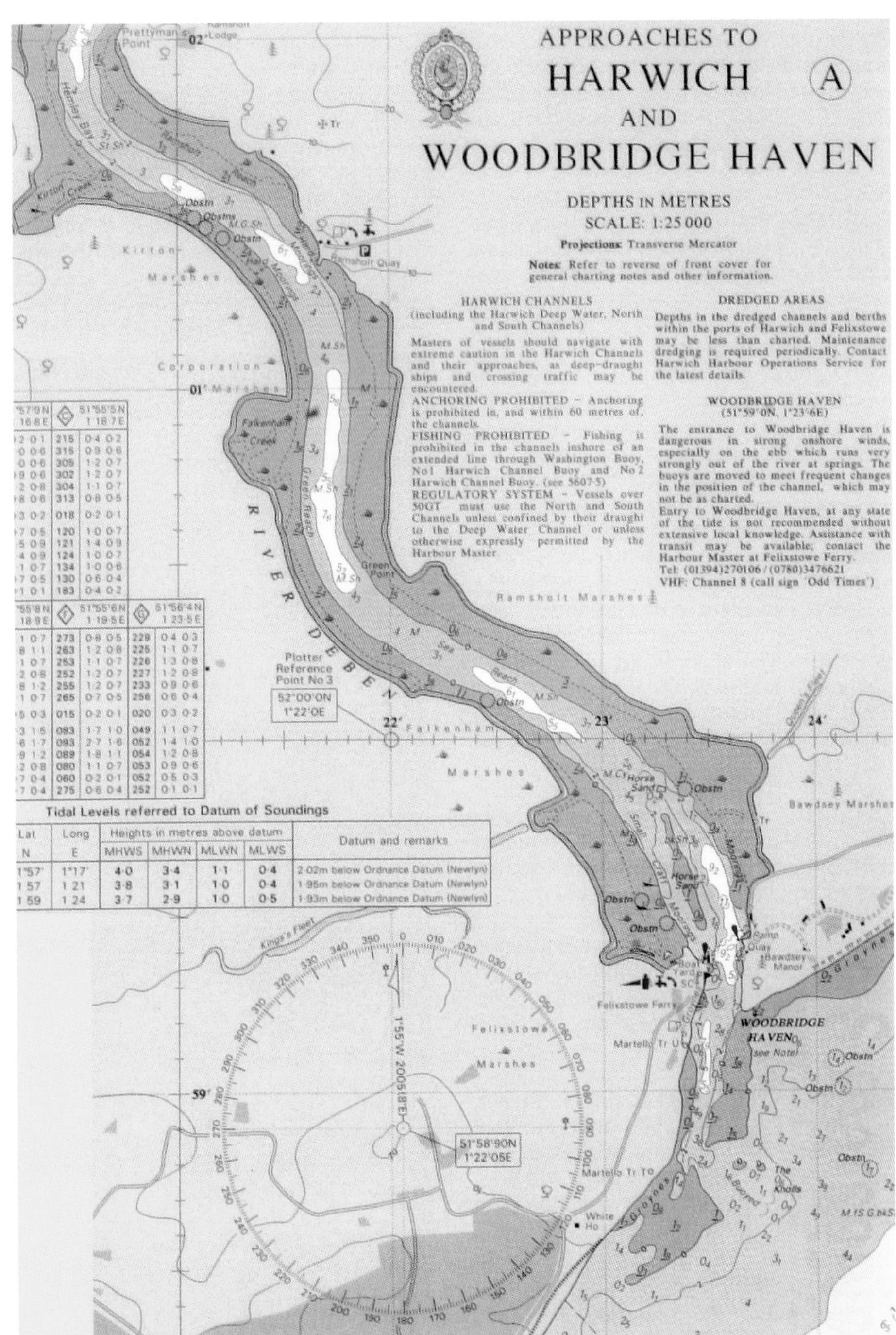

Tidal Levels referred to Datum of Soundings

Lat N	Long E	Heights in metres above datum				Datum and remarks
		MHWS	MHWN	MLWN	MLWS	
1°57′	1°17′	4·0	3·4	1·1	0·4	2·02m below Ordnance Datum (Newlyn)
1 57	1 21	3·8	3·1	1·0	0·4	1·95m below Ordnance Datum (Newlyn)
1 59	1 24	3·7	2·9	1·0	0·5	1·93m below Ordnance Datum (Newlyn)

Not to be used for navigation

Before entering you should first make sure you locate the Woodbridge Haven buoy and then follow the latest pilotage. At the time of writing, the recommended course is marked by a new red West Knoll can buoy and the green Mid Knoll conical buoy, which you should pass close to. Remember not to use lateral buoys like 'join the dots' and to ensure you know where to turn onto a new course. I have witnessed a few surprised faces as people round up on Mid Knoll buoy, only to find themselves in shallow water. There is also a PH buoy where the entrance to the river narrows to keep you off the shoals to port. The ebb tide can be particularly strong through this narrowest point and the newcomer is advised not to try to negotiate it against the tide. The depth over the bar at LWS can be less than a metre, so the best time for entry is between half-tide and HW. Once past the entrance, the drying Horse Sand is in mid-stream and for a visitor it is safer to take the better defined main channel to the eastern (Bawdsey) side of it until past the Horse Sand buoy, even if it is then necessary to turn back for a mooring on the Felixstowe-ferry side.

The latest information and a downloadable chart of the entrance can be found at www.debenentrance.com, where updates and information are also regularly posted. This is also available in printed form from local chandlers, harbour masters, clubs and marinas. If in any doubt you should contact the Harbour Master John White, or his assistant Stephen Read, prior to attempting to enter.

When leaving the river heading north, it is best to do this around HW or on the very early ebb, but when heading south this would leave a long slog against the tide, so if your auxiliary is up to stemming the flow (and you will often need to achieve more than 5 knots) you may choose to leave a couple of hours before HW and use the last of the tide to push you towards Landguard Point.

FELIXSTOWEFERRY

Felixstoweferry is too often passed by, which is a pity. It is a hive of waterside activity where professionals and amateurs share the river and shore-based facilities alike. There are a cluster of fishing huts on the shore rubbing shoulders with the club house, whilst fishing boats are moored in the bay alongside assorted odd house-boats and cruising and racing boats of all types and sizes. Ashore there is the boat-yard run by Andrew Moore, whose family

FELIXSTOWEFERRY SKIPPERS INFORMATION	
Harbour Master	John White, Tel: 01394 270106 Mobile: 07803 476621 or VHF Ch08 call-sign "Odd Times", or his assistant Stephen Read on Mobile: 07860 191768
Water	Standpipe at the top of the slip, or alongside by arrangement with the boatyard
Fuel	Available in cans from the boatyard or alongside by arrangement with the boatyard
Facilities	WC behind the sailing club. Showers may be available on request at FFSC when open
Boatyard	Felixstoweferry Boatyard, Tel: 01394 282173
Chandlery	At boatyard, currently limited but being expanded for 2007 season
Slips	By arrangement with boatyard for its slip where it can handle up to 14 tons, or for use of the Felixstoweferry Foreshore Trusts' slip, contact ESWSC or ask in the café
Scrubbing Posts	By arrangement with boatyard
Water Taxi	VHF Ch08, call-sign "Deben Ferry"

FELIXSTOWEFERRY SHORESIDE INFORMATION

Stores	The Ferry Café may be able to offer limited stores, otherwise the nearest shops are in Old Felixstowe where there is a Spar supermarket, butchers and bakers. There is also a good range of stores in Felixstowe town centre
Banks, PO	None, nearest Felixstowe
Public Tel.	On the roadside, 100 yards up past the sea wall
Club	Felixstoweferry Sailing Club is a small club focusing on dinghies, but also has many cruising members. The bar is open weekend afternoons and Mon, Wed, and Fri evenings. Website: www.ffsc.co.uk Email: enquiries@ffsc.co.uk (Sec. Gina Cooper), Tel: 01394 272466. The premises are shared by East Suffolk Water Ski Club whose members ski on the Deben upriver from Felixstoweferry, Website: www.eswsc.co.uk
Taxis	Coastal Taxis, Felixstowe, Tel: 01394 277777; AM Taxis, Trimley St. Mary Tel: 01394 285677
Accommodation	Fishermans Hall B&B near the Ferry Boat Inn, Tel: 01394 670909; otherwise in Felixstowe, where a variety is available
Tourist Info.	Nearest in Felixstowe, 91 Undercliff Road West. Tel: 01394 276770 Email: ftic@suffolkcoastal.gov.uk
Police	32 High Road West, Felixstowe. Tel: 01473 613500
Doctor	Dr. Davenport & Ptnrs., 201 Hamilton Road, Felixstowe. Tel: 01394 283197
Hospital	(A&E) Ipswich Hospital, Heath Road. Tel: 01473 712233
Dentist	Walton House Dental Practice, 218 High Street, Felixstowe. Tel: 01394 283419
Pharmacy	Nearest, Felixstowe town centre
USEFUL NUMBERS	
Yacht Surveys	Marine Surveys (East & South) Ltd. (Stephen Read), Tel: 01394 212512; T. J. Davey, Tel: 01394 282033

have run the yard for over 40 years, together with its chandlery (to be significantly extended in 2007), an art gallery next to the boatyard, fresh and smoked fish stalls, a café, public toilets, the sailing club and further along a couple of dozen interesting houses, two pubs and a small church.

MOORINGS

Felixstoweferry Boatyard will often be able to find you a vacant mooring for a short stop. If going ashore in your dinghy, it would be wise to ensure you have a reliable outboard due to the strong tidal flow which can run at up to 5 knots. The Boatyard now runs the foot ferry which will also act as a water-taxi for the mooring area on request. The Felixstoweferry Harbour Master, or his assistant, may also be able to offer assistance in finding a vacant mooring, but may alternatively direct you to anchor just upstream of the moorings on the western side, which will mean a fairly long dinghy trip to the ferry hard (please ask permission of the ferrymen prior to using it), or the shingle shore off the boatyard for landing.

CREW CHANGES AND TRAVEL

By car Felixstowe is easy to reach at the end of the A14 and Felixstoweferry just a short distance further on. There are four or

Felixstoweferry foreshore

five buses during the day (Mon-Sat) to Felixstowe and Woodbridge. For bus information contact Traveline East Anglia, Tel: 08706 082608 Website: www.traveline.org.uk. In peak season an open top bus runs on Sundays to Felixstowe. There is an hourly train service from Felixstowe to Ipswich for onward connections to London Liverpool Street and Norwich and coach connections. See Ipswich section in River Orwell chapter for further information. For train information contact 'One' Customer Services, Tel: 08456 007245 Website: www.onerailway.com

EATING AND DRINKING

The Ferry Café is well known for its excellent all-day breakfasts, kippers, fresh fish and chips and afternoon teas. It also offers a full menu of hot and cold meals and light snacks and is open all day Mon-Fri 0900-1600 and weekends 0730-1630. The café also has fresh milk and bread always available, as well as newspapers and magazines. Tel: 01394 276305. The Ferry Boat Inn, with real ales, is the first pub you come to standing back behind the green on the right of the road. Food is available for lunch and dinner every day. The bar is open 1100-1500 and 1730-2300, Sat 1100-2300, Sun 1200-2230 and food is served 1200-1400 and 1830-2100 (Sun evening 1800-2030). Tel: 01394 284203.

Further down, set back on the left towards the sea, is the friendly locals pub The Victoria Inn, serving real ales and excellent food, both downstairs and in the upstairs Seaview Restaurant with its magnificent views over the sea wall (also available for private functions). The bar is open 1100-1500 and 1800-2300 (Sun 2230) and food is served 1200-1430 and 1800-2100 (Fri and Sat 2130). Tel: 01394 271636.

TO SEE AND DO

There is an interesting walk of about eight miles around the Kings Fleet, which does however, require a map. Follow the sea wall north for a mile or so from the car park, then cut inland along a track to the north of the fleet marked Stour and Orwell Walk. The path bears away from the fleet after about a mile and passes through Deben Lodge Farm and onto a lane, where after a few hundred yards you turn left along another footpath, which branches left at a brook and back towards Old Felixstowe along Gulpher Road. You can then either follow this lane back to Felixstoweferry, or branch off short of the golf club and follow the sea wall. Alternatively, it is a pleasant dry-footed walk along the sea wall into Old Felixstowe about one and a half miles away.

There is a pleasant bathing beach backed by rows of beach huts just past the golf course about a mile along the sea wall. The Harbour Master John White, runs one-hour river trips on his launch 'Odd Times' in season. Tel: 01394 270106 Mobile: 07803 476621.

In Felixstowe you will find a range of entertainment and all the usual facilities you would expect in an English seaside town, including the Spa Pavilion Theatre, Box Office: 01394 282126; the pier, and a leisure centre (opposite the pier) with swimming pool, Tel: 01394 670411.

At the far end of Felixstowe is Landguard Fort which is an English Heritage site of 18th, 19th and 20th century fortifications and the site of the last opposed invasion of England in 1667. Landguard Fort is open daily, April to October, 1000-1700 (1800 in peak season), Tel: 01394 277767. Nearby is the Felixstowe Museum with a range of exhibits, open 1300-1730, Tel: 01394 674355.

BAWDSEY

Bawdsey lies across the mouth of the Deben from Felixstoweferry and can be reached by dinghy (landing on the beach, or by the foot ferry which runs on demand daily from April to September and week-ends in October. Ashore, Bawdsey Manor now offers accommodation in the manor and estate cottages, function facilities and a range of educational courses, including watersports (dinghy and powerboating) from the riverside watersports centre it shares with the yacht club, Tel: 01394 411633. On the waterside is Bawdsey Haven Yacht Club, Tel: (Secretary) 01394 410258, which is located in the premises of the old RAF Yacht Club.

Slip – apply at estate gatehouse, Tel: 01394 411633. For all other facilities and further information please refer to the Felixstoweferry section.

HISTORY

If you have time to look around whilst negotiating the entrance you will see two Martello towers from Napoleonic times very close to the beach to the south of the river mouth.

High on the right bank, standing out from the trees, is Sir Cuthbert Quilter's Victorian Bawdsey Manor, which became an RAF base shortly before the Second World War. At that time it played an important part in the development of radar and RDF equipment and until very recently Bawdsey Manor was still owned by the RAF, but they have now gone and the building is now used for functions and education. There are open days to see what remains of the radar research station and a group is hoping to create a permanent exhibition (see Bawdsey – To See and Do).

Behind Felixtoweferry lies Kings Fleet marshes now dammed off from the river but in early medieval times this was once the southern arm of a major naval port. For many centuries fishermen from here have departed the Deben in search of a living, some in locally built boats and in times past, travelling as far as Iceland.

CREW CHANGES AND TRAVEL

There are hourly buses during the day Monday to Saturday to Woodbridge and Ipswich. For information contact Traveline East Anglia. Tel 08706 082608 Website: www.traveline.org.uk

TO SEE AND DO

The experimental radar station in the grounds of Bawdsey Manor is open to the public on Sundays and some Bank Holidays in the summer months. Tel: 07821 162879. The buses from Bawdsey to Woodbridge stop on route at Sutton Hoo making a visit from here possible. Refer to Woodbridge section for Sutton Hoo information.

FELIXSTOWEFERRY TO RAMSHOLT

After Felixstoweferry there is no speed limit until nearing Ramsholt, although craft travelling at speed would soon feel rather out of place on such a peaceful, relaxing river. The local water-ski club uses the first reach, known as Sea Reach, with jumps which can be entertaining. From above the Felixstoweferry moorings to Ramsholt, the deepest water is generally towards the west bank. As you approach the bend in the river known as Green Point, the saltings and marshes give way to a more rural scene. As you turn into Green Reach you will pass Falkenham Creek to port and the speed limit reduces to 8 knots here. Some bring up to anchor hereabouts, although holding has been reported as variable. Ahead the Ramsholt Arms and the old barge quay will come into view on the eastern bank, together with numerous moorings, which the channel passes between.

RAMSHOLT

Ramsholt is considered by those fortunate enough to keep their boats here to be the best place on earth. It is, however, all private land belonging to the estate, but has a good pub, the well known Ramsholt Arms. There has been talk about starting to charge a landing fee and although this makes the yachting fraternity nervous, one could understand it, if the monies were to be used to maintain the quay and landing. A public footpath leads along the bank of the river here and a lane runs out to the north. The barge quay is one of many on the river that has seen much busier days of loading farm produce and bricks and unloading coal and other commodities from Newcastle and London. The flint tower on the big red brick church that can be seen just upstream of Ramsholt, has been used frequently in the past both as a beacon and a watchtower.

RAMSHOLT SKIPPERS INFORMATION	
Harbour Master	George Collins. Tel: 07930 304061 or 01394 384318
Water	Tap at Ramsholt Arms

MOORINGS

The Mooring Master at Ramsholt Quay, the helpful George Collins, is the man to see for a mooring and he is almost always around during the summer, often on his yacht 'Brio'. If he cannot find you a vacant buoy, which is rare, he may recommend you anchor at the edge of the fairway, or a mile upstream at The Rocks. The river wall footpath leads back to Ramsholt, but you will need stout shoes and a torch at night. This path extends from opposite Woodbridge virtually all the length of the river.

CREW CHANGES AND TRAVEL

You would need to walk the two and a half miles into Shottisham for hourly buses during the day (Monday to Saturday) to Woodbridge and Ipswich. For information contact Traveline East Anglia. Tel: 08706 082608 Website: www.traveline.org.uk

EATING AND DRINKING

The Ramsholt Arms is in a wonderful riverside setting and offers real ales and good food in pleasant surroundings lunchtimes and evenings. The bar is open for meals and drinks lunchtimes and evenings, seven days a week. Tel: 01394 411229.

RAMSHOLT SHORESIDE INFORMATION	
Stores	None
Banks, PO	None
Public Tel.	By Ramsholt Arms on the roadside
Club	None
Taxis	M & R Cars, Woodbridge, Tel: 08001 694269 or 01394 386191; Atlas Cars, Woodbridge, Tel: 08000 747094
Accommodation	B & B available at Ramsholt Arms. Tel: 01394 411229
Police	Grundisburgh Road, Woodbridge. Tel: 01473 613500
Doctor	Yates, Ball, Perkins & Stevens, Mill Hoo, Alderton. Tel: 01394 411641
Hospital	(A&E) Ipswich Hospital, Heath Road. Tel: 01473 712233
Dentist	The Dental Surgery, 5 Elm Street, Ipswich. Tel: 01473 231199
Pharmacy	Nearest, Woodbridge town centre

If you are feeling energetic, a two and a half mile walk along lanes and paths will take you to Shottisham where you will find the Sorrel Horse Inn with a range of real ales and excellent food in the restaurant. The bar is open 1200-1500 and 1800-2300 (Sat 1200-2300, Sun 1200-2230) and food is served every day 1200-1500 and 1800-2100, although booking is a good idea. Tel: 01394 411617.

TO SEE AND DO

There are many interesting walks along the river and one is a pleasant circular walk of about seven miles upriver, cutting inland along indistinct paths, to the village of Shottisham. Sustenance can then be sought at the delightful Sorrel Horse Inn, and you can make your way back via paths and lanes to Ramsholt Quay.

Woodbridge Haven ©PRPA

RAMSHOLT TO WALDRINGFIELD

Continuing upstream you shortly pass Kirton Creek to port soon after the Ramsholt moorings end. It is hard to believe that this and the tiny hamlet of Hemley beyond were once, in medieval times, a port significant for its salt production. Soon after the creek, the river bends sharply to starboard around Prettyman's Point and the buoyed channel follows the starboard bank past the popular anchorage known as The Rocks. Apart from the aesthetics of the location with its small sandy beach and tree-lined shore, this anchorage offers an alternative to Ramsholt Reach when the rare circumstance of wind strength and direction make this a bit lumpy. You should take care not to damage the fragile cliffs if landing here.

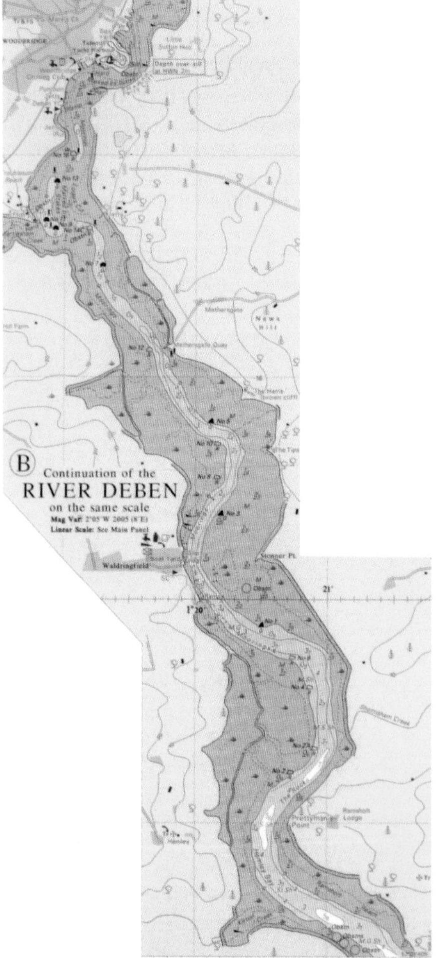

Not to be used for navigation

From The Rocks onwards the channel becomes considerably narrower and twists and turns its way. The visitor should ignore the banks and carefully follow the channel markers past Shottisham Creek to starboard before easing over to the port bank as you start to come into the moorings at Waldringfield. Dinghies and small craft occasionally use the water behind the tidal island off Stonner Point, but the main channel passes between the moorings, so don't be tempted to follow them.

WALDRINGFIELD

The moorings off Waldringfield spread for about a mile up the river, both before and after the waterside of the village. The scene here can vary from a peaceful haven in the calm of a weekday evening, to a frantic hive of activity on a Saturday afternoon or evening with dinghy races, sight-

WALDRINGFIELD SKIPPERS INFORMATION

Harbour Master	Mr. A. Davidson, Tel: 07944 586874
Water	Standpipes at boatyard and sailing club
Fuel	Diesel available from the boatyard around HW or from the garage one mile away at the other end of the village
Facilities	Showers may be available at WSC by arrangement
Boatyard	Waldringfield Boatyard, Tel: 01473 736260
Chandlery	At boatyard
Slip	40 ton crane at boatyard
Scrubbing Posts	For up to 30 feet (only suitable for fin keels) and can be booked at the bar of the The Maybush Inn

WALDRINGFIELD SHORESIDE INFORMATION

Stores	None
Banks, PO	None
Public Tel.	By The Maybush Inn
Club	Waldringfield Sailing Club open Wed evenings and Sat afternoons, Tel: 01473 736633; (Sec. Margaret Lake), Tel: 01394 283347 Website: www.waldringfieldsc.com
Taxis	M & R Cars, Woodbridge, Tel: 08001 694269 or 01394 386191; Atlas Cars, Woodbridge, Tel: 08000 747094
Police	Grundisburgh Road, Woodbridge. Tel: 01473 613500
Doctor	Dr. Haigh & Ptnrs., The Village Hall, Waldringfield. Tel: 01394 382157
Hospital	(A&E) Ipswich Hospital, Heath Road. Tel: 01473 712233
Dentist	Walton House Dental Practice, 218 High Street., Felixstowe. Tel: 01394 283419
Pharmacy	Nearest Woodbridge town centre

seers picnicking and swimming at the beach in front of the beach houses, and the 'Jahan' trip boat setting off full of passengers to cruise the river.

The waterside of the village of Waldringfield seems to purely exist for The Maybush Inn and the sailing club and boatyard that support the many dinghy sailors and yachtsmen here. They even provide a special church service for sailors during Deben Week when the Bishop comes across from Ramsholt on a yacht dressed overall. Local yachts and dinghies anchor in front of the clubhouse for the service whilst the brass band provides the music so that 'For those in peril' can sound out across the anchorage. The waterside of the village is very attractive and certainly shows no signs of the once thriving cement works here that was based on the local mud and chalk imported by barges from the Medway.

MOORINGS

Many of the moorings at Waldringfield belong to the local Fairways Committee or the club, but there are a number under the control of the boatyard. Visitors moorings are difficult to find in peak season, but you can either report ashore to find out whether any are vacant, or call the boatyard or Harbour Master who may be able to help. There is a little space in front of the sailing club where it is possible to anchor, otherwise you have to anchor above, or below the moorings. It is possible to land on the shingly beach at any time, but do not land directly in front of the club house, as this is reserved for bathers only (signs here indicate the prohibited stretch).

CREW CHANGES AND TRAVEL

Waldringfield is not a convenient place for transfers by public transport, but is only a 20 minute taxi ride from Woodbridge.

EATING AND DRINKING

The Maybush inn is a very popular venue by land and river as it is only three miles from Woodbridge and is situated right on the banks of the Deben. Although the scene has hardly changed through the years, the pub has had a recent major facelift. This has sadly stripped it of much of its old character, but somehow the increased amenity it now offers, together with the friendly service and the timeless bankside terrace, combine to quickly dispel any negative feelings. The pub has its own slipway where it is possible to land at any state of tide. The bar is open all day, seven days a week and serves food 1200-1430 and 1830-2130 (all day at weekends). Tel: 01473 736215.

TO SEE AND DO

Waldringfield Boatyard runs river trips in summer on MV Jahan, enquire at boatyard.

WALDRINGFIELD TO WOODBRIDGE AND WILFORD BRIDGE

Above Waldringfield the river steadily shallows and increasingly twists and turns its way to Woodbridge, requiring careful attention both to pilotage and the state of tide as you pass through the attractive countryside. Just upstream of Waldringfield at the first bend are two popular anchorages at The Tips and The Hams, with dry landing towards high water on the east bank. These are followed shortly after by the moorings off Methersgate Quay. This is another of those used by barges until the beginning of the 20th century, but it is now a private quay with no public access from land, or river. There is a short gap in the moorings before the Woodbridge moorings start again just as you start the sharp turn to port into Troublesome Reach. Actually, with sufficient tide and attention to the lateral buoys, this reach is no trouble at all. The same cannot be said of the short cut here called Loders Cut, which although clearly marked, I would not recommend to other than shoal draft craft near high water.

At the end of Troublesome Reach you pass the entrance to Martlesham Creek to port, just as the river turns sharply to starboard past Kyson Point and onto Woodbridge. After Kyson Point the density of moorings increases, although most of them dry at low water and Woodbridge itself comes into view, with the bright white tide mill ahead. With the clubs and boatyards crowding the waterside and strollers promenading on the riverside walk, on a calm summer day it can feel like you are sailing across the village green. You almost expect to have to duck for a cricket ball.

The scene can appear quite busy with moorings all over the river, most of them drying at low water and although the channel is clearly marked, it can be difficult for the visitor to follow amongst the mooring buoys. For guidance, the channel tucks in quite close to the west bank by the yards and quay before turning sharply to starboard to round the Tide Mill and Tide Mill Yacht Harbour.

Beyond the Tide Mill the channel is buoyed to the head of navigation at Wilford Bridge for those wishing to continue on the tide. The channel is very tortuous but well marked and carries about 2 metres on a neap tide as far as the Granary Yacht Harbour. In fact the buoyage upstream has been improved in recent years and some of the buoys have been given back their old names from barging days.

MARTLESHAM CREEK

For those who seek a quiet haven a little away from civilisation and can happily take the mud, the marks can be followed up the tortuous Martlesham Creek, to the boatyard here. In times past this place was infamous for its band of smugglers and nobody seems to have told them about changing fashions, as rumour has it

MARTLESHAM CREEK SKIPPERS INFORMATION	
Harbour Master	Mike, Tel: 01394 384727 or Mobile: 07850 754726
Water	Standpipe at the top of the slip and on staging berths
Electricity	On staging berths only
Fuel	Available in cans or alongside at high water by arrangement with the boatyard
Facilities	WC and shower at boatyard
Internet	Broadband available for permanent berths only
Boatyard	Most boatyard facilities available on request – contact Harbour Master
Chandlery	None, although calor gas available
Slips	Slip and crane for up to 10 tons and 37 feet at boatyard

MARTLESHAM CREEK SHORESIDE INFORMATION	
Stores	Nearest in Martlesham Heath, village store one and a half miles, Tesco superstore two miles, open 24 hours (1000-1600 Sun)
PO	At village store
Bank	Nearest, Woodbridge but cash machines at Tesco
Public Tel.	Near The Red Lion pub
Taxis	M & R Cars, Woodbridge, Tel: 08001 694269 or 01394 386191; Atlas Cars, Woodbridge, Tel: 08000 747094
Police	Grundisburgh Road, Woodbridge. Tel: 01473 613500
Doctor	Dr. A. Schurr & Ptnrs., 23 The Square, Martlesham Heath. Tel: 01473 610028
Hospital	(A&E) Ipswich Hospital, Heath Road. Tel: 01473 712233
Dentist	The Dental Surgery, 5 Elm Street, Ipswich. Tel: 01473 231199
Pharmacy	Nearest, Woodbridge town centre

that this continued right into the early 20th century. The upper parts of the creek hold a mere trickle at low tide, so you will need to ensure adequate height of tide to explore here. If in doubt about your depth, check with Martlesham Creek Boatyard before negotiating the creek, or go in towards the top of the tide.

At the boatyard at the top of the creek you will find yourself in a tranquil rural setting among 32 acres of woodland presided over by the ever helpful Mike, who jealously protects the friendly and traditional atmosphere. Mike's father started the yard in the 1960's when he bought the land and quay purely as somewhere to keep his own boat, but over the years this has extended to the boatyard we see today, with 60 to 70 moorings, hard-standing and simple facilities.

MOORINGS

There are mud berths here on pontoons, staging and moorings and often space for a visitor, either alongside the pontoon or on the trots off the yard. Call to make prior arrangements.

CREW CHANGES AND TRAVEL

Although a little away from Woodbridge, it is only five minutes by taxi to Woodbridge Station for trains to Ipswich and onward connections to Norwich or London Liverpool Street, or coaches nationwide. See Ipswich section of River Orwell chapter for further information.

EATING AND DRINKING

Martlesham is well served for eating and drinking and The Red Lion pub is only 10 minutes walk from the boatyard. Take the track up through the woods to the lane and turn right, the pub is at the T-junction at the end of the lane and offers real ales and an extensive menu. The bar is open every day 1100-2300 (2230 Sundays) and serves food 1100-2200 (1200-2130 Sundays). Tel: 01394 382169.

Turning left at the Red Lion will take you up the hill into Martlesham Heath. Take the right fork for the village (left for the superstore) where just short of the village store is The Black Tiles pub, which is of a trendy modern appearance and again offers real ales and an extensive menu. The bar is open every day 1100-2300 (2400 Friday and Saturday) and serves food 1200-1430 and 1730-2130 (all day weekends). Tel: 01473 624038.

TO SEE AND DO

It is possible for the energetic to take a very pleasant riverside two mile walk into Woodbridge directly from the boatyard. For those without the time, or inclination, just up the track through the woods from the boatyard and left on the lane is Martlesham church with its ancient wall painting of St. Christopher.

For those looking for a longer walk, there is a well way-marked five mile circular walk from the boatyard, past the church and out through Walk Farm Woods and across Martlesham Common with its tumuli to The Black Tiles. You can then either head back down the lane, or round the back of the village through Broomfields Farm to The Red Lion where a path leads back to the boatyard. On a Sunday this walk could be extended by a mile to take in the aviation museum at Martlesham Heath Control Tower Museum not far from the superstore, open Sundays, April to October, 1400-1630 admission free. Tel: 01473 624510.

WOODBRIDGE

Woodbridge is an historic town with a very traditional feel and many interesting buildings and has a certain charm to it. It offers good shops and many excellent places for eating and refreshment, as well as a number of visitor attractions.

As you come into Woodbridge on the river, the first building of note is the pavilion-style structure of the Deben Yacht Club on the sea wall, recently raised to protect it against flooding. Then comes the pontoons, jetties and buildings of Everson's boatyard and the Deben Rowing Club. Run by the Everson family from 1889 until 1969, the boatyard has been taken over in recent years by a local consortium of enthusiasts to protect the services it offers and the site itself from development. Here

WOODBRIDGE SKIPPERS INFORMATION

TIDE Mill YACHT HARBOUR ⚓⚓⚓⚓

Harbour Master	Tel: 01394 385745 or VHF Ch80 call-sign "Tide Mill Yacht Harbour" (VHF Ch37 is sometimes also used for berthing operations) Email: info@tidemillyachtharbour.co.uk
Water	On pontoons
Electricity	On pontoons
Fuel	Diesel berth just inside entrance
Facilities	WC, showers and laundry (new 2007)
Internet	Free wireless
Boatyard	Full range of boatyard services at marina. Tel: 01394 385745
Chandlery	Some at marina, otherwise nearest are Seamark Nunn in Trimley St. Martin (15 miles), Tel: 01394 451000 or Fox's, Ipswich (20 miles), see Bourne Bridge section of River Orwell chapter
Slips	Crane up to 16 tons

OTHER

Moorings	Everson's, Tel: 01394 385786; Charter Marine, Tel: 01394 610993; Robertson's, Tel: 01394 382305
Water	At yards
Facilities	Public WC by sea wall, showers available at Deben Pool (see To See and Do section)
Boatyards	Everson's, Tel: 01394 385786; Charter Marine, Tel: 01394 610993; Robertson's, Tel: 01394 382305; Mike Clark, Tel: 01394 387838
Slips	Everson's (crane 7 tons), Tel: 01394 385786; Charter Marine (crane 6 tons), Tel: 01394 610993; Robertson's (travel hoist 60 tons), Tel: 01394 382305
Scrubbing Posts	Everson's, Tel: 01394 385786

WOODBRIDGE SHORESIDE INFORMATION

Stores	Woodbridge has a diverse and extensive range of shops, but for general supplies there is a Budgens supermarket in the Turban Centre (five minutes walk) open 0800-2000 (1000-1600 Sun). The Woodbridge Fine Food Company's delicatessen in New Street is worth a visit if you have time.
Banks	All main banks in town
PO	At Budgens
Public Tel.	At Railway Station
Clubs	Deben Yacht Club, Tel: 01394 384440; Woodbridge Cruising Club, Tel: 01394 386737 Website: www.woodbridgecruisingclub.co.uk
Taxis	M & R Cars, Woodbridge, Tel: 08001 694269 or 01394 386191; Atlas Cars, Woodbridge, Tel: 08000 747094
Accommodation	There is a wide range of accommodation in and around the town from guest houses to inns and hotels. Enquire at the Tourist Information Centre
Tourist Info.	At the Railway Station. Tel: 01394 382240
Police	Grundisburgh Road, Woodbridge. Tel: 01473 613500
Doctor	Dr. Haigh & Ptnrs., Framfield House, 42 St Johns Street, Woodbridge. Tel: 01394 382157
Hospital	(A&E) Ipswich Hospital, Heath Road. Tel: 01473 712233
Dentist	The Dental Surgery, 5 Elm Street, Ipswich. Tel: 01473 231199
Pharmacy	Nearest Woodbridge town centre

USEFUL NUMBERS

Charts and Navigational Equipment	Small Craft Deliveries, Wilford Bridge Rd. Tel: 01394 382600
Riggers	Atlantic Rigging operates from the Tide Mill Yacht Harbour. Tel: 01394 610324
Sailmakers	Suffolk Sails is next to the Tide Mill and specialises in cruising sails and offers a repair service (often open seven days in season). Tel: 01394 386323
Traditional Yacht Fittings	Classic Marine. Tel: 01394 380390 Website: www.classicmarine.co.uk
Yacht Brokers	Temple Marine, Tel: 01394 383108; Andy Seedhouse Boat Sales, Tel: 01394 387833
Yacht Deliveries	Small Craft Deliveries. Tel: 01394 382600

they concentrate on moorings and storage, but offer some general yard services as well. Further up the sea wall and set back a little is Woodbridge Cruising Club. Passing the bandstand-like shelter we come to the recently restored town quay and the yard of Charter Marine Engineering, which in addition to engineering, offers a full range of boatyard services. As the river swings to starboard you pass the large white structure of the tide mill and the tidal ponds, which now form the Tide Mill Yacht Harbour. Shortly after the harbour the next boatyard you come to at Lime Kiln Quay is Robertson's Boatyard. The yard was established in 1887 and offers all general boatyard services with

Woodbridge Quay and Tide Mill

one of the largest slips in the area capable of handling up to 60 tons with its travel hoist. There is also a workshop and the yard can make timber spars and prepare and repair rigging. They have dredged the area of its jetty berths making them particularly suitable for the Dutch and Thames barges often to be seen here.

Mike Clark is also to be found in the Kestrel Shed at Robertson's yard, where he offers repair services for small craft in GRP or wood. Just behind Robertson's yard is Classic Marine, a chandlery dealing in traditional yacht fittings, where there is also a fabrication shop for bronze and stainless fittings if it can't be found in the company's catalogue.

MOORINGS

Woodbridge often has over 1,000 visiting yachtsmen a year, partly as it is possible to make a weekend visit from neighbouring rivers, despite the restrictions imposed by timing the tricky river entrance. Everson's Boatyard may be able to assist with drying moorings and there are several dinghy landing places along the river wall and since the works on the town quay, it may be possible by prior arrangement with Charter Marine, to lay alongside there. Robertson's Boatyard has drying jetty berths, best suited for Dutch and Thames barges, but berths can be found for visitors wishing to take to the mud.

Otherwise, moorings afloat can be found in the Tide Mill Yacht Harbour, where even deep fin keeled yachts can lie afloat on finger pontoons in this recently extended, peaceful and well sheltered harbour. The sill at the entrance carries over 2.5 metres at HWS and the tide gauge is marked in metres to give the depth over the sill.

There are waiting buoys off the entrance to accommodate early arrivals. There has never been much negative comment possible about this harbour, with its high standards and almost inland waterways feel among grassy banks, together with its close proximity to the town, except the constant gripe that its facilities let it down. Now director Richard Kember has shown me the plans and around the building site for a new state-of-the-art block to contain offices, showers, WC's and laundry, opening for the 2007 season, which should make this a standard-setting marina in every respect.

CREW CHANGES AND TRAVEL

Woodbridge is a convenient place for crew changes with regular trains to Ipswich and onward connections to Norwich or London Liverpool Street, or coaches nationwide. See Ipswich section of River Orwell chapter for further information. For train information contact 'One' Customer Services. Tel: 08456 007245 Website: www.onerailway.com

EATING AND DRINKING

Woodbridge has a good range of eating and drinking establishments, so I shall just provide information on a selection, but would advise having a look round the town as there are many more.

The Quayside Café located on the quay near the station provides teas, coffee, snacks and English breakfasts. The Waterfront Café by the Tide Mill is far from an ordinary café and particularly known for its seafood, open in season 0900-1730 every day, Tel: 01394 610333. The Captain's Table is a well thought of brasserie in pleasant surroundings with a varied menu and has been awarded the Michelin Bib Gourmand. It is at 3 Quay Street and is open Tues to Sat (and Bank Holiday Sundays) for morning coffee, lunch, afternoon tea and dinner, Tel: 01394 383145. The Galley is another up-market restaurant in Market Hill open every day for lunch and Mon to Sat for dinner, Tel: 01394 380055.

There are also a variety of pubs and inns in Woodbridge to suit all tastes, many serving food, including The Anchor Inn in Quay Street, The Cherry Tree Inn in Cumberland Street, the ancient Kings Head in Market Hill and The Old Mariner in New Street.

TO SEE AND DO

Woodbridge Tide Mill is open 1100-1700 at Easter, weekends in April and October and every day May to September. Although it no longer produces flour, it has been restored and the wheel is turned occasionally when tides are right. Admission £2.00, children free. Tel: 01728 746959.

Woodbridge Museum is a local and town museum in Market Hill and is open Easter to October, Thurs to Sun (and Bank Holiday Mon), 1000-1600. Admission £1.00, children £0.30. Tel: 01394 380502.

Suffolk Punch Heavy Horse Museum telling the story of these beautiful local working horses, is on the first floor of the Shire Hall in Market Hill and is open Easter to September, Tues, Thurs and Sat 1400-1700. Tel: 01394 380643.

Buttrums Windmill still has turning sails and is regarded as one of the finest remaining tower windmills. It is five minutes walk from the town centre in Burkitt Road and is open on Sundays and Bank Holidays in April to September (and Saturdays May to August) 1400-1730. Tel: 01473 264755.

If you have the time, no visitor to Woodbridge should miss a visit to the Sutton Hoo site and exhibition. The finding in 1939 of ships' rivets in an ancient burial mound by archaeologist Basil Brown, led to the discovery of an Anglo-Saxon burial ship. The site had fortunately been missed by grave robbers and had lain undisturbed for some 1300 years. Careful excavation unearthed what is now believed to be the burial ship of King Raedwald, containing his most treasured possessions and

HISTORY

Although the area is best known for the Sutton Hoo burial ship dating from the Anglo-Saxon period, finds have been made around the Deben dating back to the Neolithic era 2500-1700 BC. The town of Woodbridge can date itself back to a settlement in the 10th century. Walking through the town one can see evidence of more recent history in the buildings in the centre, where the Kings Head claims to be the oldest building.

The maritime history of the town can be dated back at least as far as the first record of it as a port in 1350, but its importance peaked at the height of its shipbuilding boom in the 17th century. Woodbridge then saw the launching from local yards of many sailing ships over 400 tons, including records of fourth rate men-of-war of 600 tons and 70 guns being improbably launched from Lime Kiln Quay. Although shipbuilding then went into decline, it continued with the building of trading brigs and schooners right up to the 19th century.

By the end of the 18th century the port was silting and in decline, but even after the railway came in 1859 it still recorded 400 ship movements a year. An interesting local story is that Henry Loder, a local printer, was forced to pay £100 libel damages in the 1870's, which so incensed the people of Woodbridge that they set up a fund to pay the damages for him. He felt unable to accept the money, so instead paid for the dredging of a cut, since known as Loder's Cut, to try to make access easier and so help keep the ailing port alive, but it was to no avail and it continued to rapidly decline until in 1882 it was declassified as a port.

giving an insight into everyday life in these times. The site is now under the management of the National Trust with a magnificent visitor and exhibition centre and well worth a day trip. Although it is possible to take a dinghy across to Ferry Cliff and walk up via footpaths to the visitor centre and site, this is not a very practical proposition. Buses run from the town centre to either the entrance or right to the visitor centre. For bus information contact Traveline East Anglia, Tel: 08706 082608 Website: www.traveline.org.uk and it is only a five minute taxi ride. The site is open every day 1030-1730, but the visitor and exhibition centre is only open 1100-1700 every day during school holidays, in season Wed-Sun (otherwise weekends only). Admission £5.50, children £2.50. Tel: 01394 389700.

The Riverside Theatre is by the station and comprises a complex of theatre, restaurant and bar. The theatre is most

The Upper Deben

MELTON SKIPPERS INFORMATION	
Harbour Master	Mel Skeet, Tel: 01394 386327 Email: mel@granary-yacht-harbour.co.uk
Water	On pontoons
Electricity	On pontoons
Facilities	WC's and showers
Boatyard	Full range of boatyard services at Melton Boatyard, Tel: 01394 386327; R. Larkman Ltd., Tel: 01394 382943
Chandlery	Small chandlery at Melton Boatyard
Slips	Melton Boat Club has a slipway, Melton Boatyard a huge 36 ton travel hoist and Larkman's a 12.5 ton crane

commonly used during the season as a cinema and offers dinner and film packages. Tel: Box office 01394 382174.

To lose a little youthful energy, Deben Swimming Pool is in Station Road (and also offers showers for non-swimming visitors). For opening times and prices, Tel: 01394 384763.

Many good walks can be had around the interesting town itself, but if you favour countryside, there is good walking to be had following the river north to Wilford Bridge and if feeling particularly energetic, the path continues on along the river and around fish ponds before returning to the town, or to Wilford Bridge. The Tourist Information Centre has pamphlets on a variety of walks.

MELTON

Woodbridge runs into Melton at its northern boundary, but Melton maintains a fierce independence. Melton has much to offer the inquisitive boat owner, particularly those looking for somewhere to leave or haul out a boat, or needing repairs. As already advised, if going past Woodbridge, care is needed to stick to the marked channel, although this carries about 2 metres even at neaps as far as the Granary Yacht Harbour. After Lime Kiln Quay, the next place of note is New Quay now occupied by Melton Boat Club, a DIY-style club for motor and sail cruisers with yard, tidal moorings and slipway.

Beyond here you will see the large former granary building which gives its name to the small Granary Yacht Harbour. Here the friendly and jovial Mel Skeet presides over both this and the adjacent Melton Boatyard, which in addition to general repairs and maintenance, specialises in slurry and grit blasting, osmosis treatment and the epoxy treatment of metal boats. Close by on the upstream side is Larkman's yard which offers boat storage in several acres of well organised yard and maintenance and repair services, including rigging.

MOORINGS

Granary Yacht Harbour has some mud berths, but the harbour itself has been dredged so many can lie afloat here to pontoons. Although there are only about 25 berths, visitors can often be accommodated by prior arrangement.

EATING AND DRINKING

The Wilford Bridge pub and restaurant is just across the road from the landing steps to port before the bridge. It offers real ales and a huge choice of home-cooked lunchtime and evening meals. The bar is open 1100-2300 (Sun 1200-2230) with food available 1145-1400 and 1830-2130 (weekends and Bank Holidays all day). Tel: 01394 386141.

MELTON SHORESIDE INFORMATION

There is a newsagent in Melton supplying basic groceries. Otherwise refer to Woodbridge section.

HARWICH HARBOUR

Harwich Harbour and Shotley ©PRPA

⊕ **52°55'.3N 01°18'.5E** *(off Landguard Buoy on recommended yacht track)*
Tides +0:00 *(differences from Harwich)*

Harwich Harbour is a good refuge port for the area and forms the entrance to both the rivers Orwell and Stour (the subject of separate chapters). This chapter will deal with the areas up to the end of Felixstowe container terminal in the Orwell and the end of Parkeston Quay in the Stour, above which you should refer to the relevant chapter for the river in question. As yachts are excluded from much of the Felixstowe shore and from the Parkeston Quay area, there are only two places of interest to the yachtsman, Harwich itself and Shotley Point opposite on the Shotley Peninsula which separates the two rivers.

When I first visited Harwich harbour in the 1970s, it was a very different place. Felixstowe Container Terminal stretched little further north than the old dock and there was room to drop the hook in the Orwell just to the north of it for a short stop (as they did in Arthur Ransome's: "We Didn't Mean to Go to Sea", although I don't know where they got the fuel after they rowed ashore!). Having extended the terminal as far north as it reasonably can, they are now in the process of extending south almost to Landguard Point. Parkeston Quay was also then much smaller and on the opposite shore HMS Ganges was only just closing down. Shotley Marina didn't exist, meaning there was again a useful anchorage at Stone Heaps, I believe about where the northern end of the marina now extends to. However, Harwich itself has changed very little in the time I have been sailing here, with just a little development here and there. Despite all the changes and considerably more traffic, the harbour is still of great use to the boating visitor, although in a different and perhaps more convenient manner.

Now just a short rant from my soapbox. With the separation of the life and industry of the harbour by that very harbour itself into the Harwich, Felixstowe and Shotley shores, it would seem to be in the interests of all parties to ensure efficient passenger transport between the three, both for work and leisure purposes and to maintain a harbour community. Since the demise of a full service many years ago, this has been restricted to a small seasonal passenger ferry running half a dozen services a day. Plans have been made to extend this to a year-round regular ferry with a capacity of I believe, some 120 persons, but I understand the landing pontoons will not be suitable for the disabled and will be positioned such that the planners accept that up to 20% of days will be lost to bad weather. A ferry service will not be regularly used unless it has a very high level of reliability, but I have no doubt that when the service fails they will put it down to lack of support rather than poor planning and lack of investment in landings. One also hopes that the operators who have struggled to make a success of the seasonal ferry will either be involved in the new service, or be looked after when the new service comes in.

APPROACH AND ENTRANCE

Due to the needs of commercial shipping, the deep-water channel into Harwich is very well marked by lit buoys from well outside the harbour, but there is also a recommended track for yachts entering the harbour which you should follow. The harbour authorities here are fairly helpful to, and forgiving of, small craft despite the commercial nature of the port, so we should co-operate and keep to the recommended tracks, unlike some I have seen coming in under spinnaker down the main channel and then tacking up river too close to the docks.

Port operations are managed by Harwich Radio, call-sign "Harwich VTS" on VHF Ch71 and it is recommended that yachts listen in on this channel for information on ship movements, particularly those of the high speed ferry. It is not necessary for yachts to report to Harwich VTS (unless you are over 50 tons) and in fact you are requested not to do so unless in emergency (e.g. you hear of a ship movement and do not think you will be able to get out of the way in time, or you are in poor visibility and have serious concerns). They can also be telephoned in extreme circumstances on 01255 243000.

Approaching from the north you will need to cross the main shipping channel off Landguard Point and you are asked to do this at right angles near Inner Ridge PH buoy (between Rolling Ground SH and Platters south cardinal buoys on the north side), before proceeding in to the south of the channel on the recommended track to Landguard buoy. This is in any case the most appropriate place to cross, as if any closer to landward, Landguard Point may obscure some outbound ship movements.

If approaching from seaward you need to identify and pass between the Cork Sand PH beacon and Cork Sand Yacht beacon (north cardinal), before heading in to the south of the main channel towards Inner Ridge PH and Landguard buoys.

From the south after passing The Naze, do not stray too far into the shallows of Pennyhole Bay. In the summer a Yellow buoy is placed here to remind us. Also keep a good look out for the sometimes very poorly marked pot-markers here. Although the majority are well marked, I have come across half submerged two-pint milk bottles. You should make for and identify Landguard buoy before proceeding into the harbour.

Once you have identified Landguard buoy from whatever direction, you should keep to landward of the PH buoys as far as Grisle and Guard. To port you should note the dangers of Cliff Foot Rocks off the breakwater at Blackman's Head which have little more than a metre over them at

LAT and further in Harwich Shelf, although the latter is marked from April to October by a small east cardinal buoy. If heading for Harwich itself you can then head in directly from short of Guard to the harbour, making sure you keep south of the main channel and north of Harwich Shelf. If heading to Shotley, or up the Orwell or Stour, cross the main channel directly between Guard and Shotley Spit south cardinal buoy. Then if heading for Shotley, or the Stour, keep to the north of the main channel.

HARWICH

Harwich is a vibrant international port with the bustling Parkeston Quay to the west and the lively seaside town of Dovercourt to the south. However, the attractive old town has for some time seemed to struggle for a purpose of its own despite the prosperity of its near neighbours and Trinity House having its main operational centre here. Harwich does however have its own tourism industry and an active local community and there are now a number of plans in the pipeline for regeneration.

Firstly, there are plans to fill in Bathside Bay to massively extend the port facilities at Parkeston. If this happens, agreement has been reached that a new small boat harbour will be built prior, both to separate the dock operations from the town and to provide replacement moorings, largely for the Harwich and Dovercourt Sailing Club. These plans would involve the demolition of the outer two-thirds of the old railway pier, construction of a new breakwater with an entrance near the Trinity House pier and the dredging and fitting out (with pontoons) of the new harbour. The club has told me that the local authorities and the port owners Hutchison Ports have been helpful and co-operative in putting together a plan that all can accept, which is a rare good news story and to be applauded. This would radically change the area to the west of Harwich Old Town, but not necessarily for the worse. The changes would also in time create a very different sailing club from the friendly DIY-style former railway workers club, but after some 80 years in existence it is good to hear the club's future and the amenity appears protected, particularly as it has already been moved a few years back from Patricks Quay for a previous port extension and road building programme.

In addition, there are further ambitious plans for the waterside of Harwich Old Town. As Trinity House now has its new operational offices and workshops, this releases large areas of land and waterside it previously occupied, which if put together with the old Navyard Wharf, provide a hugely valuable area for potential development. Ideas include a marina and waterside residential development. Again we shall watch in interest and let us hope that this will not become purely another expensive high-rise second-home development and that it will contribute not only financially, but actively to the life of Harwich. We shall also watch with interest to see if Harwich Town Sailing Club by the green is affected by the development and if so, we hope suitable arrangements are made to ensure its existence and the amenity it provides are protected.

MOORINGS

The harbour authority has recently put in a yacht mooring pontoon on Halfpenny Pier which is a great boating asset, whether for a short stop or for overnight and again highlights the authorities continuing efforts to accommodate those in small boats wherever possible, despite the commercial pressures on the area. The L-shaped pontoon has been placed to the west of the pier and also accommodates the foot ferry landing and an area where small fishing boats can load and unload. As you approach the pontoon, the yacht moorings are the outer 50 metres on the outside and between the piles on the inside and the first part of the inner leg and all are clearly marked. You may raft up to three deep and it's first come, first served, with no bookings. The pontoon can be a bit bouncy with all the passing traffic, so you should fender well, the inside

Not to be used for navigation

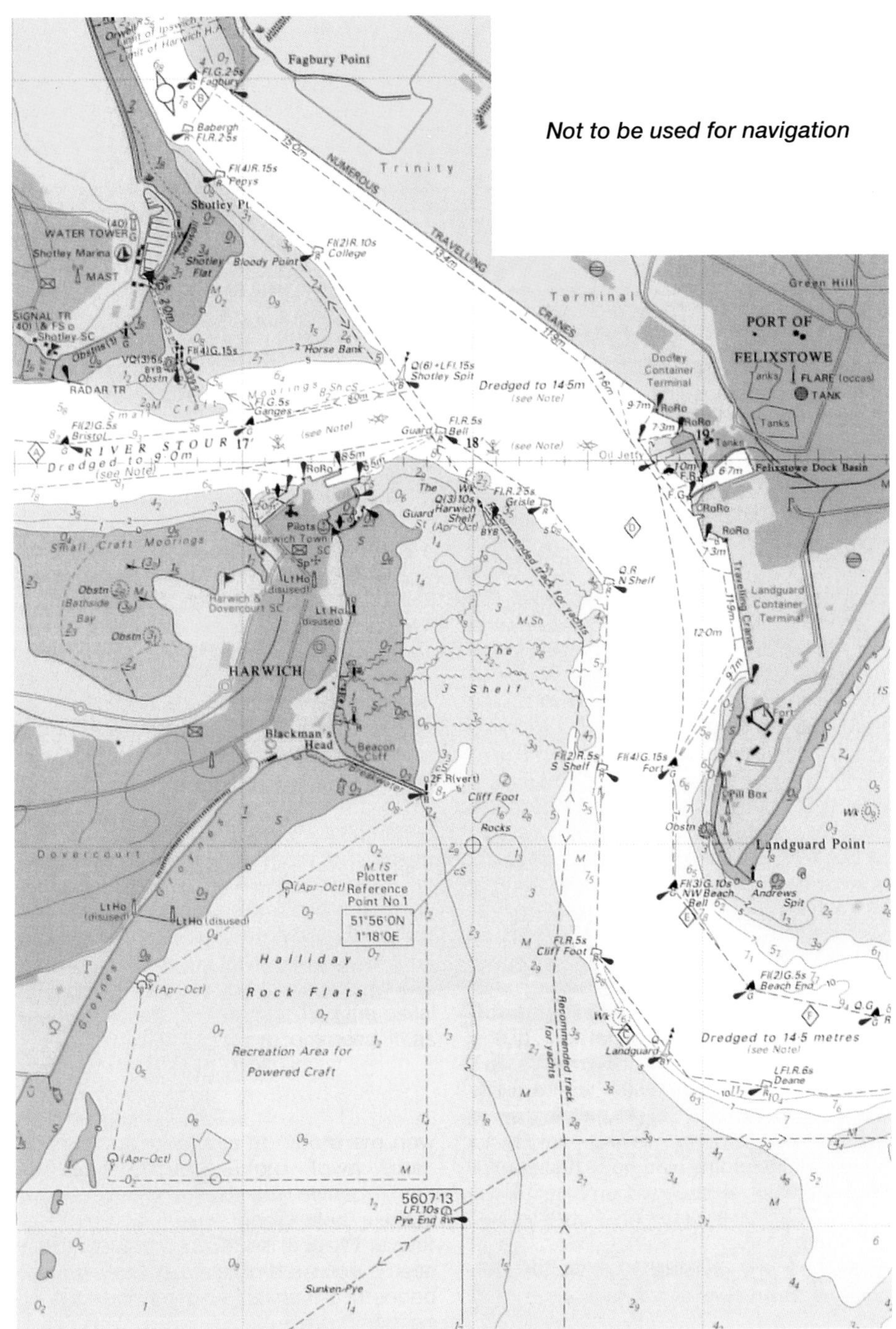

HARWICH SKIPPERS INFORMATION

Harbour Master	Tel: 01255 243030 Email: harbourmaster@hha.co.uk
Water	Tap for filling cans at foot of Halfpenny Pier
Electricity	None
Fuel	None convenient
Facilities	New blocks offering WC and showers for those staying overnight, plus public WC across the road opposite the pier
Boatyard	None
Chandlery	Harwich Chandlers Ltd. in Kings Head Street opposite the pier. Tel: 01255 504061
Slip	Crane at HDSC
Website	www.hha.co.uk

berths being slightly more comfortable. The pontoon is free for stops during the day, but from 1600-0900 you will be charged for an overnight stop (£10 for a 10 metre in 2006). Otherwise Harwich and Dovercourt Sailing Club may be able to let you use a drying mooring in Bathgate Bay.

CREW CHANGES AND TRAVEL

Both the train and bus stations are five minutes walk away at the south west end of the Old Town, which combined with it's proximity to the sea, makes Harwich a good place for a crew changeover. There are regular buses throughout the day to the villages along the south of the Stour to Manningtree and to Clacton. For bus information contact Traveline East Anglia, Tel: 08706 082608 Website: www.traveline.org.uk. There are regular trains, hourly or better (slightly less on Sundays) to Manningtree and onwards to London Liverpool Street. For information contact 'One' Customer Services, Tel: 08456 007245 Website: www.onerailway.com or National Rail Enquiries, Tel: 08457 484950 Website: www.nationalrail.co.uk

There is a seasonal foot ferry to Shotley and Felixstowe, running half a dozen trips every day from Easter to early September and then at weekends to the end of September. This service can also offer a river trip or water taxi service. Tel: 07919 911440 Website: www.harwichharbourferry.com
Harwich also has regular ferry links to the continent, see Travel section in Introduction.

HISTORY

In case you've ever wondered why Harwich hasn't had more historical prominence, this is because it really didn't exist until the 12th century. Up to that time the rivers exited further north directly following the line of the Stour out to sea. This also explains why the Roman Saxon Shore fort of Walton to guard what was then known as Orwell Haven was at Felixstowe (now under the sea off it). A severe storm closed this entrance and opened the current one south of Landguard Point and the town soon developed into a borough and major sea and naval port. From the 17th century onwards, the sea and naval ports slowly declined, although the later development of the nearby ports at Parkeston and Felixstowe have continued the importance of the harbour if not the Old Town.

Now there are ships coming and going all the time with container freight, roll-on roll-off cargoes, passenger and fast ferries. In 1999, over 357 million tons of shipping entered the Haven ports. Felixstowe docks are the result of the vision of one man, Colonel Tomline, in the 19th century who imagined a seaside resort and harbour. The old town of Felixstowe itself grew as a popular resort when the railway arrived in Victorian times but the docks have progressed more slowly and steadily through two centuries. Eventually it was the frequent labour disputes in the London docks and elsewhere that diverted shipping to Felixstowe, which now handles a continuous stream of cargoes from Europe and around the world.

HARWICH SHORESIDE INFORMATION

Stores	Howlett's Convenience Store in Market Street, two blocks back from the quay down either Kings Head Street or Kings Quay Street, offers a free delivery service to the yacht berth. Open Mon to Sat 0700-1300 and 1415-1800 and Sun 0700-1300. Extensive stores in Dovercourt
Banks	Nearest in Dovercourt and the only cash machine in the Old Town is in The Billy pub in West Street (turn off the quay to the west of the pier)
PO	In Church Street (turn off the quay to the west of the pier)
Public Tel.	Opposite foot of pier
Clubs	Harwich and Dovercourt Sailing Club in Gashouse Creek just past the old railway pier, Tel: 01255 508041 and Harwich Town Sailing Club on the shore to the eastern side of the town past Navyard Wharf, Tel: 01255 503200
Accommodation	There is a range of accommodation around the town, from hotels and inns to guesthouses. Details at Visitor Centre on pier
Tourist Info.	The Tourist Information centre is a mile away on the road to Parkeston, but there is a helpful Visitor Centre on Halfpenny Pier
Taxis	Harwich Taxis, Tel: 01255 551111; Starlings Taxis, Tel: 01255 503000
Police	88-92 Main Road, Harwich. Tel: 01255 221312
Doctor	Dr. Child & Ptnrs., 77 Fronks Road, Dovercourt. Tel: 01255 556868
Hospital	(A&E) Colchester General, Turner Road, Colchester, Tel: 01206 747474 (A&E) Clacton Hospital, Tower Road, Clacton, Tel: 01255 201717
Dentist	Dovercourt Dental Practice, 120 Fronks Road, Dovercourt. Tel: 01255 503570
Pharmacy	A number in High Street and Main Road in Dovercourt

USEFUL NUMBERS

Boatbuilder	Harwich Boatcraft, where Bob Fenton specialises in restoration, repairs and new work in timber. Tel: 01255 551396
Marine Electronics	PRS Communications Ltd., Tel: 01255 240523
Sailmakers	Dolphin Sails, Tel: 01255 243366

EATING AND DRINKING

There is a café on Halfpenny Pier offering a range of snacks and there is a wide selection of places to eat in the town. The Pier Hotel opposite has two restaurants, the ground floor family friendly bistro-style Halfpenny Pier Restaurant and a very smart first floor Harbourside Restaurant specialising in seafood, Tel: 01255 241212. There are many other less pricey restaurants and pubs further back from the quayside and a Chinese takeaway open evenings only (closed Tuesdays).

TO SEE AND DO

The Harwich Society manages a Visitor Centre on Halfpenny Pier which is full of useful information on things to see in the Old Town, where there is ample to keep you busy for a day or so and offers a pleasant place to just take a stroll round, although the beach over by the green is little more than a shingle boat park and for a decent beach you will need to travel further to Dovercourt.

In Kings Quay Street there is the restored 1911 Electric Palace cinema which shows films on Wednesdays, Fridays, Saturdays and Sundays and holds occasional jazz concerts. Tel: 01255 553333.

On, or near the green, is the Lifeboat Museum, the Maritime Museum in the Low Light and the Treadmill Crane which was moved many years ago from the wharf to the green. This crane was operated by manpower, much like hamsters in a wheel. My favourite historical place of interest is The Redoubt Napoleonic fort off Main Road which houses an eclectic collection. All these are open every day from May to September 1000-1600.

Landguard Fort (reached by the foot ferry from Halfpenny Pier) is an English Heritage site of 18th, 19th and 20th century fortifications and the site of the last opposed invasion of England in 1667. Open daily April to October 1000-1700 (1800 in peak season).

Further afield in Dovercourt you will find a swimming pool, Tel: 01255 508266 and roller-skating rink, Tel: 01255 551909.

An interesting, though not all rural, longer walk of about 14 miles, can be had following the sea wall and Essex Way South out of Harwich, round the creeks and marshes, striking inland on the Essex Way to Ramsey, before again following the Essex Way round the back of the refinery to Parkeston and back into Harwich.

SHOTLEY POINT

The future of Shotley Point is still undetermined. Ever since the closure of the Royal Navy training establishment HMS Ganges at Shotley, the majority of the site has stood empty and decaying. Despite the marina development at Shotley Point Marina, the area still seems to waiting to see what will happen. The latest residential development plans have been turned down as too dense for the local infrastructure to cope, but it seems some kind of mixed redevelopment of the site will be inevitable – we wait with interest.

MOORINGS

Most of the moorings off Shotley Village are for fishing boats, tugs and pilot vessels, although there are a few yacht moorings, one of which you may find free for a short stop. Shotley Marina offers a locked basin with 350 pontoon berths and full marina facilities. Although not the prettiest outlook over Felixstowe Docks, the convenience of location and friendliness of staff, far outweigh this one negative.

SHOTLEY SKIPPERS INFORMATION	
Harbour Master	Lock Control VHF Ch80 Call-sign "Shotley Marina", Tel: 01473 788982 Email: sales@shotley-marina.co.uk
Water	On pontoons
Electricity	On pontoons
Fuel	To starboard as you enter marina
Facilities	WC, showers (and baths!) and launderette
Internet	Free wireless
Boatyard	A full range of marine services, including marine and electrical engineers, grp repairs and spray centre
Chandlery	Extensive on-site chandlery
Slip	40 ton travel hoist and 20 ton crane
Website	www.shotleymarina.co.uk

SHOTLEY SHORESIDE INFORMATION

Stores	Some basic stores can be obtained from the mini-market in the chandlery or from a mini-market in the Bristol Arms. More extensive stores can be obtained from the store up the hill in the village
Banks, PO	PO in village, no bank
Public Tel.	By the showers and The Shipwreck
Club	Shotley Sailing Club, mainly dinghies. Tel: 01473 787500 Website: www.sailingclub.shotleygate.com
Taxis	JR Travel, Belstead. Tel: 01473 730291
Police	Civic Drive, Ipswich. Tel: 01473 613500
Doctor	Dr. Dineen & Ptnrs., Kingsland, Shotley. Tel: 01473 787435
Hospital	(A&E) Ipswich Hospital, Heath Road (a mile and a half to the east of the town centre). Tel: 01473 712233
Dentist	The Dental Surgery, 5 Elm Street, Ipswich. Tel: 01473 231199
Pharmacy	Nearest, Ipswich

USEFUL NUMBERS

Boatyard & Workshop	Shotley Marine Services. Tel: 01473 788982
Brokerage	Fox's Yacht Sales. Tel: 01473 788772
Chandlery	Harwich Chandlers. Tel: 01255 504061
Sailing School	Britannia Sailing. Tel: 01473 787019

The recommended yacht track from south of Shotley Spit buoy is parallel to the deep water channel, passing close to the north of Ganges buoy to the marked approach channel leading to the lock. Before locking in you should contact the lock control for berth allocation and to get the lock gates opened. At the lock entrance there is an Inogen leading light on the starboard side. When a vessel is on the correct line of approach, vertical black lines are seen on an orange screen. Any deviation from the correct bearing will cause the black lines to change to arrows pointing back into the line of deep water. The lock is manned 24 hours a day enabling access to and from the marina at all states of the tide (although those vessels that draw over 1.8 metres should contact the lockmaster for advice at LWS). Traffic lights control the lock movements and boats are requested not to enter the lock against a red traffic light unless specifically advised to do so by the lock master.

CREW CHANGES AND TRAVEL

Hourly buses to Ipswich (less on Sundays) for train connections. For bus information contact Traveline East Anglia, Tel: 08706 082608 Website: www.traveline.org.uk. For train information contact 'One' Customer Services, Tel: 08456 007245 Website: www.onerailway.com or National Rail Enquiries, Tel: 08457 484950 Website: www.nationalrail.co.uk

There is a seasonal foot ferry to Harwich and Felixstowe, running half a dozen trips every day from Easter to early September and then at weekends to the end of September. This service can also offer a river trip or water taxi service. For further information Tel: 07919 911440 Website: www.harwichharbourferry.com

EATING AND DRINKING

The Shipwreck bar and restaurant is in the marina. Open 1100-2300 (Sun 1200-2230) and offers food Wed to Fri 1000-

Halfpenny Pier

1400 and 1800-2100, Sat 1000-1430 and 1800-2130 and all day Sun 1000-2000. Tel 01473 788865.

The bar at Shotley Sailing Club on the sea wall is open Wednesday, Friday and Saturday evenings and Sunday lunchtime.

Surprisingly, The Bristol Arms further along the sea wall dates in parts from the 12th century and offers excellent bar and restaurant meals. It houses a small shop and is lively, friendly and has a certain eccentric charm. Open Mon to Fri 1100-1430 and 1730-2300, Sat 1100-2300, Sun 1200-2230, and for food lunchtimes and evenings to 2100 every day. Tel: 01473 787200.

TO SEE AND DO

The HMS 'Ganges' Association has a small museum at Shotley Point Marina. Open at weekends and bank holidays from Easter to October from 1100-1700. Tel: 01473 684749. Other than some pleasant walks there is little to do or see at Shotley, so if you are staying over I would suggest utilising the foot ferry for a visit to Harwich.

There are some excellent walks from Shotley. One is to head west along the Stour from The Bristol Arms (although due to erosion of the riverside path you initially have to deviate inland to the first road on your left up the hill and follow on from this until it rejoins the riverside path a few hundred yards on). A mile along Erwarton Bay, a path leads inland and joins the Stour and Orwell Walk where you turn right and follow the path back into the top end of Shotley Gate. A second short circular walk is to head out north along the sea wall from the marina, cutting back inland on a path half a mile on, until this reaches the road, where you turn left back into Shotley Gate. A third and much longer circular walk of 15 miles, but one I would recommend for the strong walker, is to walk out along the Stour, striking inland after about three and a half miles past the sadly dilapidated Sparrow Hall and joining the Stour and Orwell Walk into Harkstead. From here there are a number of road and path routes across the peninsula to Chelmondiston and from there to Pin Mill, where just short of the Butt & Oyster, you turn off to the right through the woods and onwards along the sea wall back to the marina.

THE RIVER ORWELL

Ipswich Wet Dock

Tides Pin Mill +0:20 Ipswich +0:30
(differences from Harwich)

From the end of Felixstowe container terminal the Orwell provides eight miles of cruising grounds through marsh and rolling countryside, right into the heart of the county town of Suffolk. The river is served by a large number of moorings, from the tranquil to the aesthetic, from simple drying moorings to marinas with state-of-the-art facilities. After the container terminal, control of navigation passes from the Harwich Haven Authority to the Ipswich Port Authority. The main channel is dredged to 5.6 metres at Chart Datum all the way to Ipswich, as fairly large shipping regularly use Ipswich docks and listening in on Ipswich Radio (Ch68) can give you advance warning of large ship movements in the river. Although there is often plenty of depth for small craft outside the channel, it is important to keep an eye on the sounder, as depths can shelve more quickly than you may expect and catch out the unwary. Nearly all the eastern side of the river comes within the Suffolk Coasts and Heaths Area of Outstanding Natural Beauty and there are a number of bird sanctuaries within this. Hence the speed limit in the Orwell is just 6 knots (other than in the designated water-ski area), but why anyone would want to speed through such surroundings defeats me anyway.

SHOTLEY TO LEVINGTON

Once past the container terminal, the Orwell changes character from wide and open port to a gentle river passing through areas of marshland and creeks interspersed by rural and wooded countryside. On the starboard hand immediately after the container terminal are the Trimley Marshes, followed soon after by Trimley Retreat Bird Sanctuary. This was created by the Harwich Harbour Authority by breaching the sea wall to replace the marshes lost when the terminal expanded, to allow the area to flood. Both areas are now protected and managed by the Suffolk Wildlife Trust. For the ornithologists among you, clean landing is possible between the gap in the sea wall and Trimley SH buoy near High Water, just downstream of the clump of trees, or you can take a pleasant walk down the sea wall from Suffolk Yacht Harbour. The river now turns to port as you round Collimer Point and opposite in the bay to starboard is the designated water-ski area and from here onwards the masts inside Suffolk Yacht Harbour become very clear.

An east coast sunrise ©Claudia Myatt

LEVINGTON

Suffolk Yacht Harbour is still independently owned and run and despite now being the largest marina on the east coast (it was recently extended to 550 berths), it has to be one of the friendliest. Although there is still a waiting list for permanent berths, visitors can usually be accommodated somewhere. The entrance to Suffolk Yacht Harbour is indicated by a red and white Safe Water buoy a couple of cables upstream of Stratton green conical buoy (flashing Q.G.) and then runs in towards the harbour down a dredged channel between lateral marker posts with appropriate top-marks. Although well dredged and wide enough for yachts to pass, this channel does not hold enough water for all deeper draft craft at LWS, so if in doubt seek the advice of the Harbour Master, or pick up a mooring and wait for enough range of tide. There are yellow leading lights for a night-time entry, isophase to front and occulting to rear.

MOORINGS

Either call the Harbour Master, or once in the entrance, go on the pontoons immediately in front of you and report to his office in the cabin at the head of them. In the rare circumstance that no moorings are available in the marina, you may be directed to one of the moorings off the marina, also managed by Suffolk Yacht Harbour. East Anglian Sailing Trust operates from the marina offering sailing for the disabled in both dinghies and yachts and is always looking for volunteers to assist in its valuable work. Website: www.east-anglian-sailing-trust.org.uk

CREW CHANGES AND TRAVEL

Levington would not be the easiest place for crew changeovers unless you intend to do this by car, in which case the A14 is only a mile or so from the marina. For public transport there is a daily bus to Trimley, Felixstowe or Ipswich for connections, otherwise I would suggest a taxi to the station at Trimley, which has hourly services to Ipswich. For bus information contact

Traveline East Anglia, Tel: 08706 082608 Website: www.traveline.org.uk and for the trains and coaches see Ipswich section.

EATING AND DRINKING

The Haven Ports Yacht Club in the old lightship is an active club with some 700 members and welcomes visitors. Both bar and restaurant are open lunchtimes and evenings, Tel: 01473 659658. The club is in the process of extending its facilities with a new clubroom opposite the lightship, which will house a substantial function room and facilities with disabled access, something the old lightship is not best at providing, despite its wonderful character.

A mile away (see To See and Do), the thatched Ship Inn in Levington provides reasonably priced food from an extensive menu, both lunchtimes and evenings, seven days a week. Open Mon to Fri 1130-1500 Sat 1030-2300 and Sun 1200-2230, with food served Mon to Sat 1200-1400 and 1830-2130 and Sun 1200-1500 and 1830-2100. Tel: 01473 659573.

LEVINGTON SKIPPERS INFORMATION	
Harbour Master	VHF Ch80 call-sign "Suffolk Yacht Harbour", Tel: 01473 659465/659240 Email: enquiries@syharbour.co.uk
Water	On pontoons
Electricity	On pontoons
Fuel	To port as you enter marina
Facilities	New blocks offering WC, showers and laundry
Boatyard	A full range of marine services, including marine and electrical engineers, climate controlled spray centre, riggers, sailmakers and stainless steel fabricators
Chandlery	Extensive on-site chandlery
Slip	Slip, crane and travel hoist to 60 tons, plus scrubbing posts (enquiries to Harbour Master)
Website	www.syharbour.co.uk

Suffolk Yacht Harbour

LEVINGTON SHORESIDE INFORMATION

Stores	Some basic stores can be obtained from the mini-market and off-licence in the chandlery. It is open 0800-1730, seven days a week, all year round, except over the Christmas period and public holidays
Banks, PO	None nearby, nearest Felixstowe or Ipswich
Public Tel.	By the chandlery
Club	The Haven Ports Yacht Club in the converted Cromer lightship in the marina welcomes visitors. Tel: 01473 659658 Email: secretary@hpyc.com
Taxis	Coastal Taxis, Felixstowe, Tel: 01394 277777; AM Taxis, Trimley St. Mary, Tel: 01394 285677
Police	32 High Road West, Felixstowe. Tel: 01473 613500
Doctor	Dr. Davenport & Ptnrs., 201 Hamilton Road, Felixstowe. Tel: 01394 283197
Hospital	(A&E) Ipswich Hospital, Heath Road (a mile and a half to the east of Ipswich town centre). Tel: 01473 712233
Dentist	Walton House Dental Practice, 218 High Street, Felixstowe. Tel: 01394 283419
Pharmacy	Nearest, Felixstowe town centre where there are several

USEFUL NUMBERS

Marine Engineers	French Marine Motors Ltd. Tel: 01473 659882 Bob Spalding Marine and Leisure. Tel: 08000 854643
Marine Electronics	R & J Marine Electronics. Tel: 01473 659737
Riggers	Rig Magic. Tel: 01473 655089
Stainless Fabrications	Mr Stainless. Tel: 01473 659295
Sailmakers	Quantum Sail Design (incorporates Parker and Kay). Tel: 01473 659878
Brokers	Clarke & Carter Interyacht. Tel: 01473 659681
Sea School	East Anglian Sea School, Tel: 01473 659992; East Coast Offshore Yachting, Tel: 01480 861381

For something different you could use the grassed BBQ area set aside at the downstream end of the marina, overlooking the countryside, Loompit Lake and the river.

TO SEE AND DO

The yacht harbour is placed at the centre of some very pleasant walking and birdwatching country. To the south and east you can join a footpath at the inner end of the marina by the BBQ area that passes Loompit Lake and follows the sea wall to Trimley Retreat. Although only a couple of miles there and back, you will lose any ornithologist for a good couple of hours. For the energetic, it is possible to construct a very pleasant longer circular walk of eight to ten miles by continuing on to the Trimley Marshes and cutting up into Trimley St. Mary. You then need to follow the road west into Trimley St. Martin, passing (or not) on the way, the Three Mariners and Hand in Hand pubs, before following a footpath along a lane branching off on the left back to Loompit Lake.

To the north and west it is a very pleasant walk of about a mile past Levington Lagoon (created by Suffolk Yacht Harbour to replace the habitat taken over by the marina) into Levington. From the end of the marina near the river, follow the sea wall path past the lagoon and along the banks of Levington Creek to near the head where you can follow a concrete track branching right, until you reach the lane where you turn left into Levington. I can think of nothing nicer early on a summer's evening, than taking this short walk into Levington to The Ship Inn next to the church for dinner, followed by a gentle stroll back. For a slightly different return walk, why not take the footpath down the lane opposite the inn, across a field to where it joins the sea wall. Turn left back to the head of the creek across a footbridge and back the way you came. Again for the more energetic, you can add three miles by continuing along the footpath on the sea wall past the creek and past Home Wood until it goes inland towards Nacton. Where the path branches before the school, take the right fork and when you join the lane, turn right back in to Levington.

If you wish to be more adventurous by water, just past the yacht harbour opposite the next SH buoy is Levington Creek, where the remains of a Viking ship were discovered some time ago in the mud. There used to be a few drying moorings in here, but these have long since gone, however the creek is still navigable on the

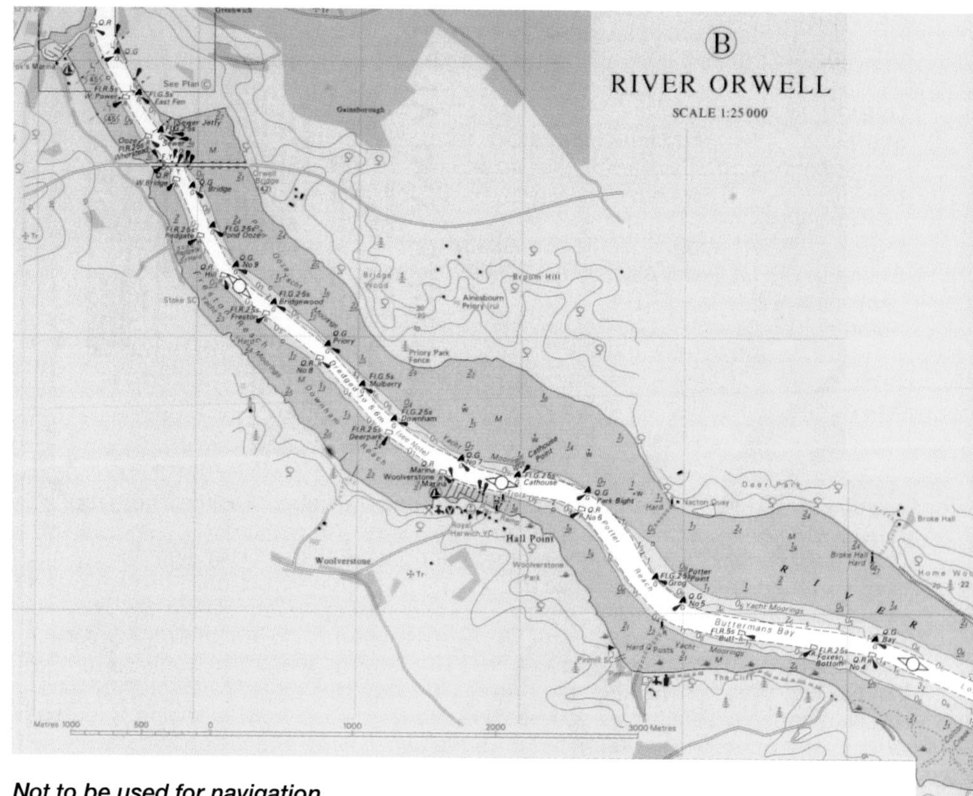

Not to be used for navigation

tide for shoal draft craft, although I have never had the courage to try it. It is possible to take a dinghy in on the tide with care as the withies and staves marking the channel seem to be eccentrically placed. Take care to give a wide berth to the port hand side of the entrance as a spit intrudes here, so stay to starboard until the creek opens up to port and then follow the channel roughly in the centre of the banks. At the head of the creek to starboard there is an old ruined timber wharf that was once used by barges to unload their cargoes and here, a couple of hours and more either side of high water, you can scramble ashore (with good fortune, dry footed).

Felixstowe can also be visited easily by taxi (see the Deben section for information).

LEVINGTON TO PIN MILL

Once past Levington Creek and on the port bank of the river just upstream of the creek, there are the remains of a hard where barges used to berth to collect produce from the farms destined for London. Further on past Colton Creek, just between the Levington moorings ending and the Pin Mill ones starting, there is still room to anchor, although this anchorage is often used by sailing barges. On the opposite side of the river is the intermittently wooded Nacton shore, where it is possible to land

A traditional east coast fishing smack ©Claudia Myatt

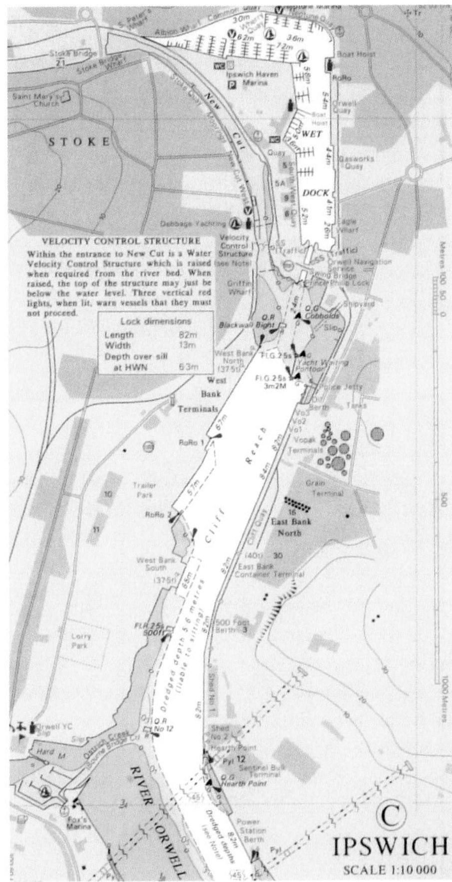

PIN MILL SKIPPERS INFORMATION

Harbour Master	Tony Ward, Tel: 01473 780621 Mobile: 07714 260568 Email: moorings.pinmill@virgin.net
Water	Tap alongside the sailing club
Facilities	Public WC at the top of the hard
Boatyards	Harry King & Sons Ltd., Tel. & Fax: 01473 780258 Email: info.kingsboatyard@virgin.net Website: www.kingsboatyard.co.uk F. A. Webb, Tel: 01473 780291
Slip	Both yards have mobile cradles, consult Harbour Master for use of the scrubbing posts

on a narrow beach near high water. From here onwards rows of moorings flank the river on both sides and as you turn into the reach known as Butterman's Bay, Pin Mill will become evident on the port hand side.

PIN MILL

Orwell Park School with its observatory, can be seen up on the starboard bank among the woods and opposite this is the cluster of buildings and barges that make up Pin Mill. Before the channel was dredged and Ipswich Dock improved, ships would moor here in Butterman's Bay to be unloaded by lightermen, so over the centuries the bars in the Butt & Oyster must have heard many a foreign sailor's yarn.

Pin Mill hard must be one of the longest on the east coast. It is accessible at most states of the tide and there is a convenient stream, the Grindle, running down its starboard side in which you can tow your dinghy to save a long haul at low water. The Grindle has claimed many a returning visitor to the Butt & Oyster whose gait has become less sure, so take care when homeward bound. This is a public hard with no charge made for its use and no

PIN MILL SHORESIDE INFORMATION

Stores	Nearest at Chelmondiston half a mile away. Walk up the lane to the main road and turn right. A little way down on the right-hand side you will find Hollingsworth Butcher and Grocer. Here, in addition to a fine grocers and butchers, there is also a green grocers and an extensive off-licence with a wine selection to put to shame many a wine merchant. Open 0800-1300 and 1415-1730, closed Wed afternoons and Sun. There is also another newsagents and store, Orwell Stores, further along again on the right, next to the Chinese takeaway.
Public Tel.	100 yards up the lane from the hard
Club	Pin Mill Sailing Club welcomes visiting yachtsmen and is open in the summer Wed 2030-2300, Fri 2000-2300, Sat and Sun 1200-1500 and 2000-2300 (weekends only in the winter). Tel: 01473 780271
Taxis	Alton Green Cars, Holbrook, Tel: 01473 328689; Hawk Express Cabs, Ipswich, Tel: 01473 222222
Police	Civic Drive, Ipswich. Tel: 01473 613500
Doctor	Dr. Dineen & Ptnrs., Kingsland, Shotley. Tel: 01473 787435
Hospital	(A&E) Ipswich Hospital, Heath Road (a mile and a half to the east of the town centre). Tel: 01473 712233
Dentist	The Dental Surgery, 5 Elm Street, Ipswich. Tel: 01473 231199
Pharmacy	Nearest, Ipswich

permission needed. The top of the hard is very wide and hard enough to drive over and this is where several barges can usually be seen undergoing repairs at low water. On the hard are scrubbing posts and barge blocks and you often see yachts and other vessels dried out for repairs.

Pin Mill is almost a compulsory stop for those cruising the area, largely due to its timelessness – everything changes and yet stays the same. The Butt & Oyster has changed hands and is now owned by the same people as The Maybush in Waldringfield, but there seems little difference. The famed yard of Harry King & Sons which was run until recently by Harry's grandson Geoff, is now Harry King & Sons Ltd. and run by Gus Curtis who has worked at Harry King's for some time and shares Geoff's love of things nautical especially if old and wooden, and Geoff is still to be seen wandering the yard.

The F. A. Webb boatyard that has been boat building and repairing barges since 1838, is now run by the dry-humoured brothers Jonathan and Richard Webb. The yard has some moorings and hard standing for over-wintering and can undertake minor repairs, although they no longer do many major works due to a return to the yard's origins in restoring the Thames sailing barge Melissa, now looking resplendent in her new paint at the head of the hard. The Melissa was built at the end of the 19th century and traded under sail until the 1940's, when in common with many other barges, she suffered the ignominy of being converted to a motor barge in which form she continued until the 1970's. She was then further converted into a houseboat and went into sad decline until rescued by the brothers a few years ago. Built of steel, the brothers inform me she needed nearly every plate renewed and at times they wondered why they hadn't just built a new barge! Now nearing completion of restoration, they intend to start chartering her in 2007 and proudly boast she'll be the fastest barge afloat, so keep an eye on the barge match results. To make enquiries about chartering the Melissa, contact Jonathan Webb at the yard.

Pin Mill

For stores and a change of scene, you will need to walk half a mile up the road to Chelmondiston and even if you don't need to, I would recommend the pleasant walk anyway.

MOORINGS

It is often possible to find a spare mooring overnight and Tony Ward is the man to see about a berth as he has some set aside for visitors. You may well find him in his yellow launch among the moorings, but otherwise just give him a call (try his mobile first if you can't see his launch on its mooring off the end of the hard). In 2006 visitors moorings were £6.00 a night, as they have been for a number of years.

EATING AND DRINKING

No visit to the east coast can be complete without a visit to The Butt & Oyster which has hardly changed since the Thames barge was in its heyday. Open all day every day 1200-2300 (Sundays 2230) and serving food seven days a week 1200-1430 and 1830-2130 (all day at weekends). Tel: 01473 786764.

If you fancy a change, there are two pubs in Chelmondiston up the lane. Having turned right at the top of the lane into the village, you first come to The Forresters Arms Inn on the right, very much a local's pub, open all day, every day 1200-2300 (2230 Sundays) and offering real ales. Food is limited to lunchtime bar snacks, but there are plans to possibly develop a Thai restaurant within the premises. Tel: 01473 780930.

Further down on the other side of the road is The Venture, a Pubmaster establishment again open all day, every day and serving food at lunchtimes and evenings. Further down still on the right, next door to Orwell Stores, is a Chinese takeaway open 1700-2230 (Fridays and Saturdays 1200-1400 and 1700-2330), closed Tuesdays. Tel: 01473 780327.

TO SEE AND DO

For some visitors it is enough to sit and soak up the atmosphere of this famous boating spot, with its tiny cottages tucked away across the common, but there are also some pleasant walks for the more energetic. There are good walks along the river in both directions and through the woods of Woolverstone Park.

There is a particularly pleasant circular walk of a couple of miles downriver through Cliff Plantation to Clamp House and back, taking a different path (higher and lower) for much of the way and providing a variety of views of the river. Just enough of a walk to build up an appetite and thirst.

CREW CHANGES AND TRAVEL

Chelmondiston is on the bus route from Shotley to Ipswich and is therefore provided with an hourly daytime service, with a couple of buses in the evening and a reduced service on Sundays. Good connections from Ipswich. For bus information contact Traveline East Anglia, Tel: 08706 082608 Website: www.traveline.org.uk and for the trains and coaches see Ipswich section.

PIN MILL TO WOOLVERSTONE

From Pin Mill, the wooded Potters Reach leads to a slight bend to port in the river from where the Orwell Bridge can be seen two miles ahead. About a mile from Pin Mill the channel moves towards the port bank and here the wooded escarpment provides a sheltered backdrop to the white building of the Royal Harwich Yacht Club with its pontoon moorings, closely followed by Woolverstone Marina.

WOOLVERSTONE

The Royal Harwich Yacht Club is one of the oldest yacht racing clubs in the country, founded in 1843. It backed the first two challenges for the America's Cup

WOOLVERSTONE SKIPPERS INFORMATION

ROYAL HARWICH YACHT CLUB

Harbour Master	Marina Master, Tel: 07742 145994
Water	On pontoons
Electricity	On pontoons
Facilities	WC and showers
Website	www.rhyc.demon.co.uk

WOOLVERSTONE MARINA ⚓⚓⚓⚓⚓

Harbour Master	VHF Ch80 call-sign "Woolverstone Marina", Tel: 01473 780206 or Email: woolverstone@mdlmarinas.co.uk
Electricity	On pontoons
Fuel	Downstream of pontoons (diesel)
Facilities	WC, showers and laundry
Internet	wireless available at a charge
Boatyard	A full range of marine services
Chandlery	On-site chandlery (up steps through the trees behind the marina)
Slip	Mobile crane 9.5 tons
Website	www.mdlmarinas.co.uk/marinas/woolverstone

and organises the North Sea Race for the RORC each year. Apart from members competing in the Haven Series and EAORA Races, the club has two fleets of keelboat day racers, the Royal Harwich One Designs and the more modern Ajax class. Dinghy fleets include a strong fleet of National Twelves together with Laser, Topper, Optimist and Handicap fleets as well as a large contingent of Wayfarers which both race and cruise. The club has run several national and international dinghy championships in Dovercourt Bay. It has its own marina arranged on two pontoons in front of the clubhouse, recently extended to 54 all-tide berths, with water, electricity and sewage disposal facilities. It also has a number of swinging moorings mingling with those of Woolverstone Marina. As is often the case, despite the apparent grandeur of the club, visiting yachtsmen are made very welcome here, with the clubhouse open every day from April to November.

Just upstream and set in 22 acres of parkland, the MDL-owned Woolverstone Marina has 235 deep water pontoon berths and 110 swinging moorings with a launch service. There are plans to extend the marina by another 70-75 berths and install a new hoist with greater capacity at the downstream end of the marina.

Between the RHYC and Woolverstone Marina is Suffolk County Council's Neptune Water Sports, offering young people aged 10 and above, training and experience in dinghy sailing.

MOORINGS

The Royal Harwich has spaces for eight visiting yachts at the river end of the pontoons, as indicated by signs, or by arrangement. Visitors berths on both

WOOLVERSTONE SHORESIDE INFORMATION

Stores	Reasonable selection of essentials and more in mini-mart in the chandlery, otherwise the nearest store is at Chelmondiston
Public Tel.	By chandlery
Club	Royal Harwich Yacht Club. Tel: 01473 780319
Taxis	JR Travel, Belstead, Tel: 01473 730291; Hawk Express Cabs, Ipswich, Tel: 01473 222222
Police	Civic Drive, Ipswich. Tel: 01473 613500
Doctor	Dr. Dineen & Ptnrs., The Street, Holbrook. Tel: 01473 328263
Hospital	(A&E) Ipswich Hospital, Heath Road (a mile and a half to the east of the town centre). Tel: 01473 712233
Dentist	The Dental Surgery, 5 Elm Street, Ipswich. Tel: 01473 231199
Pharmacy	Nearest, Ipswich

USEFUL NUMBERS

Boatbuilders/ Repairers	Medusa Marine, Tel: 01473 780090; Nigel Waller, Tel: 07899 903982
Chandlery	Woolverstone Chandlery, Tel: 01473 780206
Marine Engineers	Volspec Marine Ltd. Tel: 01473 780144
Sailing School/ Brokerage/ Charter	Blue Baker. Tel: 01473 780111
Sailmakers	Sail and Cover. Tel: 01473 780075

Royal Harwich Yacht Club

pontoons and trots are also available at Woolverstone Marina and you should call on VHF, or by telephone, for a berth. Access to both marinas is possible at all states of tide.

EATING AND DRINKING

The RHYC bar is open lunchtimes and evenings (all day at weekends) offering snacks and light meals to members and visiting yachtsmen. More substantial meals are available at weekends. Tel: 01473 780219.

Buttermans is a smart bistro-style bar and restaurant with riverside view at Woolverstone Marina open to the public and offering meals and bar snacks. Open Mon to Thurs 1200-1500 and Fri to Sun 1200-2300 (Sun 2230). Tel: 01473 780886.

The Boot at Freston (see Freston section) is a pleasant two mile walk, or short taxi ride away and the Butt & Oyster at Pin Mill, a little closer.

TO SEE AND DO

Woolverstone is a peaceful rural location and there are good and varied walks from here both up and downstream. Downstream there is a pleasant three mile walk along the shore to Pin Mill, returning by a footpath near the sailing club and across Woolverstone Park coming out onto the lane above St. Michael's Church, Woolverstone and following the lane back down to the marina.

To walk in the opposite direction, I recommend the walk to The Boot at Freston, two miles away. Walk up the lane from the marina until you come to a path on your right opposite the end of the sports field by the church. Follow this path through the edge of the woods past Woolverstone House on the left, across a lane following the path with a hedge on your right. When you reach a further lane, follow this straight on and it will peter out after a while into a track.

When you come to yet another lane you can either turn left onto this and follow the main road right to the pub, or turn right taking the path to the left just before the wood (straight on will take you on a detour to the Freston Tower). Skirt the woods until you drop down through the corner of the woods and up a lane through a cluster of houses to emerge opposite The Boot.

CREW CHANGES AND TRAVEL

At the top of the lane, the main road is on the bus route from Shotley to Ipswich and is therefore provided with an hourly daytime service, with a couple of buses in the evening and a reduced service on Sundays. Good connections from Ipswich. For bus information contact Traveline East Anglia, Tel: 08706 082608 Website: www.traveline.org.uk and for information on trains and coaches see Ipswich section.

WOOLVERSTONE TO FRESTON

The landscape of the Orwell from Butterman's Bay to the Orwell Bridge consists of rolling hills, fields and woods. Occasionally manor houses can be seen among groups of trees. These are the great estates of Orwell, Woolverstone and Freston.

The Woolverstone moorings extend for some way upstream and there is a short stretch before those of Stoke Sailing Club are reached. The club's hard is just after Freston Tower on the western bank a mile or so upstream of Woolverstone.

FRESTON

Stoke Sailing Club moved here in the 1970's from its original site in Ipswich where the Ro-Ro ferry terminal now stands. A small friendly club of mixed sailing and motor cruisers, it opens when a club member is there and has little in the way of facilities and no bar. It has 86 moorings of which only the outer 16 do not take the mud, but it does have an excellent hard accessible at most states of the tide. Tel: 01473 780260. If the club is closed, follow the sea wall to the upstream end of its compound where a footpath to the side of the compound will access the lane.

A half a mile walk up the lane and turning left at the main road up the hill, will bring you to The Boot at Freston, where you will find a good selection of real ales and a restaurant with a varied menu (with vegetarian and vegan options). The bar is open Mon to Fri 1200-1500 and 1700-2300 and all day 1200-2300 at weekends (2230 Sun). The restaurant opens Mon to Sat 1200-1430 and 1800-2130 and Sun 1200-1600 and 1800-2030. Tel: 01473 780277.

FRESTON TO IPSWICH

After Stoke Sailing Club moorings there are a number of buoys belonging to Orwell Yacht Club before the bridge. The mighty structure of the Orwell Bridge was built in 1983 to take the Felixstowe and Yarmouth traffic south of Ipswich. It is 38 metres high and dominates the view, although as modern bridges go it's quite elegant. The bridge can cause some odd wind shifts, although there is plenty of width for yachts between the piers. This is not so for the container ships and ferries that use the channel, so keep well away if one is approaching and let him through before you.

The bridge acts as a dividing line in the appearance of the river, where green, rural scenery gives way to chimneys, main roads and the buildings and wharfs that make up the dock area.

BOURNE BRIDGE

After the bridge there are three more pairs of channel buoys and several yacht moorings to port belonging again to Orwell Yacht Club. The red can buoy, No12, serves to indicate the entrance to Ostrich Creek and thereby the friendly

Fox's Marina and equally friendly Orwell Yacht Club. There is now a small Safe Water Buoy positioned just before it and to enter the creek and marina, pass close to the Safe Water Mark leaving the buoy No12 to starboard and pass between the port and starboard hand marker piles.

As there seems to be constant confusion over the name of the creek round here, I shall follow the example of the local bus timetables and refer to the area as Bourne Bridge. Bourne Bridge is actually the bridge over Belstead Brook where it becomes Oyster, or Ostrich, Creek. It is always marked on charts as Ostrich Creek, but locals tell me that this is only because nobody could understand what the old locals with their strong Suffolk accent were saying and that it should always have been Oyster Creek (as in Oyster Yachts) and hence they are delighted that on becoming a Beefeater, the local pub reverted to it's old name of The Oyster Reach from The Ostrich Inn, a name I understand it only acquired temporarily.

MOORINGS

Don't be tempted to pick up a mooring hereabouts without checking with the Orwell Yacht Club, as I have been told some have become problematic. It seems that the prop-wash of passing commercial vessels has washed away the soft mud, leaving a pretty solid bed. Not only does this reduce the holding for the moorings, but should you take the bottom, it is no longer as forgiving as it was. Following advice, the Orwell Yacht Club are trialing some fore and aft trot moorings just after the bridge and these may solve some of the problems if successful.

It looks improbable, but there is all-tide access for up to 1.8 metres draft in the creek, both to the marina and the club's visitor berths and you have these two choices when looking for a mooring here. The mooring master at Fox's will always try his best to find you room in one of the 100 pontoon berths in the marina, but as the channel here is quite tight to turn in, I would recommend calling their Harbour Master before entering the creek. Alternatively, Orwell Yacht Club also welcomes visitors and you can follow the line of pile moorings to starboard until you come across three bays right in front of the Orwell

BOURNE BRIDGE SKIPPERS INFORMATION

FOX'S MARINA

Harbour Master	VHF Ch37 and 80 call-sign "Fox's Marina", Tel: 01473 695126
Water	On pontoons
Electricity	On pontoons
Fuel	Pontoon to port as you enter marina
Facilities	WC, showers and laundry
Internet	Free wireless
Boatyard	A helpful Marine Service Centre on-site offering a full range of marine services
Chandlery	Extensive on-site slip – travel hoist and crane (capacity 70 tons) at boatyard
Website	www.foxsmarina.com

USEFUL NUMBERS

Workshop	Tel: 01473 689111
Rigging	Tel: 01473 691235
Chandlery	Tel: 01473 688431 (Electronics, Tel: 01473 695099)
Sailing School	East of England Sailing School, Tel: 01480 463737

ORWELL YACHT CLUB

Harbour Master	Call club when open, Tel: 01473 602288
Water	On landing pontoon
Facilities	WC's and showers
Fuel	At Fox's, or garage near entrance to club
Website	www.orwellyachtclub.org.uk

BOURNE BRIDGE SHORESIDE INFORMATION

Stores	Nearby convenience store open 0800-1900
Banks	Nearest, Ipswich
PO	Nearest, Ipswich
Public Tel.	At both yacht clubs and box nearby
Club	Fox's Yacht Club and Orwell Yacht Club, visiting yachtsmen welcome at both if on their moorings
Accommodation	Premier Inn at The Oyster Reach pub. Tel: 01473 692372
Tourist Info.	Nearest, Ipswich
Taxis	Hawk Express Cabs, Ipswich, Tel: 01473 222222; Four One Seven Cabs, Tel: 01473 417417

For emergency information refer to Ipswich section

Yacht Club building and its all-tide landing pontoon. Here you will stay afloat at most times in around 2 metres, but if you take the ground at low water the mud is so soft that you probably won't notice unless you try to move. They are quite happy to have three boats rafted up in each bay and if a workboat is in one, you may raft alongside. Around high tide you may go onto the pontoon in order to enquire at the club, but stays here for yachts are limited to 30 minutes. This pontoon provides an all-tide dinghy landing.

CREW CHANGES AND TRAVEL

Bourne Bridge is on a number of bus routes connecting Ipswich with Shotley and Manningtree. Regular buses run a number of times an hour, throughout every day until late evening, from a stop in Wherstead Road (across Bourne Bridge) to Ipswich, for train and coach links. Good connections from Ipswich. For bus information contact Traveline East Anglia, Tel: 08706 082608 Website: www.traveline.org.uk and for the trains and coaches see Ipswich section.

EATING AND DRINKING

Fox's Yacht Club, bar and meals opening times – Mon to Wed 1000-1500, Thur 1000-1500 and 1730-2230, Fri 1000-1500 and 1700-2230, Sat 1000-2230, Sun 1000-2000. Orwell Yacht Club, bar open most evenings in season.

The Oyster Reach Beefeater, open all day and for meals 1200-2200, Fri & Sat 12-2300. Tel: 01473 692372.

IPSWICH

Not so many years ago Ipswich was a place only visited if in dire need of major stores, or in order to transfer crews, and then excuses were made for stopping at Fox's and making them take the bus. Now things are very different as Ipswich is undergoing a renaissance and is an interesting cruising destination in its own right, although it can still be pleasant to stay over at Bourne Bridge and bus in if the bright lights beckon.

Continuing past Bourne Bridge you enter Ipswich docks with its container and Ro-Ro ferry terminals, the port hand side of the channel being marked by port hand channel buoys. You then pass a waiting pontoon to starboard and then between a pair of red and green channel marker buoys to the lock gates if you wish to lock through to the Wet Dock.

LOCKING THROUGH

The Prince Philip Lock has recently been refurbished allowing 24 hour access, with access almost on demand. Call up the lock on VHF Ch68 call-sign "Ipswich Port Radio" or Tel: 01473 213526, as you pass under the Orwell Bridge inbound (and before leaving your berth outbound) and follow instructions. There are red and green traffic lights on the control tower for guidance. You must moor to the pontoon to starboard in the lock, raft up there or go alongside the port hand wall, securing by passing warps around the tubes or through the thimbles in the orange buoys. Leading up to high tide the gates will sometimes be left open for 'free flow', but you will still need to call the lock for permission to go through and follow the traffic signals. There are times on extreme high tides when flood protection gates are closed preventing lock entry, when you may need to wait on the pontoon a short while.

THE WET DOCK

With the transformation of Ipswich's waterfront over the last few years and the on-going work, the Wet Dock takes another step in its history. As you enter the dock there are still some commercial wharves on either side, soon giving way to the marinas, although there are plans to redevelop even these areas to allow further residential and leisure expansion.

Once past these there are two marinas in the Wet Dock, Ipswich Haven Marina to port on the island and Neptune Marina to starboard on the north (town) side of the dock. Ugly concrete grain silos have been demolished to be replaced by modern buildings and once tired and derelict maltings have been renovated and transformed into luxury apartments and offices. A number of new blocks of luxury apartments have been built, with many more in the pipeline and in the middle of it all the Old Customs House has been restored to an imposing grandeur.

Even though there is still much to be completed, the waterfront is again coming to life, although dancing to a very different tune. Outstanding plans include educational and cultural buildings on the waterfront, as well as further commercial, leisure and residential development. Sadly, one can't help thinking that the island site of the Haven Marina may prove too tempting to developers to stay as hardstanding and boatyards for long and that these too will eventually be squeezed out and that would be a shame.

IPSWICH SKIPPERS INFORMATION

IPSWICH YACHT HAVEN ⚓⚓⚓⚓⚓

Harbour Master	VHF Ch37 or 80 call-sign "Ipswich Haven Marina", Tel: 01473 236644 Email: ipswichhaven @abports.co.uk
Water	On pontoons
Electricity	On pontoons
Fuel	Pontoon to port by slip
Facilities	WC and showers (2 blocks), laundry
Boatyard	Peters plc has a workshop on-site as do marine engineers Volspec Marine Ltd. (Volvo main dealer) and the helpful R & J Marine Electronics Ltd. for electronics
Chandlery	Peters plc operates the on-site chandlery
Slip	Travel hoist (capacity 70 tons) at marina with storage ashore

NEPTUNE MARINA

Harbour Master	VHF Ch37 or 80 call-sign "Neptune Marina", Tel: 01473 215204, Fax: 01473 215206 Email: enquiries@neptune-marina.com
Water	On pontoons
Electricity	On pontoons
Fuel	At the eastern end of the marina
Facilities	WC, showers and laundry
Internet	Wireless planned for 2007 (details not known)
Boatyard	All usual services available
Chandlery	None as yet
Slip	Travel hoist and cranes up to 30 tons with short-term storage ashore
Website	www.neptune-marina.com

IPSWICH SHORESIDE INFORMATION

Stores	A great variety of shops in the town centre, from the usual multiples to specialist shops in the side streets. If staying in the Ipswich Haven Marina (or New Cut) there is a Co-op convenience store a short way down Vernon Street (left over the road bridge as you exit the dock area) open 0800-2100 (0900-1800 Sun)
Banks	All banks in the town centre
PO	Nearest, Fore Street (one road back from the Neptune Marina), but three further in town centre
Public Tel.	At Ipswich Haven Marina offices and many nearby in town
Club	Newly started Ipswich Haven Yacht Club, no premises
Accommodation	A variety of accommodation in town, the nearest being the Salthouse Harbour Hotel on the north quayside and just beyond the dockside a Novotel
Tourist Info.	In town centre (St. Stephens Lane). Tel: 01473 258070
Taxis	A number of local companies including: Hawk Express Cabs, Ipswich, Tel: 01473 222222; Four One Seven Cab Company, Tel: 01473 417417
Police	Civic Drive. Tel: 01473 613500
Doctor	Barrack Lane Medical Centre (10 minutes walk north west of town centre). Tel: 01473 252827
Hospital	(A&E) Ipswich Hospital, Heath Road (a mile and a half to the east of the town centre). Tel: 01473 712233
Dentist	The Dental Surgery, 35 Berners Street (10 minutes walk north west of town centre). Tel: 01473 252519
Pharmacy	A number in town centre
USEFUL NUMBERS	
Boat Builders	Spirit Yachts Ltd. Tel: 01473 214715
Boatyard, Brokerage & Sales	Peters plc has a workshop on-site, Tel: 01473 225710
Chandlery	Peters plc, Tel: 01473 232649; Boat Gear Direct specialises in anchoring and mooring equipment, Tel: 07900 988355
Electronics	R & J Marine Electronics Ltd. Tel: 01473 659737
Marine Engineers	Volspec Marine Ltd., Tel: 01473 219651; Harvey Marine Services, Tel: 01473 328870; Diesco Group, Tel: 01473 251800; Seapower (Lindsay Rufford) based in the New Cut, Tel: 07768 772359; PBS Marine Services (for outboards), Tel: 01449 720095

Also on the island site are Fairline's testing operations and next door the fascinating yard of Spirit Yachts, builders of classically styled wooden yachts (including the one in the James Bond film Casino Royale), built and finished to a standard that gladdens the heart, brings tears to the eyes and makes your wallet go into hiding. Sean McMillan and Michael Newman brought their team to Ipswich Haven a couple of years ago and it's worth a few minutes just to poke your head round the corner and see what they're working on and what's on the pontoons nearby – and don't drool too much.

MOORINGS

The moorings in the dock are administered by Neptune Marina and the ABP owned and run Ipswich Haven Marina. Neptune Marina has 150 berths and will usually be able to find a space for visitors and Ipswich Haven Marina 250, with 30 reserved for visitors, right in front of the offices, bistro and facilities. Currently there should be no problem finding a berth despite Ipswich's new found popularity.

CREW CHANGES AND TRAVEL

Ipswich is an ideal place for crew changes with good train and coach links. Ipswich Railway Station is 15 minutes walk away from the Wet Dock (to the west across the other side of the River Gipping) with fast connections to Norwich (40 minutes) and London Liverpool Street (80 minutes). For information contact 'One' Customer Services, Tel: 08456 007245 Website: www.onerailway.com, or National Rail Enquiries, Tel: 08457 484950 Website: www.nationalrail.co.uk. Scheduled coach services are operated from Ipswich nationwide by National Express, Tel: 08705 808080, Website: www.nationalexpress.com. Ipswich is a hub for bus services which are operated by Ipswich Buses locally and First Eastern Counties to places out of town. A number of smaller operators also run services to and from Ipswich. For information contact Traveline East Anglia, Tel: 08706 082608 Website: www.traveline.org.uk

EATING AND DRINKING

Ipswich has every variety of eating and drinking establishment you could possibly want and you could undertake a gastronomic tour of the world all within 10 minutes walk if you had the time to spare. I shall purely list a few suggestions. Last Anchor, a bistro-style bar and restaurant right by the visitors pontoons in the Ipswich Haven Marina. Can get busy, Tel: 01473 214763. Bistro on the Quay, a very pleasant and moderately priced bistro restaurant on Wherry Quay. Very popular, so you will probably need to reserve a table, Tel 01473 286677. Il Punto is The Brasserie floating restaurant on Neptune Quay, Tel: 01473 289748.

Loch Fyne at Mortimers, 1 Duke Street, one road back from the Neptune Marina office, is large and very chic. A friendly and moderately-priced restaurant, with outside terrace and a private room, specialising in seafood (linked to the Scottish Loch Fyne company), but also has a variety of other non-fish dishes. Can get very busy on Fridays and Saturdays when there is entertainment. A tip is that they do very reasonable set meals (£10-£13) between 1200-1900, Tel: 01473 269810. The Lord Nelson pub restaurant in Fore Street just back from the quay, has an extensive menu (including an unusual vegetarian selection) and serves Adnams beers on gravity straight from the cask, Tel: 01473 254072. If the family are pining for theme food, a variety from MacDonald's to Frankie & Benny's can be found at Cardinal Park, five minutes walk west.

For the real ale drinker (and for their reasonably priced food) there are two Wetherspoons in town, one in the centre, but a more pleasant one just to the north in Crown Street opposite the local bus station. If you seek real ale emporia dedicated to the hop, there are two going out of town along St. Helens Street to the east, The Dove Street Inn (20 minutes walk) and further along (30 minutes) in Spring Road, The Fat Cat, both open all day and featuring fine and wide varieties of beer, some on gravity.

TO SEE AND DO

Ipswich is becoming a centre for culture and the arts and offers a variety of live music and two theatres (pamphlets available at Tourist Information). The New Wolsey Theatre is in Civic Drive to the

Ipswich Wet Dock and New Cut ©PRPA

north west of the town centre, Tel: 01473 295900 Website: www.wolseytheatre.co.uk. The Regent Theatre is at the top end of St. Helens Street to the north east of the town centre, Tel: 01473 433100 Website: www.ipswichregent.com

Ipswich Museum in High Street to the north west of the town centre has a variety of family friendly interesting displays, including Roman, Anglo-Saxon and from the time of Nelson. Also to the north of town is Christchurch Mansion, a 16th century house with rooms decorated in styles from Tudor to Victorian and an important collection of works by John Constable and Thomas Gainsborough. Admission to both is free and they are open 1000-1700 Tuesday to Saturday, with Christchurch also open Sundays from 1200-1630 and Bank Holiday Mondays from 1000-1700. In the summer, guided walking tours operate from the Tourist Information Centre on Tuesdays and Thursdays.

To burn off energy, Crown Pools swimming complex in Crown Street is to the north of the town centre and has three pools, including a leisure pool for the family with wave machine, Tel: 01473 433655. There is also a Cineworld Multiplex Cinema at Cardinal Park five minutes walk west. For information and booking call 0871 200 2000.

Sadly, the Tolly Cobbold brewery was taken over in 2002 by Ridley's (and subsequently by Greene King) and the brewery closed, bringing an end to over 250 years of brewing on the site and the brewery tours that many used to enjoy. The semi-derelict brewery and maltings stand, no doubt awaiting development, to starboard as you enter Ipswich, so doff a cap as you pass.

NEW CUT

As you pass the pair of red and green buoys that mark the entrance to the Prince Philip Lock, to port is the tidal New Cut that leads up to Stoke Bridge and the River Gipping, built when the Wet Dock was created. If entering, don't cut the corner – stick to the middle as the mud

HISTORY OF IPSWICH

There is no evidence of a settlement prior to, or in the period of Roman occupation, but following their withdrawal, the Saxons who had plagued the area with raids previously, established settlements around 450AD. These joined together and by around 600AD had become one of England's oldest towns Gypwic or Gyppeswick. Locals seem to favour the meaning of this as the place of someone called something like Gyp, but with a river called the Gipping and 'wick' also meaning an opening or widening place, the widening of the Gipping, seems to me more probable. Following difficult periods of mixed fortunes including Viking invasions and Danish rule, the port started to develop and from 1100 to 1650, Ipswich thrived as a port exporting wool, textiles and agricultural products. The town's seal, associated with the charter granted by King John in 1200, depicts the first ship to have a fixed rudder, not a simple oar! Later that century, the town's important maritime industry was engaged in building war galleys for Edward I.

As time went on, there were problems with silting of the river and this was why, in the 18th century, ships were unloaded downriver onto barges until operations took place to restore access to the quays. When the Wet Dock was first built between 1839 and 1842, it failed to revive the shipbuilding industry but was the largest wet dock in the country and handled cargoes from all over the world, although the majority came from across the North Sea.

builds on both sides of the entrance. Within the entrance to New Cut is a water velocity control structure that is raised, when required, from the river bed. When raised, the top of the structure may be just below the water level. Three vertical red lights, when lit, warn vessels that they must not proceed. Along New Cut on the port hand side, are Debbage Yachting's pontoons.

MOORINGS

Debbage Yachting has pontoon berths and is happy to accommodate visitors for short stays. Most boats will dry out but the mud is very soft and they have 2 metre draft fin-keelers berthed here. The family-run company's rates are very reasonable and useful to know if you need to leave a boat somewhere for a few days, or weeks, and they will undertake minor repairs. There is a yard crane for up to 20 tons and a 12 ton mobile crane available for hire. Diesel, fresh water and electricity are available alongside, but no facilities. There is a locked compound beside New Cut for boat storage and the company also offers a yacht transport service with a speciality of delivery to home lay-up with a purpose-built trailer. Tel: 01473 601169.

Orwell Bridge

ABP HAVEN MARINAS

IPSWICH

The Marina in the heart of Ipswich

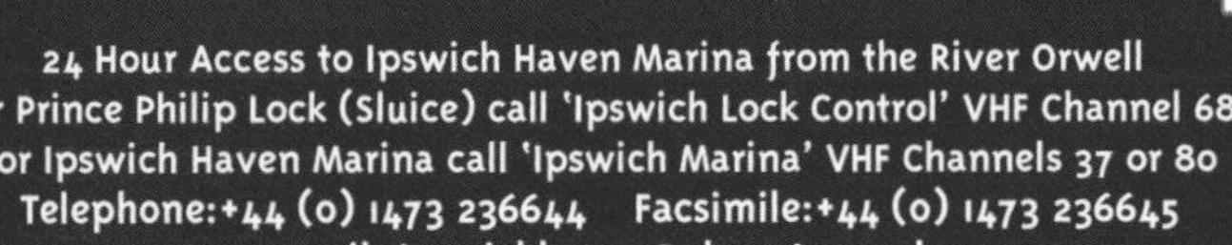

24 Hour Access to Ipswich Haven Marina from the River Orwell
For Prince Philip Lock (Sluice) call 'Ipswich Lock Control' VHF Channel 68
for Ipswich Haven Marina call 'Ipswich Marina' VHF Channels 37 or 80
Telephone:+44 (0) 1473 236644 Facsimile:+44 (0) 1473 236645
e-mail: Ipswichhaven@abports.co.uk

LOWESTOFT

Situated on Lake Lothing
with access to the broads and open sea

For more information just contact:
Telephone:+44 (0) 1502 580300
Facsimile:+44 (0) 1502 581851
e-mail: lowestofthaven@abports.co.uk
www.lowestofthavenmarina.co.uk

THE RIVER STOUR

Wrabness sunrise

Tides Wrabness +0:20, Mistley +0:35, Manningtree +0:45 *(differences from Harwich)*

The Stour, with its south bank in Essex and north in Suffolk, meets the River Orwell between Shotley Point and Harwich before the waters pass through Harwich Harbour into the North Sea. People have differing opinions of the Stour, but from the first time I sailed it, I have found it both beautiful and intriguing. It can change its face with a veer of the wind and demands skills in estuarial sailing to make the most of it, but a casual visit can still be made to some parts, without going into the intricacies of mud-larking. For those with sturdy shoal draft craft, it is in this river that your vessel will come into it's own.

The Stour has about 8 miles of buoyed channel as far as Mistley and Manningtree, although it almost dries out completely in the upper reaches. The river offers fairly wide expanses of uncluttered water with few facilities for yachtsmen beyond Shotley (details of Shotley and Shotley Marina are covered in the Harwich Harbour section). This is in marked contrast to the neighbouring Orwell and endears it to those who seek peace and quiet away from commercialisation.

SHOTLEY TO WRABNESS

From the Guard PH buoy the recommended course is for yachts to cross to the north side of the main channel to Shotley Spit south cardinal buoy before navigating up the first part of the Stour. You should then keep outside the main channel until past Parkeston to avoid the commercial traffic, including ferries, the Harwich-Hook HHS, cruise-liners and cargo ships. Until well clear, keep a listening watch on CH71 Harwich V.T.S. for warning of ship movements.

After you pass the piers at Shotley there are trees and fields on the north bank, which slowly eases away from channel into Erwarton Bay, which contrast strongly with the docks and passenger terminals at Parkeston on the south side. The original quay was built in the late 19th century and named after Charles Parkes who was then Chairman of the Great Eastern Railway. Its immediate success was due to the quick rail links, making it ideal for both passengers and perishable goods. After Parkeston, the south bank curves away into Copperas Bay, although the channel continues on a fairly straight course westwards towards Erwarton Ness south cardinal beacon some two miles further up river.

From Erwarton the channel continues to the west, although slightly easing south for a time until the green lateral buoy No1 is passed. Be careful not to stray into the big ship moorings to the south side of the channel, as they are unlit and an anti-pollution boom is strung between them. After No1 buoy the channel heads due west again and begins to narrow, but the two cardinal beacons, Holbrook south cardinal and No2 north cardinal, should now be in sight (as will be the moorings at Wrabness slightly to south of them) and you should aim to pass between the two beacons before turning a little to the south to leave the green lateral No3 buoy to starboard and the moorings and subsequent red lateral No4 to port.

ERWARTON

Just past the Erwarton south cardinal beacon, there is excellent holding in mud in line with the beacon going west from it and this is a popular anchorage, comfortable in most winds and giving good shelter in winds with any north in them. As you are close to the channel used by coasters, don't forget a riding light at night. It can however become exposed if the wind is strong westerlies, easterlies or southerlies. If strong winds spring up from the south, better shelter can be found across the river off Copperas Bay, although one should not encroach into the bay too much, as it becomes shallow quite quickly and there are some obstructions charted hereabouts. Copperas Bay is an RSPB reserve, which when combined with the Copperas Wood reserve on the shore, provides a haven for wildlife, cheek by jowl with the industrialised Parkeston Quay.

Landing is possible on Erwarton Ness for most of the tide just upstream of the remains of an old barge jetty. The shingle shelves gradually, so it is best to row in at least for the final part. A little paddle in a couple of inches of water may be necessary to drag the dinghy to shore, so one person should go bare-footed, or take some boots. From here, there are walks along the sea wall both to east and west and also to Erwarton village about a mile

ERWARTON INFORMATION	
Facilities	None
Stores	There are no shops in the village
Public Tel.	None
Taxis	P&S Taxis, Manningtree. Tel: 01206 396321
Police	Civic Drive, Ipswich, Tel: 01473 613500
Doctor	Dr. Dineen & Ptnrs., Kingsland, Shotley, Tel: 01473 787435
Hospital	(A&E) Ipswich Hospital, Heath Road (a mile and a half to the east of the town centre). Tel: 01473 712233
Dentist	The Dental Surgery, 5 Elm Street, Ipswich. Tel: 01473 231199
Pharmacy	Nearest, Ipswich

and a half away to the north. From the ruined jetty follow the track north across the field, going through the farm gate and then following the track as it turns to the north east again through fields coming to another farm gate, after which you follow the road to the left past the farm which winds on gently uphill to The Queens Head at the T-junction, where you can turn right to the village.

EATING AND DRINKING

The Queens Head is a 17th century inn sensitively modernised, and although now largely taken over by the restaurant area, it retains a friendly traditional bar with bar billiards and darts, serving Adnams ales. The pub closes in the afternoons between 1500-1830, but offers both lunch and dinner from an extensive menu, seven days a week and is well worth the pleasant walk. Tel: 01473 787550.

CREW CHANGES AND TRAVEL

There are occasional buses throughout the day to Shotley, Ipswich and Manningtree from Erwarton. For bus information contact Traveline East Anglia, Tel: 08706 082608 Website: www.traveline.org.uk. For trains from Manningtree see the Manningtree section and for trains and coaches from Ipswich see the Ipswich section of the River Orwell chapter.

HOLBROOK BAY

Holbrook Bay, where the Royal Hospital School stands out to the north, contains several small creeks that are popular anchorages and it is possible for shallow draught boats or a dinghy to make their way across the mudflats by following the buoys and withies to a landing near Harkstead and Holbrook. The school was originally founded in 1712 in Greenwich for the sons and grandsons of seafarers injured or killed in maritime service. The school moved from Greenwich to Holbrook in 1933 following a generous gift from a benefactor who admired the contribution former pupils had made in the First World War. Until the 1940's it was a condition that on leaving, boys entered a maritime service, but in the 1940's the school dropped this and is now a co-educational boarding school accepting pupils from all backgrounds, although it still has strong connections with the Royal Navy.

Not to be used for navigation

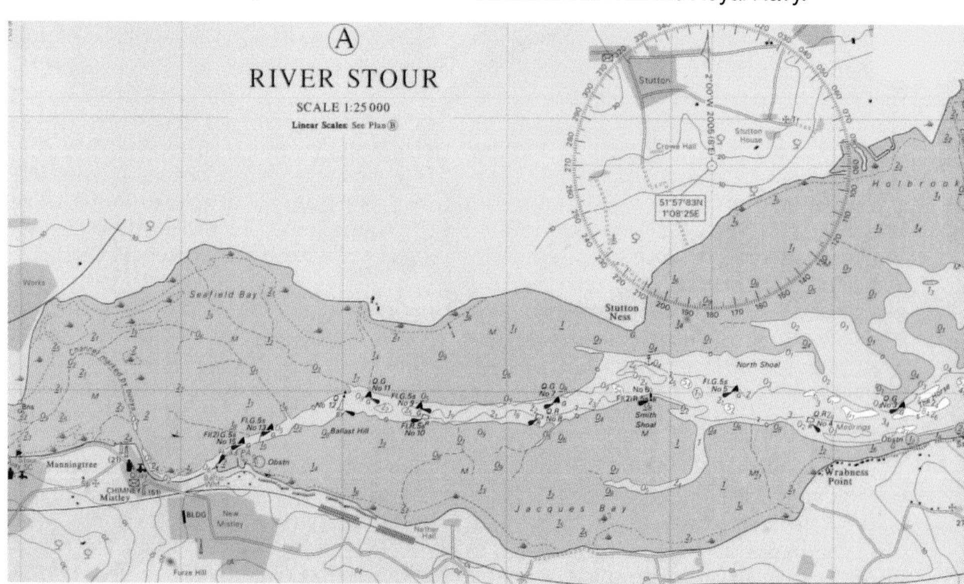

HOLBROOK BAY INFORMATION	
Facilities	None
Stores	There are no shops in Harkstead, but Holbrook has a Post Office and village stores open Mon to Fri 0900-1730 and Sat until 1200
Banks	Cash machine in The Compasses at Holbrook
Public Tel.	There is a telephone up a back street opposite the pub in Harkstead and directly outside the one in Holbrook
Taxis	P&S Taxis, Manningtree. Tel: 01206 396321
Police	Civic Drive, Ipswich. Tel: 01473 613500
Doctor	Dr. Dineen & Ptnrs., The Street, Holbrook. Tel: 01473 328263
Hospital	(A&E) Ipswich Hospital, Heath Road (a mile and a half to the east of the town centre). Tel: 01473 712233
Dentist	The Dental Surgery, 5 Elm Street, Ipswich. Tel: 01473 231199
Pharmacy	Nearest, Ipswich

Gallister Creek is the first anchorage you come to and can be found by sounding in on rounding Harkstead Point into Holbrook Bay and creeping up as far as you dare, but is best done before the tide covers all the flats. It is not easy to find the head of the creek, but landing is possible on the beaches here for about two and a half hours either side of high tide. If you wish, you can then find a way up the low cliffs where Harkstead will be seen less than half a mile away and by following one of the many paths, find your way onto the lane and into the village.

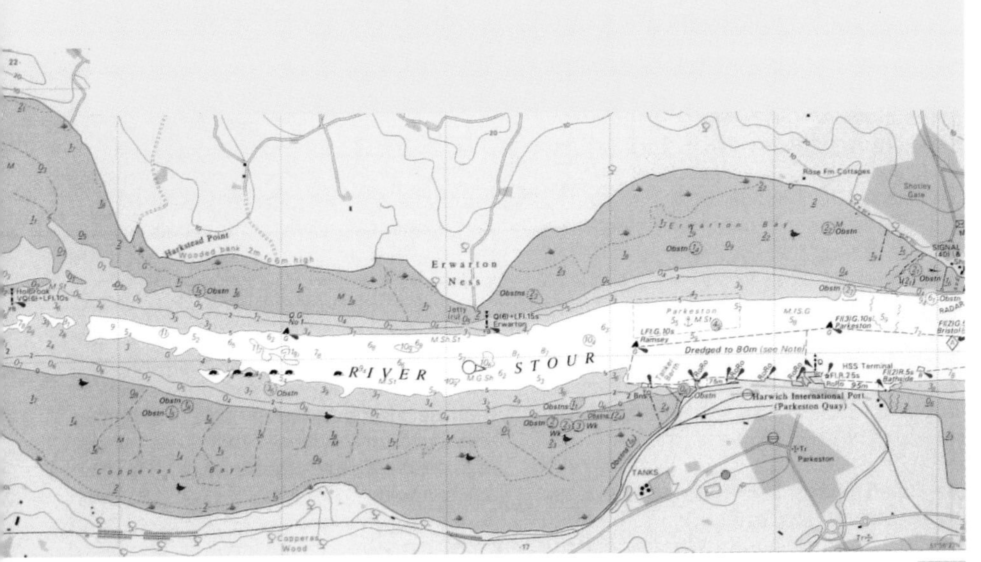

A coaster passing Erwarton Ness

Holbrook Creek opens up northwards immediately after Holbrook Beacon and again is easiest before the tide covers all the flats. The upper reaches are marked by lateral buoys and withies and shoal draft craft can find their way close to the head. Otherwise anchor as far in as you want to go and take the dinghy ashore. There is dry landing on staging at the head of the creek for easily the top half of the tide. From there you can follow the well marked path out past the car park into the lane and turn left for Holbrook about a mile away, or right for Harkstead a little less. Alternatively, you can follow the footpaths along the shore and across the fields into Harkstead.

EATING AND DRINKING

There is a pleasant country pub in Holbrook called The Compasses with real ales and meals served lunchtimes and evenings every day and a landlord who has sailed and therefore understands our strange requests. Tel: 01473 328332. Bar open 1130-1430 and 1800-2300 (Sun 1200-1500 and 1800-2230) and restaurant 1200-1415 and 1800-2115 every day.

The Bakers Arms in Harkstead has been taken over by new landlords in 2006 and they tell me they intend to start serving food both lunchtimes and evenings every day. Bar open Mon to Thurs 1200-1500 and 1800-2300 and all day Fri to Sun (Sun to 2230), Tel: 01473 328595.

CREW CHANGES AND TRAVEL

There are occasional buses throughout the day to Shotley, Ipswich and Manningtree from Holbrook and Harkstead. For bus information contact Traveline East Anglia Tel: 08706 082608 Website: www.traveline.org.uk. For trains from Manningtree see the Manningtree section and for trains and coaches from Ipswich see the Ipswich section of the River Orwell chapter.

WRABNESS

At Wrabness there are many trots of moorings but no club to contact for a vacant one, so the visitor must be prepared and available to move if necessary. There is clean landing on the beach at the foot of the cliff and in front of the beach huts and chalets. There are no facilities or services at Wrabness and the two pubs have long since closed. This is a place to enjoy the peace and splendid scenery, sharing it with those in the stilted beach huts ashore. Wrabness Nature Reserve in Oakfield Wood above Wrabness has recently been licenced as a Woodland Burial Site. Were it not for the absence of a house of

WRABNESS INFORMATION

Facilities	None
Stores	None
Public Tel.	None
Taxis	Manningtree Taxis, Mistley, Tel: 01206 393333; Harwich Taxis, Harwich, Tel: 01255 551111
Police	88-92 Main Road, Harwich. Tel: 01255 221312
Doctor	A. R. Alldrick & Partners, Harwich Road, Wix Village. Tel: 01255 201299
Hospital	(A&E) Colchester General, Turner Road, Colchester, Tel: 01206 747474; (A&E) Clacton Hospital, Tower Road, Clacton, Tel: 01255 201717
Dentist	Manningtree Dental Practice, 17a High Street, Manningtree. Tel: 01206 393744
Pharmacy	Alliance Pharmacy, Station Road, Manningtree. Tel: 01206 393134

refreshment for my many mourners, the peace and beauty of the location would almost make me want to change my funeral plans from scattered ashes from a 'penny sick' off Clacton, to tucking them away in a cornflakes packet under an oak tree here.

CREW CHANGES AND TRAVEL

There are regular buses throughout the day at Wrabness to Harwich and Manningtree. For bus information contact Traveline East Anglia, Tel: 08706 082608 Website: www.traveline.org.uk. There are regular trains, hourly or better, from Wrabness Station (one mile) to Harwich and Manningtree and direct onwards to London Liverpool Street (90 minutes). For information contact 'One' Customer Services, Tel: 08456 007245 Website: www.onerailway.com or National Rail Enquiries, Tel: 08457 484950 Website: www.nationalrail.co.uk

WRABNESS TO MANNINGTREE

Although the channel is well buoyed from Wrabness onwards, consulting a chart and/or pilot book is essential for the rest of the navigable river as the channel is narrow and shallow. For the newcomer it is best attempted well after half flood and unless you are staying, a quick turn around should be planned to avoid being left on the mud when the water runs away, which it does quickly. But if you can take the mud, you'll be glad you stayed, as both places have something to offer the cruising yachtsman.

Leaving PH No4 buoy off Wrabness behind, the river bends slightly north towards the Suffolk shore and you should leave SH buoy No5 close to starboard before heading west again towards No6 PH beacon, opposite Stutton Ness, leaving this to port. Trees and fields flank the river on both sides above Wrabness, but the warehouses, chimneys and maltings of Mistley are soon seen in the distance. After No6, you will pass between two pairs of lateral buoys and then a further green starboard hand buoy will be seen. This is No11 and you should leave this close to starboard, before heading for No12 north cardinal buoy. Do not be tempted to treat these two as a pair and cut the corner, or Ballast Hill to port will catch you. If you are too early on the tide, or this is close enough for you, it is possible to anchor to north of the channel just past the cardinal buoy in the first part of Cross Reach in the entrance to Lowercraft Fleet where there is a hole where a small yacht can stay afloat, but don't forget a riding light at night.

From here the channel bends towards Mistley and you should leave the two starboard channel buoys close to starboard, before turning in towards the quay itself. The best water is to be found very close to the quay, with a bank half-way along the quay only about 30 metres off (often evidenced by swans airing their knees on it), which should be left to starboard before slightly coming away from the quay for the very last wooden faced section. If you ever try to chance it across the flats here, beware of the unmarked barge wreck, which can be seen clearly at low tide, lying to the north of the quay.

From this point onwards the channel is marked by a series of small lateral buoys right up to head of navigation at Manningtree and these should be followed as if joining dots if you wish to stay off the mud. The channel goes off in a big loop to the northern side of the estuary before heading back towards Manningtree. Do not be tempted to follow local yachtsmen through small channels across the mudflats, until you've taken the time to gain their local knowledge. On reaching the moorings at Manningtree, the best water is to be found by feeling and sounding your way between and through the moorings.

JACQUES BAY

Jacques Bay is a good anchorage often forgotten by all but locals and sailing barges. From No5 SH buoy feel in southwards towards the farm buildings on the shore. The creek turns 90° to the west after a short distance to bring you into a pool with over one and a half metres at LWS and good holding behind No6 beacon. Locals in shoal draft craft sometimes use Netherhall Fleet further up the Stour and take the mud further westward in the bay. An hour or so either side of high water, clean landing is possible towards the western end of the bay on what is known locally as Bradfield Beach.

BRADFIELD

For those in Jacques Bay taking the dinghy ashore, Bradfield is reached after half a mile by following the lane which exits the bay at Bradfield Beach under the railway line and up to the main road, where you turn left up Ship Hill.

EATING AND DRINKING

Soon after you come into the village the first pub you come to is The Strangers Home. The pub serves both evening meals and lunches and just evening meals at weekends. The bar is open all day at weekends. Tel: 01255 870304.

Further on through the village you will come to the pleasant and friendly second pub, The Village Maid, which has real ales and is open all day, every day 1200-2300 (Sun 2230) serving food all day 1200-2100. Tel: 01255 870329.

BRADFIELD INFORMATION	
Facilities	None
Stores	Follow the lane through to the other end of the village (one mile), where there is a village store and Post Office open Mon to Sat 0800-1800, Sun 0930-1230
Bank	Cash machine in The Strangers Home pub
Public Tel.	Outside The Strangers Home pub and a further one outside the village store
Accommodation	There is bed & breakfast accommodation at Emsworth House on Ship Hill with stunning views over the river. Tel: 01255 870860
Taxis	Manningtree Taxis, Mistley, Tel: 01206 393333; Riverside Taxis, Station Road, Lawford, Manningtree, Tel: 01206 397563

For emergency and medical services refer to Manningtree and Mistley section

CREW CHANGES AND TRAVEL

There are regular buses throughout the day from Bradfield to Harwich and Manningtree. For bus information contact Traveline East Anglia, Tel: 08706 082608 Website: www.traveline.org.uk. For trains from Manningtree see the Manningtree section.

STUTTON

Between No6 beacon and Stutton Ness there is a wide expanse of deep water in which to anchor with good holding in this pleasant location. Due to the coaster traffic, anchor as far north in this pool as you can and don't forget a riding light at night. Clean, dry landing is possible here on the Ness at most states of tide and if you follow the lane from the Ness downstream along the shore and branching away after a short while, this will take you up to the main road where you can turn right into Stutton just over a mile from the river.

STUTTON INFORMATION	
Facilities	None
Stores	None
Public Tel.	In the centre of the village
Taxis	P&S Taxis, Manningtree, Tel: 01206 396321
Police	Civic Drive, Ipswich. Tel: 01473 613500
Doctor	Dr. Dineen & Ptnrs., The Street, Holbrook. Tel: 01473 328263
Hospital	(A&E) Ipswich Hospital, Heath Road (a mile and a half to the east of the town centre). Tel: 01473 712233
Dentist	Manningtree Dental Practice, 17a High Street, Manningtree. Tel: 01206 393744
Pharmacy	Nearest, Manningtree or Ipswich.

EATING AND DRINKING

As you come into the village on the left-hand side there is The Kings Head Inn, open lunchtimes and evenings, seven days a week for both bar and restaurant. Tel: 01473 328898.

CREW CHANGES AND TRAVEL

There are occasional buses throughout the day to Shotley, Ipswich and Manningtree from Stutton. For bus information contact Traveline East Anglia, Tel: 08706 082608 Website: www.traveline.org.uk. For trains from Manningtree see the Manningtree section and for trains and coaches from Ipswich see the Ipswich section of the River Orwell chapter.

MISTLEY AND MANNINGTREE

Although Mistley and Manningtree are separate places I will deal with them here as one, as it's only a very pleasant half-mile walk along the riverside road known as The Wall between them, passing waterside punt racks and the famous swans that reside here. Mistley is an odd mixture of the industrial (still with a working maltings) and the genteel, whilst Manningtree is a typical small English town, with narrow streets, minute market square and even a small beach by the quay on which children play and bathe on hot summer days at high tide.

MOORINGS

There are three choices of moorings in this area. The first place you will come to is Mistley Marine just before the quay. Although this is the boatyard from which Mistley Marine runs its engineering and dredging operation, there is also a parallel leisure operation from the pontoons. There are plans to further develop the leisure facilities into a small drying marina here and I wish them well, as this would be a valuable facility. Although space for visitors is limited, the friendly proprietors will always try to find you room for a very moderate fee against a pontoon or barge, but you will dry out here. Due to their commercial operations, visitors should always seek agreement with Mistley Marine prior to mooring and you will need to

Manningtree Hard

do this during normal working hours. By making your way through the boatyard and up Anchor Lane, you will join the main road at the downstream end of Mistley.

The second place to moor is against Mistley Quay. After much argument between local sailors and the commercial users of the quay, it seems that the rights of this public quay have been established. Locals tell me the public portion is past the commercial quay and the constricted part of the quayside, where it opens up and you can see through to The Mistley Thorn. The quay here is fine for a short stop, but is not very yacht friendly if staying a tide and for this you will need to carry a board or similar to prevent top-side damage. Also, at the time of writing, the quayside ladders had been cut off (I understand during the period of dispute), making the quay difficult to access from the deck of a small yacht, but there are plans to resolve this situation.

Above Mistley Quay the moorings are the responsibility of Stour Sailing Club and the third place for visitors to moor are the two drying moorings provided just off the end of the club hard. Visitors are welcome here without prior arrangement if the club is closed, although it is often to be found open around high tides. I have also been told that small yachts may now go alongside the end of the quay just past the hard at high tide as the mud has been levelled here. I cannot vouch for this personally, although it is clear the mud has been levelled and I would suggest making local enquiries prior.

CREW CHANGES AND TRAVEL

There are regular buses throughout the day at Mistley to Harwich and Manningtree. There are also regular trains, hourly or better, from Mistley Station (near the quay) to Harwich and Manningtree and direct trains onwards to London Liverpool Street. Manningtree station is half a mile from Manningtree town centre, with regular fast services to London Liverpool Street (80 minutes), Ipswich and Norwich, although buses run regularly from the town to the station. For bus information contact Traveline East Anglia, Tel: 08706 082608 Website: www.traveline.org.uk For train information contact 'One' Customer Services, Tel: 08456 007245 Website: www.onerailway.com or National Rail Enquiries, Tel: 08457 484950 Website: www.nationalrail.co.uk

MISTLEY & MANNINGTREE SKIPPERS INFORMATION

MISTLEY

Harbour Master	Mistley Marine, Tel: 01206 392127 Mobile: 07850 208918 Public quay at Mistley, no Harbour Master
Facilities	None

MANNINGTREE

Harbour Master	Stour SC, Tel: 01206 393924 or Email: timjgoodwin@mac.com
Water	At the top of hard, enquire at SSC
Fuel	None close by
Facilities	WC and showers at SSC and public WC and launderette in town

MISTLEY & MANNINGTREE SHORESIDE INFORMATION

Stores	If at Mistley Marine, turn left at the top of Anchor Lane and you will find a general store open seven days a week 0800-1800 (Sun 0830-1300). From the quay, there is a PO and stores in the High Street, or turn right to Manningtree (half a mile). Manningtree has the variety of shops expected of a small town. In the High Street there is a Tesco Express open seven days a week 0600-2200 and at the far end of town there is a Co-op supermarket for a slightly greater range of goods
Banks	Barclays and National Westminster in town, plus a cash machine at the Co-op supermarket
PO	One in the High Street, Mistley, one in the High Street, Manningtree and another in the Co-op supermarket
Public Tel.	Public telephones at the top of Anchor Lane in Mistley and in the High Street in Manningtree
Clubs	The very friendly and welcoming Stour Sailing Club is on the quay at Manningtree. Tel: 01206 393924 Website: www.stoursailingclub.co.uk. The East Coast branch of The Old Gaffers Association is active in the area, as evidenced by some fine old classics moored hereabouts. Website: www.eastcoastclassics.co.uk
Accommodation	A variety of accommodation in the area, a few examples being Dry Dock B&B in Quay Street, Manningtree, Tel: 01206 392620; The Cross Inn, Manningtree, Tel: 01206 396391; The Mistley Thorn, Mistley, Tel: 01206 392821
Taxis	Manningtree Taxis, Mistley, Tel: 01206 393333; Riverside Taxis, Station Road, Lawford, Manningtree, Tel: 01206 397563
Police	New Road, Manningtree. Tel: 01206 392611
Doctor	Dr. Hoskyns & Prtnr., Station Road, Manningtree. Tel: 01206 397070
Hospital	(A&E) Colchester General, Turner Road, Colchester. Tel: 01206 747474
Dentist	Manningtree Dental Practice, 17a High Street, Manningtree. Tel: 01206 393744
Pharmacy	Alliance Pharmacy, Station Road, Manningtree. Tel: 01206 393134
USEFUL NUMBERS	
Rigging fittings	Sta-Lok Terminals Ltd., Station Road, Lawford, Manningtree. Tel: 01206 391509

EATING AND DRINKING

MISTLEY

The Mistley Thorn on the High Street was completely refurbished in 2004 and is now a truly 'foodie' chic restaurant and bar that recently became the first restaurant in Essex to get a Michelin Bib Gourmand award. Moderately priced for the quality, and unlike some of its Chelsea cousins, not at all pompous, this place is well worth digging out your cleanest smock aboard for a visit. The walk to and from Manningtree is a very pleasant one if you are moored there and there's always a taxi back if you lack post-prandial energy. Under the guidance of Californian chef Sherri Singleton, The Mistley Thorn specialises in serving local and organic fare, including unusually, real ales and organic lager and cider. The bar is open Mon to Fri 1200-1500 and 1830-2300

HISTORY

The settlement of Manningtree pre-existed Roman times and the name derives from the Manni tribe that inhabited the area. Shakespeare described Falstaff as: "that roasted Manningtree ox", and the infamous Matthew Hopkins, Witchfinder General, lived in the town and commenced his terrible deeds in Manningtree and Mistley and is buried at Mistley Heath. Many of his trials took place in what is now The Mistley Thorn and his ghost is said to appear by the pond on a full moon. The 16th century Weavers, who fled the Netherlands, constructed many cottages in Mistley and Manningtree and the French Huguenots, following in the 17th century, added further buildings that reflected another architectural style, both still in evidence. Mistley almost became a spa town when Richard Rigby started to develop the town in the 18th century, but the combination of a collapse of his funds and his reputation put an end to this. However, the architecture in Mistley still provides a glimpse of these aspirations as do the best remnants of Robert Adam's work Rigby commissioned for the town – the Swan Fountain opposite The Mistley Thorn and Mistley Towers.

and all day at weekends 1200- 2300 and the restaurant opens for lunch and dinner seven days a week. Tel: 01206 392821.

There is also a fish and chip takeaway near the top of Anchor Lane to the east of town and a small teashop above the Mistley Quay Workshops.

MANNINGTREE

Manningtree has a variety of places to eat and drink with a couple of restaurants and a number of pubs. A few examples are the Mogul Indian Restaurant in the High Street, Tel: 01206 394102, the more up-market Stour Bay Restaurant, also in the High Street, Tel: 01206 396687 and The Crown pub which backs onto the quay next door to the yacht club, open all day and serving lunch and dinner seven days a week (and Sunday breakfast!). The Stour Sailing Club has a friendly upstairs bar with real ales and a balcony overlooking the river, open at weekends and some other times in season when the tide's in! There is also a fish and chip shop and a Chinese takeaway in town.

TO SEE AND DO

Other than a trip to the miniature beach at Manningtree, the area offers only quite genteel pursuits. There is a museum in Manningtree High Street, but this is only open for a couple of hours Wednesday morning, Friday afternoon and Sunday morning. Both Mistley and Manningtree however are worth exploring on foot and have some well preserved old houses and you can see the Adams Swan Fountain and Mistley Towers, which are the remaining twin towers of an Adams church (keys can be obtained from the Mistley Quay Workshops). There is a craft centre on the quay at Mistley Quay Workshops, which includes workshops for bookbinding, pottery, stained glass, painting and the making of harpsichords. For the walkers among you, there is a pleasant three mile walk with good views following the Essex Way out of Mistley (starting between The Mistley Thorn and the station), going under the railway and then up onto Furze Hill and into Mistley Heath before returning along the road.

THE RIVER STOUR TRUST

The River Stour Trust was established in 1968 to protect the rights of navigation on the Stour to Sudbury in which it has been completely successful, and to strive to restore navigation from the sea to Sudbury. This second aim is slower in coming to fruition, although the Trust has restored sections and three locks and continues to press for further. The Trust has a new Visitor and Education Centre at Cornard Lock, near Sudbury. Website: www.riverstourtrust.org

THE WALTON BACKWATERS

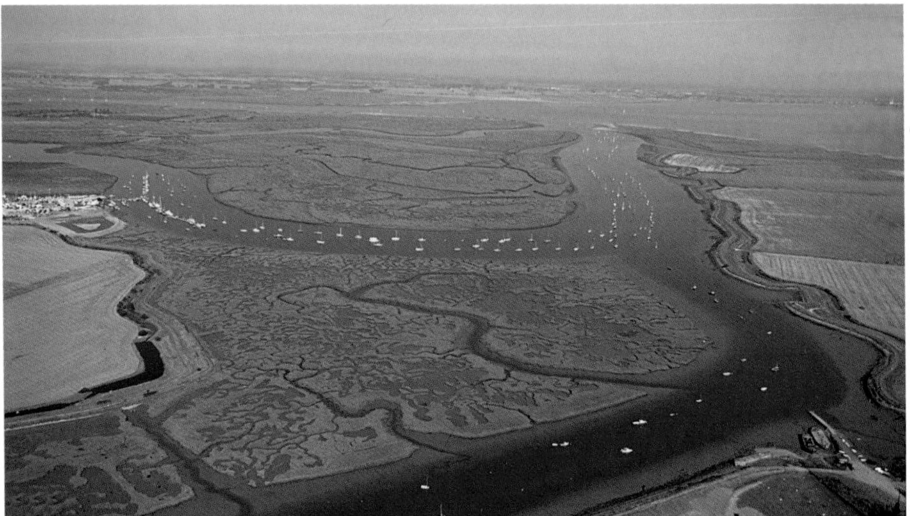

Walton Channel and Titchmarsh Marina ©PRPA

51°55'.0N 01°17.9'E *(off Pye End buoy)*
Tides entrance to Walton Backwaters: 0:00 *(difference from Harwich)*

The Walton Backwaters are a protected site of special scientific interest and a haven for wildlife. It is not the place to cruise if in search of dramatic scenery and interesting landmarks, as the vistas consist mainly of saltings and creeks with the occasional topsail glimpsed across land. Some days it can even seem quite bleak, but once in amongst the islands, it is a place to escape from civilisation and commercialism. Many will have 'visited' the Walton Backwaters as children when reading Arthur Ransome's 'Secret Water', and for some, the magic kindled by the book never goes away. Much of The Backwaters are within sight of Felixstowe docks, yet are a haven for wildlife.

APPROACH AND ENTRANCE

Approaching from any direction it is vital for the newcomer to locate Pye End safe water buoy before attempting to enter The Backwaters. Once found, the entrance is fairly straightforward, except in strong easterly winds when a chop can build up quickly to dangerous proportions. Thanks to the efforts of the yacht club, the channel into The Backwaters is well marked and with reasonable preparation offers no particular hazards, although depths in places are only about 1.5 metres at LWS. Selected buoys are lit, but I would recommend a daytime entrance prior to a night-time one, as the newcomer can find it confusing. Up to Island Point the speed limit is 8 knots and from there onwards throughout the Backwaters, 6 knots and 4 knots past quays etc. On reaching Island Point north cardinal buoy marking the spit of the north-east end of Horsey Island,

Hamford Water curves off to starboard and the Walton Channel to port.

WALTON CHANNEL, FOUNDRY REACH AND TWIZZLE CREEK

Three more red can buoys lead into Walton Channel and depths here drop again for a time to little more than a metre at LWS in places. There is then a green conical buoy to watch out for and leave to starboard, as it marks another spit that has caught many keels around low water. If the weather is fine, there will be many boats at anchor just inside the Walton Channel, as the firm beach of Stone Point to port makes a popular landing place and this can be a delightful spot to bring up on a summers night. Stone Point is an SSSI and managed by Walton and Frinton Yacht Club which is trying to preserve the amenity for the good of all. There are notices warning of a tern nesting site which should be observed and everyone should treat this place with respect so we can all continue to be allowed this amenity. If planning a club or group visit, please speak with WFYC prior.

There are moorings to follow all along the Walton Channel to the north cardinal buoy marking the spit separating Foundry Reach and Twizzle Creek. Foundry Reach branches off to port and very soon becomes drying. By following the line of the moorings in the centre of the creek this leads to the boatyards and WFYC yacht basin. Shortly after entering Foundry Reach there is a landing to port by some steps in the sea wall from where you can walk into Walton, although it's a bit muddy and the walk is along the sea wall and then through a breakers yard! Don't use the jetty at Foundry Dock as there is no way out of the yard here. On reaching the Walton and Frinton Yacht Club buildings, the creek forks. To port is the entrance to the yacht basin and on to the town hard and to starboard the creek leads up to Bedwells yard, although just

WALTON SKIPPERS INFORMATION

WALTON YACHT BASIN

Harbour Master	Contact Bedwell & Co., Tel: 01255 675873
Water	On berths
Electricity	On berths
Fuel	In town
Facilities	WC and showers at club (open daily)
Boatyard	Bedwell & Co., Tel: 01255 675873 and Frank Halls & Son at the Town Hard, Tel: 01255 675596
Chandlery	Both boatyards have chandleries attached
Slips	Bedwells has an 18 ton crane and two slip sheds for up to 40 tons; Frank Halls has a 12 ton hoist. Websites: www.wfyc.co.uk and www.frankhalls.com

WALTON SHORESIDE INFORMATION

Stores	Good range in town quarter of a mile, including Co-op convenience store in High Street open 0700-2200 (0900-1700 Sun)
Banks	None, cash machine in Co-op
PO	In High Street
Public Tel.	At WFYC and in town
Club	Walton and Frinton Yacht Club. Tel: 01255 678161
Taxis	Walton Taxis, Tel: 01255 675910; Shore Taxis, Tel: 01255 676887
Accommodation	A range available in town including the Walton Tavern on the front and the Queens Head in the High Street, contact Tourist Information
Tourist Info.	Seasonal opening on Princes Esplanade. Tel: 01255 675542

 Not to be used for navigation

in the starboard arm to port there is a quay by the club, where you can temporarily moor to enquire.

Leaving the cardinal buoy to port and branching off to starboard into Twizzle Creek, the line of moorings lead to Titchmarsh Marina. You will soon come to some pontoons in the creek off the marina and half way along these there is a clear entrance to port into the marina. There is a sill, but if you can navigate the Twizzle you will usually have enough depth but there is a depth gauge on the pontoon to starboard to assist as you enter. The Twizzle is navigable for a short distance after the marina at high tide, but due to the oyster beds hereabouts, anchoring is not permitted.

WALTON-ON-THE-NAZE

Walton-on-the-Naze is a traditional family seaside resort with an outstanding and safe sandy beach. The narrow streets of the town contain numerous shops, restaurants and pubs overlooking the second longest pier in the country. In high summer the town is very busy, but at the end of the season it reverts to a sleepy place, with a rather old-fashioned charm.

MOORINGS

All the swinging moorings in this area belong to Frank Halls & Co., Bedwell & Co., or are privately owned and are marked H, B or P respectively, so you can easily check the availability and suitability of most with the yards. If looking for a marina berth you will surprisingly find yourself spoilt for choice in The Backwaters. Firstly, there is the limited access in Foundry Reach to the simplicity of the yacht basin by the WFYC and its closeness to town (being only five minutes walk from the High Street) and traditional surroundings. Secondly, there is the relatively simple access to the sophistication of Titchmarsh Marina with its first class facilities at reasonable prices. Although Titchmarsh is a little remote, requiring a taxi ride to town, you will find most of your requirements catered for on-site. Bikes are also available for hire.

TITCHMARSH MARINA SKIPPERS INFORMATION	
Harbour Master	Call on VHF Ch80 call-sign “Titchmarsh Marina” or Tel: 01255 672185
Water	On pontoons
Electricity	On pontoons
Fuel	Diesel pontoon and LPG to port on entry
Facilities	Full marina facilities
Internet	Wi-fi hotspot
Boatyard	Full boatyard services available on-site
Chandlery	Large, well stocked on-site chandlery, Marinestore. Tel: 01255 677775
Slips	35 ton travel-hoist and 25 ton crane
Scrubbing Posts	Available, contact Harbour Master
Website	www.titchmarshmarina.com

The Walton Yacht Basin in Foundry Reach provides sheltered moorings for 60-70 boats. The basin is managed for the Walton Yacht Trust by Bedwell & Co., who should be contacted in advance for entrance and berthing information. There is a depth of 2 metres in the basin, but the narrow 3.6 metre wide entrance is only opened for a short period up to high water when there will generally be something in excess of 2 metres over the sill. You should note that at extreme neaps the entrance can be left closed to protect depths in the basin.

Titchmarsh Marina accessed from the Twizzle, offers 490 deep water floating pontoon berths in a large, very sheltered basin. Titchmarsh & Son had been boatbuilders in Mill Lane, Walton, since the 1950s and moved to the Twizzle to construct the marina over 30 years ago. The facilities on-site include the popular Harbour Lights restaurant and bar for

TITCHMARSH MARINA SHORESIDE INFORMATION

Stores	Basic supplies carried in chandlery, otherwise in town one mile, including Co-op convenience store in High Street open 0700-2200 (0900-1700 Sun)
Banks	None, cash machine in Co-op
PO	In High Street
Public Tel.	At marina by office
Taxis	Walton Taxis, Tel: 01255 675910; Shore Taxis, Tel: 01255 676887
Accommodation	A range available in town including the Walton Tavern on the front and the Queens Head in the High Street, contact Tourist Information
Tourist Info.	Seasonal opening on Princes Esplanade. Tel: 01255 675542
Police	Martello Road. Tel: 01255 851212
Doctor	Dr. J. A. F. Geldard & Ptnrs., Vicarage Lane. Tel: 01255 674373
Hospital	(A&E) Clacton Hospital (open 0900-1700) Tower Road (A&E) Ipswich Hospital, Heath Road. Tel: 01473 712233
Dentist	Mr. Turner, 26 Elm Tree Avenue, Frinton-On-Sea. Tel: 01255 672309
Pharmacy	R. S. Wheeler, 40 High Street. Tel: 01255 675900
USEFUL NUMBERS	
GRP Repairs	Smooth Finish (Titchmarsh Marina). Tel: 01206 251080
Marine Electronics	Hurst Marine Services (Titchmarsh Marina). Tel: 01255 673171
Marine Engineers	JB Services (in Frank Halls yard). Tel: 07971 644291 Marine & Motor Services (Town Hard). Tel: 01255 679234 French Marine Motors (Titchmarsh Marina). Tel: 01255 850303
Sea School	North Sea Yachting (Titchmarsh Marina). Tel: 01473 232221
Yacht Brokers	Westwater Yacht Sales (Titchmarsh Marina). Tel: 01255 672500

berth holders and visitors alike. The sill carries 1.2 metres at MLWS, so most craft can enter at any time on the top half of the tide and some of us with shoal draft can surprisingly have all-tide access on neaps. They do not have allocated visitors berths, but with the large number of berths in the marina, they can usually find you a space, but it is important to contact them prior.

CREW CHANGES AND TRAVEL

Walton-on-the-Naze is a convenient place for crew changes with good train and coach links. The station is close to the town centre with services to Colchester and London Liverpool Street (90 minutes – changing at Thorpe-le-Soken). For information contact 'One' Customer Services, Tel: 08456 007245 Website: www.onerailway.com, or National Rail Enquiries, Tel: 08457 484950 Website: www.nationalrail.co.uk. Scheduled coach services are operated from Walton-on-the-Naze to London by National Express, Tel: 08705 808080 Website: www.nationalexpress.com. There are also regular bus services to the surrounding area. For information contact Traveline East Anglia, Tel: 08706 082608 Website: www.traveline.org.uk

EATING AND DRINKING

The Harbour Lights restaurant and bar in Titchmarsh Marina serves real ales in its small bar with extensive outside terrace with pleasant views. It is open 1200-2300 every day. The smart and busy restaurant serves breakfast, lunch, afternoon teas and dinner from an extensive menu, 0800-2100 every day. Tel: 01255 851887.

Walton and Frinton Yacht Club is situated at the head of Foundry Reach and on the site of an old mill. It welcomes visitors and has a lounge, with the bar open 1130-1430 and 1800-2230 (Sundays 1200-1500 and 1830-2200) every day. The restaurant opens 1200-1345 and 1830-2015 (Fridays and Saturdays 2100) every day. Tel: 01255 675526.

Being a seaside town, Walton-on-the-Naze has a wide variety of eating and drinking establishments from pubs and clubs, cafés and takeaways to fish and chips and restaurants of many nationalities, most within the small area bounded by the sea front and the High Street. Taking a walk round this area will usually yield something to suit most tastes.

For lovers of seafood, Naze Oysters has its packing shed by Bedwells yard by the Town Hard. Tel 01255 673123.

TO SEE AND DO

Walton has safe and sandy bathing beaches along the seaward side of the town with the pier reaching out into the northern end of the Wallet. The pier has recently been taken on by new management and is showing evidence of their interest. Apart from the usual array of amusements, there is a ten-pin bowling alley (Tel: 01255 675646) open 1000-2400 every day, a diner and a bar. The Tyne Class lifeboat is also moored against the inside of the end of the pier these days, although the crew room and RNLI gift shop are still ashore near the entrance to the pier.

Going north from the town centre there is the Columbine Centre, which is the home of the indoor bowls centre and multi-purpose hall that doubles at times as a theatre. Adjacent to this is the modern indoor swimming pool, Tel:

Sunset in the Walton Backwaters ©C. Blaney

01255 676608. Across on the seafront is the Old Lifeboat House by the new Coastguard building which houses the Maritime Museum. Open from Spring Bank Holiday to 31st August, Tel: 01255 678259. There are also wildlife spotting boat trips on The Backwaters on the launch 'Katrina', from Foundry Dock, Tel: 01255 671852.

Going further north still you will come to the grassy expanse of The Naze itself with wonderful views over the surrounding seas. Here you will also find the famous tower, built in the early 18th century as a navigational aid. It has in recent years been restored and now has tearooms, a museum and gallery with viewing platform at the top. From here you can see across The Backwaters, up to the Suffolk shoreline and on very clear days, I am told the north Kent coast comes into view. Open 1000-1700, April to October, admission £2.50 or £6 for a family ticket. Tel: 01255 852519.

For the walker there are some very pleasant walks hereabouts, along the shoreline and sea walls. One pleasant and easy walk of about three miles, starts from the Naze Tower, goes out to the cliffs (take care of the crumbly cliff edges) and north past the Fossil Cliffs to the north end of The Naze, where it turns in towards The Backwaters alongside Cormorant Creek through the John Weston Nature Reserve. The path turns south alongside the Walton Channel and the start of Foundry Creek, where you can either branch back to the Naze Tower, or continue on the Foundry Dock and the path through the breakers yard back into town.

HAMFORD WATER AND THE INNER BACKWATERS

Hamford Water is wide and open and carries plenty of water for well over a mile past Island Point and the entrance to the Walton Channel. Oakley Creek branches off to starboard marked by the Exchem east cardinal buoy after about a mile. Although anchoring is not generally recommended in this creek (and landing on the shore prohibited), it is worth exploring to see the seal colony that lives hereabouts. This is the only backwater still used by commercial shipping making their way to and from the explosives factory at Great Oakley, so keep a watchful eye out in the creek (and for that matter in the entrance to The Backwaters and Hamford Water) near high water.

Continuing past Oakley Creek up Hamford Water, Kirby Creek soon opens up to port. This top end of Hamford Water is a popular deep water anchorage in the right conditions. A spit extends from the tip of Skipper Island, so if entering Kirby Creek the recommendation is usually to follow the Horsey Island shoreline into the creek where there are a number of moorings to follow. Continuing down the creek you will come to the miniature Honey Island. Although to port of the island there are moorings, there is little water and no room to anchor clear of the oyster beds. To starboard just past the island, there is plenty of room to bring up and some pools where you can lie afloat in peaceful surroundings. You can either land from a dinghy opposite Skippers Island and follow the sea wall path to Kirby Quay a mile away, or follow the very tricky and shallow creek round to port of the headland to the head of the creek at Kirby Quay itself. Kirby le Soken is half a mile away up a lane, where you will find a village store and post office and the Ship Inn, with its friendly bar and large restaurant, open lunchtimes and evenings. Tel: 01255 674256.

Back in Hamford Water and continuing on past the north of Skippers Island nature reserve, you come into Landermere Creek. The creek shallows here to about 2 metres at MLWS and best water is found by following the line of the northern shore, as extensive shoals spread north from Skippers Island. Again this is a popular anchorage and slightly more sheltered than downstream. After about half a mile the creek swings southwest and there is a small pool of deeper water just before this. The water shallows considerably in this reach to the west of Skippers Island at times to less than a metre at LAT, yet there are pools where moorings will be found, although for shoal draft yachts there is just room to anchor clear and stay afloat on most tides.

After about a third of a mile the creek swings to starboard again into a westerly direction and soon becomes drying, although there is initially a useful deep water pool carrying about 2 metres at LWS. Landing can be made from a dinghy further up this creek at Landermere Quay on the south side, or Beaumont Quay near the head of the creek on the north side. Although there seem to be drying moorings everywhere here, the area is wonderfully remote and quiet and ideal for those with shoal draft craft able to take the ground and those who enjoy exploration by tender, especially if by sailing dinghy in Arthur Ransome style.

St. Osyth boatyard

THE RIVER COLNE

⌖ **51°44'.6N 01°02'.5E** Colne Bar Buoy
Tides Brightlingsea +0:15, Wivenhoe +0:25 *(differences from Harwich)*

The Colne has been navigated since Roman times and its towns and villages have earned a living from all kinds of nautical occupations. Yachting and fishing brought fame to the area over the years, as has smuggling, wrecking and salvaging, but now the commercial traffic has largely gone and is restricted to small quays in Rowhedge and Brightlingsea. Colchester has even stopped being a port in the last few years due to silting. The oyster cultivation industry still clings on here, as does fishing, but otherwise the rest of the Colne is now purely devoted to leisure boating.

APPROACH AND ENTRANCE
Finding the entrance to the Colne and the Blackwater is not difficult, although landmarks can be difficult for the newcomer to identify until close in. There are the Knoll and Eagle buoys and then the Colne Bar buoy to point you in the right direction, although landmarks are still too far away to use at this point. The familiar yellow light on Bateman's Tower off Brightlingsea (which you never seemed to be able to distinguish until well into the approach!) has now been replaced by a white light (Fl(3)10s), which may make approach at night easier. From the Colne Bar, there is a buoyed route to follow for deep water, with the gentler shelving side to port.

After just over a mile, you will pass between Inner Bench Head red can buoy (Fl(2)R.5s) and Colne Point green conical buoy (Fl.G.3s). It is about another mile to the next pair of lateral marks, by which time the river narrows down enough to see the beaches on both banks. Mersea Island is to the port and the beaches of St. Osyth and Point Clear to starboard.

Those familiar with this coast and particularly those with shoal draft, will be seen taking short cuts in fine weather. From the Blackwater they will skirt Mersea Island closer in and from the Wallet will go north of The Eagle before heading for Colne Bar buoy. These can be rewarding, but should not be attempted without having built up familiarity and without careful planning and detailed charts.

Heading into Brightlingsea (which is lit all the way in), stand well off Colne Buoy

No13 (where the 8 knot speed limit in the river starts) as this dries at LWS and keep the Brightlingsea Spit cardinal buoy close alongside to the port side (north) and pick up the leading lights/ boards bearing 041 degrees. There is less than a metre of water at LWS with the channel deepening to 2 metres 100 metres further on, but shallowing again later. Deeper water is to be found on the south side of the channel as you follow channel markers in and then slowly ease to starboard towards the pontoons. Stick close to the pontoons as the channel is narrow and beware of the tidal stream that can run through here at up to 3 knots.

BRIGHTLINGSEA

Brightlingsea is all many know of the Colne, but you should read this chapter further as there are other places of interest to the visiting yachtsman up river. Having said that, Brightlingsea is an interesting and convenient place for a stopover. The only Cinque Port in Essex, its history with the sea runs deep and its fishermen have sailed far and wide in locally built craft. Henry VIII made the area a naval station, having his ships built from local timber and commercial shipbuilding followed. All sorts of imports and exports have been handled here, as well as at Colchester at the head of the river and a strong link

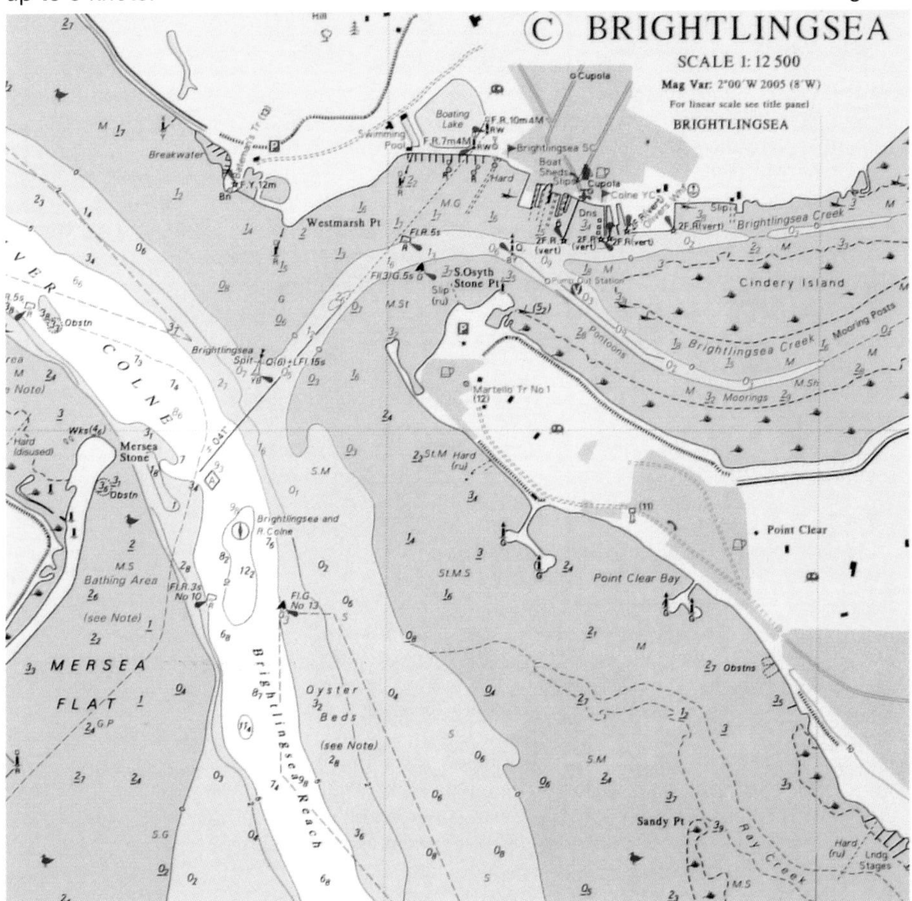

Not to be used for navigation

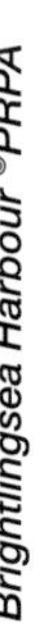
Brightlingsea Harbour ©PRPA

with the water still exists in the town, with its facilities for commercial and pleasure boating. As the commercial side diminished, the town became famous for its ocean-going and racing yachts and vied with Tollesbury for local prominence in the J-class days.

Just inside the creek is the site of the old James & Stone shipyard, now being developed into a waterside housing and marina complex. Once not the most favoured development locally, it seems to have won over the locals and the developers have told me how surprised and

BRIGHTLINGSEA SKIPPERS INFORMATION

Harbour Master	VHF Ch68 call-sign "Brightlingsea Harbour", Tel: 01206 302200
Water	Standpipes at the top of the hammerhead jetty and at Colne YC
Electricity	None
Fuel	Only in cans from garages in town, many go across to Bradwell to fill up
Facilities	Public WC near hard, WC and showers for visitors at CYC. Rubbish disposal also at CYC jetty. Oil may be emptied into the Council Boat Park waste oil tank.
Internet	CYC has helpfully created a free Wi-fi Hot Spot based at its clubhouse
Boatyard	A number, see Useful Numbers
Chandlery	Morgan Marine. Tel: 01206 302003
Slips	Enquire with boatyards (Morgan Marine has a 25 ton travelhoist) or the Hard Master, Tel: 01206 303535 and for dinghies enquire at Brightlingsea Sailing Club, Tel: 01206 303275
Scrubbing Posts	Enquire Hard Master, Tel: 01206 303535
Website	www.brightlingsea-town.co.uk/sailing/harbour_commissioners.htm
Water Taxi	Jon Brett runs the water taxi VHF Ch37, Tel: 07733 078503. This runs from mid-April to end-Oct, Fri 1700-2300, Sat 0900-2330 and Sun 0900-2100 (Fri 0900-2300, Sat 0900-2330 and Sun to Thur 0900-2200 in the school summer holidays)

BRIGHTLINGSEA SHORESIDE INFORMATION	
Stores	Good shops in town centre including a Tesco Express open 0600-2300 every day, a Co-op supermarket open 0700-2200 (0900-1700 Sun) and a Spar convenience store open 0600-1030 every day
Banks	A number of major banks in the high street and cash machine at Tesco
PO	Station Road
Public Tel.	By the shelter on the quayside
Club	Colne Yacht Club. Tel: 01206 302594 Website: www.colneyachtclub.org.uk
Taxis	Wivenhoe Station Cars, Tel: 01206 822020; Travelink Essex, Tel: 01206 828282
Accommodation	A range of accommodation in the town, enquire at HM office
Tourist Info.	In the HM office
Police	Station Road. Tel: 01206 302515
Doctor	Colne Medical Centre, Station Road. Tel: 01206 302522
Hospital	(A&E) Colchester General Hospital, Turner Road, Colchester. Tel: 01206 747474
Dentist	Figaji, Tilkeridou & Namazy, 32 Crossways, Jaywick. Tel: 01255 207620
Pharmacy	Alliance Pharmacy, Victoria Place. Tel: 01206 302029

pleased they have been at the number of locals buying the properties. Perhaps this will be the rare waterside development to have the week-round occupation it deserves and as such will add to the community and it's prosperity. The marina will have a sill and access approximately two hours either side of high water and although only having about 70 berths for residents, should help prevent extra pressure on the harbour berths.

Set up by Act of Parliament in 1928 to administer the harbour, the Brightlingsea Harbour Commissioners are representative of the Town and District Councils and all groups who have an interest in the harbour, and since the demise of Colchester as a port, have taken over responsibility for the entire Colne. The Harbour Master, Bernie Hetherington and his team, run the day-to-day activity within the harbour and river from their office just back from the quay. Facilities in the harbour have been steadily upgraded over the years. Boats of all shapes and sizes are accommodated on about 500 berths, large numbers now being on pontoons, but there are also moorings including some drying moorings, for small craft. The Harbour Master's staff make visitors very welcome, which explains why there are often nearly 100 visiting boats on a summer weekend and they always seem to find room for you somewhere. A water taxi offers an excellent service for those wishing to go ashore and explore the town, and the Colne Yacht Club welcomes visiting yachtsmen. There is also a foot ferry service between Brightlingsea, Point Clear and East Mersea.

There is a 4 knot speed limit in the harbour and this is strictly administered and jet-skis and wet bikes are not permitted. Although shallow, it is possible to navigate north of Cindery Island, but there is not much of interest beyond the island. This area is used by the last few remaining commercial vessels to visit the quay, although the gravel barges that used to frequently load here no longer do so.

MOORINGS
Up to 100 visitors can be accommodated on deep water moorings, mostly on pontoons and visitors are usually accommodated on the eastern pontoon at the end nearest the quay. These pontoons do not have shore access, but there is a regular water taxi service in season. Contact the Harbour Master's team to arrange a mooring. They will either be in the office or out on the water in one of their launches and will often lead you to a berth. During the season they will be in attendance from about 0800 to 2000 (in winter until 1600) and out of season they also offer a launch service for the moorings from 0800-1000 and 1500-1600. In emergency (not just being late in please, or we'll find the number withdrawn), Bernie can also be contacted out of hours on 07952 734814. If you're late in, try checking up and down the pontoons, the berth-holders will generally hang a "Back Tonight" notice if they don't want you to use their space. There are also some drying alongside berths at Brightlingsea Boatyard.

Near HW you can go alongside the hammerhead pontoon by the hard for a maximum of 15 minutes if you need to, but don't leave a vessel unattended here. Anchoring is prohibited anywhere in the harbour due to the lack of space, risk of fouling and commercial traffic.

BRIGHTLINGSEA - USEFUL NUMBERS

Boat Park & Launching	Brightlingsea Boat Park and Ride. Tel: 01206 304747
Boatyard, Engineers & Brokers	Morgan Marine. Tel: 01206 302003
Charter & Racing	West Quay Sailing. Tel: 07789 936439
Equipment & Fittings	Heron Yacht Services. Tel: 01206 303695
Hull Blasting, Treatment & Painting	Mick Oliver. Tel: 01255 423960
Jetskis	Personal Watercraft Centre. Tel: 01206 303333
Marine Engineers	French Marine Motors, Tel: 01206 302133; DB Marine, Tel: 01206 304391
Powerboat Importers & Brokers	Global Trade Partners. Tel: 01206 305500
Preservation Society	Colne Smack Preservation Society. Tel: (Sec.) 01206 304204
Sailing Association	North London Sailing Association. Tel: 01279 503108
Sailing Club	Brightlingsea Sailing Club. Tel: (Sec.) 01206 302676
Sailmakers	James Lawrence Sailmakers, Tel: 01206 302863; Advantage Sails, Tel: 07909 542138
Spars and Rigging	Sailspar. Tel: 01206 302679
Training (Power)	International Boat Training Centre, Tel: 01206 307777; Coastal Boating Academy, Tel: 07914 000394
Waterski Club	Brightlingsea Waterski Club. Tel: 07770 840029
Yacht Upholstery	Passmore Upholstery. Tel: 01206 384300

The beach huts at Brightlingsea

CREW CHANGES AND TRAVEL

There are regular bus services from Brightlingsea to Wivenhoe and Colchester (less frequent evenings and Sundays) for connection to rail services to London. For information contact Traveline East Anglia, Tel: 08706 082608 Website: www.traveline.org.uk. For train information contact 'One' Customer Services, Tel: 08456 007245 Website: www.onerailway.com or National Rail Enquiries, Tel: 08457 484950 Website: www.nationalrail.co.uk

There is a foot ferry service in season between Brightlingsea, Point Clear and East Mersea Stone, operated by the harbour commissioners, which runs during the day at weekends (every day peak season).

EATING AND DRINKING

Brightlingsea has many places of refreshment and is worth a walk round to explore, but I shall name a few places for reference, some near the quay and others further in towards town. Colne Yacht Club welcomes visitors to its bar and excellent restaurant overlooking the harbour and is so popular that advance booking is advised at weekends. The restaurant is open every day in season (1200-1400 and 1900-2100, all day at weekends). Tel: 01206 302594.

Just back from the quay is the new Coach House Coffee Shop, with a small outside terrace, Tel: 01206 304200. Further along is the famous (well among my crews!) Waterside Café and Fish & Chip Restaurant, where good eat-in and takeaway fish and chips and other delights, including a first class all-day breakfast may be purchased, open 1200-2130 (2100 Sundays), Tel: 01206 302710.

Following the road westwards you will come to the Yachtsmans Arms pub which is open 1100-1430 and 1800-2300 (all day

Fridays, Saturdays and Sundays) and serves food Thursday to Sunday at lunch-times only 1200-1400. Further on still is the Kovalam Indian Restaurant open every day 1200-1430 and 1800-2300 (2400 Friday and Saturday). Just up from here is The Sun pub in New Street which is open 1200-1500 and 1730-2300, weekends 1200-2400 (2230 Sundays), which serves bar food Mondays to Thursdays, 1200-1400 and 1730-2000.

Just behind the Harbour Master's office is Tower Street, which runs up to the high street. Here you will find the pleasant Raj Pavillion Indian restaurant open in the evenings 1800-2330 every day (2400 weekends), Tel: 01206 303767. A little further on towards town is the small CK Bistro open Wednesday to Saturday, 1800-2200 (last orders 2130), where you will find excellent freshly prepared food. They cater for all tastes, but you will need to bring your own alcohol and be prepared not to rush, Tel: 01206 305805.

TO SEE AND DO

Brightlingsea Museum is in Duke Street and is open from 1400-1700 Mondays and Thursdays and 1000-1600 Saturdays. If in need of more energetic entertainment there is a marvellous open-air swimming pool open daily from Whitsun to the end of the summer holidays on the road out to Bateman's Tower.

A very pleasant walk of five miles among marshes and woods can be trod from Bateman's Tower north along the sea wall to Alresford Creek, then inland along the creek for a short while before following a path inland through the sand pits to cut back to the sea wall again just above the tower. Pamphlets on this walk, with a map, are kept in the Harbour Master's office.

ST. OSYTH CREEK

Halfway along Brightlingsea Creek and just past Cindery Island, St. Osyth Creek branches off to starboard and makes a tortuous, but reasonably well marked one-mile journey to St. Osyth Quay for those able to take the ground. This creek is best negotiated towards the top of the tide, as it is very shallow in places and you may touch. As you approach the road bridge there are some quaint cottages to port at the head of the creek together with staging and the quay of St. Osyth Boatyard just beyond.

ST. OSYTH

St. Osyth is believed to have been named after a 7th century abbess killed here by Danish invaders for refusing to renounce her god. A priory was built and named in her honour in the early 12th century and the small town grew up around it. The port traces its history back to 1215 and there has been a quay here since about the same time. At the road bridge the creek has been dammed to form a lake on the far side where some boating activities occasionally take place.

For the intrepid and patient (and with drafts of less than 1.5 metres), who are prepared to take the mud, it is worth negotiating the twisting creek, as St. Osyth makes a pleasant alternative to Brightlingsea, with both its quayside facilities and those in the small town half a mile away up the road. At the boatyard you will always find a variety of traditional craft and on my last visit a wooden spritsail barge was being rebuilt – it appears from the keelson upwards!

MOORINGS

There are both staged mud-berths and a quay at St. Osyth Boatyard and it is usually possible to find a mooring there, but you should call the boatyard to check before attempting the creek. Berths were charged at a mere £5.00 per night in 2006 and visitors are made welcome.

CREW CHANGES AND TRAVEL

There are regular bus services from St. Osyth to Clacton and Colchester (less frequent evenings and Sundays) for connection to rail services to London. For information contact Traveline East Anglia,

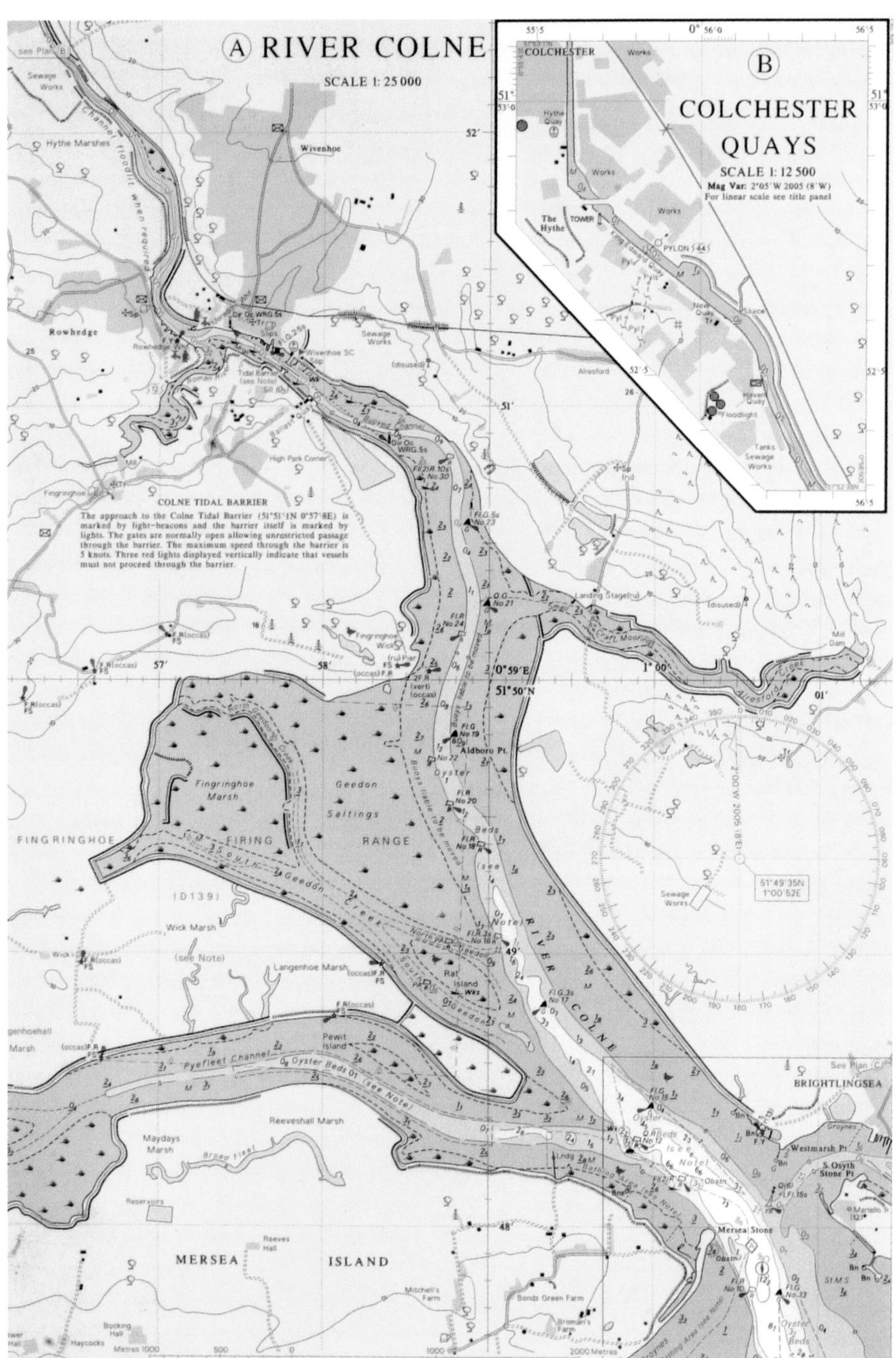

Ⓐ RIVER COLNE
SCALE 1: 25 000
Ⓑ COLCHESTER QUAYS
SCALE 1: 12 500
Mag Var: 2°05'W 2005 (8'W)
For linear scale see title panel
COLCHESTER
Hythe Quay
Works
The Hythe
TOWER
King Edward Quay
PYLON
New Quay
Sluice
Hythe Quay
Floodlight
Tanks
Sewage Works
Wivenhoe
Hythe Marshes
Channel floodlit when required
Rowhedge
Sewage Works
Wivenhoe SC
Tidal Barrier (see Note)
Ballast Quay
High Park Corner
Fingringhoe
Alresford
COLNE TIDAL BARRIER
The approach to the Colne Tidal Barrier (51°51'·1N 0°57'·8E) is marked by light-beacons and the barrier itself is marked by lights. The gates are normally open allowing unrestricted passage through the barrier. The maximum speed through the barrier is 5 knots. Three red lights displayed vertically indicate that vessels must not proceed through the barrier.
Landing Stage(ru)
(disused)
Mill Dam
Alresford Creek
0°59'E
51°50'N
1° 00'
01'
57'
58'
Fingringhoe Wick
Aldboro Pt.
Oyster Beds
Fingringhoe Marsh
Geedon Saltings
FINGRINGHOE
FIRING RANGE
South Geedon Creek
(D139)
Wick Marsh
(see Note)
Langenhoe Marsh
Rat Island
RIVER COLNE
Sewage Works
51°49'35N 1°00'52E
2°00'W 2005 (8'E)
Pewit Island
Pyefleet Channel
Oyster Beds
Reeveshall Marsh
Maydays Marsh
Broad Fleet
Reservoirs
Langenhoehall Marsh
BRIGHTLINGSEA
See Plan C
Westmarsh Pt
S. Osyth Stone Pt
Martello Tr
Mersea Stone
Obstn
Bathing Area (see Note)
MERSEA ISLAND
Reeves Hall
Mitchell's Farm
Bonds Green Farm
Broman's Farm
Bocking Hall
Haycocks
Metres 1000 500 0 1000 2000 Metres
48'
49'
51'
52'

Tel: 08706 082608 Website: www.traveline.org.uk. For train information contact 'One' Customer Services, Tel: 08456 007245 Website: www.onerailway.com, or National Rail Enquiries, Tel: 08457 484950 Website: www.nationalrail.co.uk

EATING AND DRINKING

The Lakeside View bar and restaurant is situated on the opposite side of the road to St. Oysth Boatyard and offers extensive eating and drinking facilities overlooking the lake. At present the bar is only open 1600-2100 every day, serving what my crew refer to as "fizzy-pop beers" and although snacks are provided when the bar is open, the restaurant only opens Sunday lunchtimes. At the time of writing, The Lakeside View was up for sale, so this situation may change. Tel: 01255 822313.

There is also a tearoom at the Mill House next to the quay, open 1100-1700 Wednesday to Sunday. A hundred yards up the hill on the left is the friendly traditional White Hart pub with bar open 1100-2400 Monday to Thursday (0100 Friday and Saturday! and 2230 Sundays). They provide a good pub menu and serve food in the bar or restaurant, 1200-1500 and 1800-2130 (1200-1800 Sundays). Tel: 01255 820318.

ST. OSYTH SKIPPERS INFORMATION	
Harbour Master	Contact Andy or Jane Harman at the boatyard, Tel: 01255 820005
Water	On quay
Electricity	On quay (and planned for the staging 2007)
Fuel	None
Facilities	WC on quay
Boatyard	St. Osyth Boatyard, Tel: 01255 820005
Chandlery	None
Slips	50 ton slipway, 80 feet dry dock and 8 ton crane at boatyard

ST. OSYTH SHORESIDE INFORMATION	
Stores	Two butchers, a baker and two convenience stores in the town, the Spar convenience store is open 0630-2100, seven days a week and the alternative Londis store is also open almost as often
Banks	None, but cash machine in Londis store
PO	In village
Public Tel.	On road to village
Taxis	Premier Taxis, Clacton, Tel: 01255 223344; Arch Taxis, Tel: 01255 435114
Accommodation	Bed and breakfast accommodation is offered at Mill House by the quay. Tel: 01255 820450
Police	Station Road, Brightlingsea. Tel: 01206 302515
Doctor	Dr. Mann & Ptnrs., Church Square. Tel: 01255 820309
Hospital	(A&E) Colchester General Hospital, Turner Road, Colchester. Tel: 01206 747474
Dentist	Figaji, Tilkeridou & Namazy, 32 Crossways, Jaywick. Tel: 01255 207620
Pharmacy	The Village Pharmacy, Clacton Road. Tel: 01255 820396

USEFUL NUMBERS

Although independent of the boatyard, St. Osyth Boatbuilders operates from the boatyard and specialises in traditional vessels.
Contact Alan Williams, Tel: 01255 820447.

Further up in the centre of the very small town there are a couple more pubs (the Kings Arms and Red Lion), both serving food. There is also a Chinese takeaway, a Chinese/Thai restaurant and a Mexican restaurant open for breakfast!, lunch and dinner.

The Balti House Indian restaurant is open every day, 1200-1430 and 1800-2400 and offers a delivery service to the quay, Tel: 01255 822224.

TO SEE AND DO

It is a short walk up the hill to the main part of the village with its attractive, nicely kept houses and selection of shops. The 12th century St. Osyth's Priory is just before the village centre on the left, but is not open to the public.

From the other side of the road bridge there are a choice of walks, either by road past Ray Creek (where improbably barges used to load gravel), or by the path along St. Osyth Creek to Point Clear. Alternatively, you can follow the path out to Lee-over-Sands and Colne Point.

PYFLEET CREEK

Back in the Colne opposite Brightlingsea is the popular anchorage off Mersea Stone. Here you will find clean landing on the island and Pyfleet Creek, which must be one of the most popular anchorages on the east coast and yet it has remained completely unspoilt. It is still the fattening ground of the Pyfleet oysters and care must be taken not to anchor on the beds that are clearly buoyed. The popularity of the 'native' oyster here goes back to Roman times.

There is water at all times for about one mile inside the creek as far as Pewit Island with its oyster packing huts. By continuing another two miles, keeping to port at the fork, the Strood (the causeway – a ford in Roman times – linking Mersea Island to the mainland) can be reached by dinghy at high water.

BRIGHTLINGSEA TO COLCHESTER

The River Colne can be navigated on the tide to the outskirts of Colchester. From north of Pyfleet to number 18 buoy, half way to Alresford Creek, is an unrestricted speed zone for use by members of the Brightlingsea Waterski & Powerboat Club only. Here Geedon Creek branches off to port. The north and south channels of the creek are separated by Rat Island and the creek runs between the Fingringhoe bird sanctuary and the army's firing ranges, which sadly close the area to navigation.

Having returned to the 8 knot speed limit and a little further on, the gravel works seen ahead to starboard are in Alresford Creek. Above Alresford Creek, the Colne narrows and dries to a trickle at low water and becomes more rural with woods and fields on its banks. The course winds over towards the woods on the starboard bank and then back towards the port hand. Beware the old dismantled jetty to port here, although I understand this will probably be marked by the time this book is published.

The two waterside villages of Wivenhoe (with its flood barrier) and Rowhedge follow soon after. On the starboard bank are Wivenhoe Sailing Club's clubhouse and small marina. At this point the church, cottages and other waterside buildings at Wivenhoe are clearly seen. Also obvious is the barrier, constructed in 1994. The barrier consists of a pair of lock gates that operate over spring tides and tidal surges. The barrier's piers cut down the width of navigation at this point to 30 metres and International Port Signals are used for one-way flow. After Wivenhoe, Fingringhoe Creek branches off to port. Once important enough to be named the Roman River, it is now used for little more than laying up on mudberths during the winter. The channel is very narrow from the villages onwards and commercial shipping has now ceased to make its way to the wharves at Colchester due to constant silting.

Alresford Creek

ALRESFORD CREEK

Alresford Creek to starboard can be an interesting detour on the tide for those with shallow draft, bearing in mind it does dry right out. The entrance is marked with some small green buoys after which there are quite a few moorings to help find the channel. After the jetty to port is a ford that allows a firm landing from which it is about one mile up the lane to the village. The ford dates back a long way, as Roman sites have been discovered on both shores here.

The creek continues its winding course towards the wooded slopes and Brightlingsea church until it reaches the old mill at Thorrington. Thames Barges, laden with straw and hay looking like water-borne haystacks, would have been seen leaving the creek in days gone by, as this was once the port for Brightlingsea.

MOORINGS

The moorings in the creek are owned by the Alresford Boat Club and there are no visitors moorings, but you are welcome to anchor and dry out after the channel markers, but short of the moorings.

CREW CHANGES AND TRAVEL

Alresford has regular bus services to Brightlingsea and Colchester (less frequent evenings and Sundays) and has hourly rail services (none on Sundays) to Colchester for connections to London.

ALRESFORD SHORESIDE INFORMATION	
Stores	General store and butchers near the station, both open 0930-1730 Mon to Fri (morning only Sat)
Banks	None
PO	Near station
Public Tel.	At station
Club	Alresford Boat Club
Taxis	Premier Taxis, Clacton, Tel: 01255 223344; Arch Taxis, Tel: 01255 435114
Police	Station Road, Brightlingsea. Tel: 01206 302515
Doctor	Dr. Hale & Ptnrs., The Avenue. Tel: 01206 824447
Hospital	Colchester General Hospital, Turner Road, Colchester. Tel: 01206 747474
Dentist	Mersea Road Dental Practice, 306 Mersea Road, Colchester. Tel: 01206 548386
Pharmacy	Alliance Pharmacy, Vine Parade, Wivenhoe. Tel: 01206 823605

ALRESFORD SKIPPERS INFORMATION

Harbour Master – None
There are no facilities but there is a garage in the village for fuel, one mile

For information contact Traveline East Anglia, Tel: 08706 082608 Website: www.traveline.org.uk. For train information contact 'One' Customer Services, Tel: 08456 007245 Website: www.onerailway.com, or National Rail Enquiries, Tel: 08457 484950 Website: www.nationalrail.co.uk

EATING AND DRINKING

The village pub The Pointer has recently come under new management having been closed for a time. They have now re-opened on Thursday to Sunday evenings, all day Fridays, Saturdays and Sundays and intend to start serving food at lunchtimes and evenings. This pleasant pub with beer garden deserves support, so why not make a visit, although I would suggest checking prior, Tel: 01206 822866. There is also a Chinese takeaway by the station open 1700-2300, Tuesday to Sunday and a fish and chip shop nearby open Monday to Saturday, 1200-1600 and 1930-2100.

WIVENHOE

Approaching Wivenhoe on the starboard bank you will first see Wivenhoe Sailing Club, which opened its clubhouse during 1994, just downstream of the tidal barrier. Wivenhoe has been famous since the beginning of the 19th century for its yacht building, although this period now appears to have ended. Cottages and a pub line the front, with many new houses developed on the waterfront. Mudberths still abound in front of the quay where some traditional Essex boats are usually to be found. Also on the riverside is the Nottage Institute, where courses in seamanship have been held for over a century. Wivenhoe stretches back further than one would think and is worth a walk round to explore.

MOORINGS

Although there seem to be many mud-berths in Wivenhoe, they are usually occupied so do not bank on getting one. The moorings both here and at Rowhedge are fully subscribed, with long waiting lists. Wivenhoe Sailing Club, just down-stream of the barrier, has put in drying pontoons with several reserved for visitors on a first come, first served basis. Even fin-keelers are okay here on the outside as the mud is very soft.

CREW CHANGES AND TRAVEL

Wivenhoe is a good place for transfers as it has regular bus services to Clacton, Brightlingsea and Colchester (less frequent evenings and Sundays) and has hourly rail services to Clacton and Colchester and some direct trains to London Liverpool Street (70 minutes). For information contact Traveline East Anglia, Tel: 08706 082608 Website: www.traveline.org.uk. For train information contact 'One' Customer Services, Tel: 08456 007245 Website: www.onerailway.com, or National Rail Enquiries, Tel: 08457 484950 Website: www.nationalrail.co.uk

EATING AND DRINKING

There are a number of good places to eat and drink in Wivenhoe, so I shall just name a few. The Rose and Crown on the quay opens every day 1100-2330 (1130-2230 Sundays) and serves food 1200-2000, Tel: 01206 826371. The Black Buoy pub opens 1130-1500 and 1830-2300 (all day weekends), serving food 1200-1400 and 1900-2100, Tel: 01206 822425. Valentinos Italian Restaurant in the middle of the village is open Tuesday to Saturday 1800-2200, Tel: 01206 825738. The Bengal Spice Indian restaurant is open 1200-1400 and 1800-2330 (2400 Fridays and Saturdays, closed Friday lunchtimes), Tel: 01206 823582. There is also Papas' Fish and Chip shop open lunchtimes and evenings (all day at weekends). Wivenhoe Sailing Club opens Friday and Monday evenings and Sunday lunchtimes.

WIVENHOE SKIPPERS INFORMATION	
Harbour Master	Refer to Brightlingsea
Water	At WSC
Electricity	None
Fuel	None
Facilities	WC and showers at WSC
Internet	None
Boatyard	None
Chandlery	None
Slips	For dinghies at WSC
Scrubbing Posts	None
Website	www.wivenhoesailing.org.uk

TO SEE AND DO

A couple of miles from Wivenhoe is the famous Beth Chatto Garden at Elmstead Market open Monday to Saturday (Monday to Friday in winter), 0900-1700, admission £4.50, Tel: 01206 822007. From Wivenhoe it is easy to travel into Colchester, where you will find Colchester Zoo, a three-mile bus journey to the south-west, open daily 0930-1730, admission £14.49, children £7.99, Tel: 01206 331292. The Norman Colchester Castle, museum and gardens make an interesting day out, admission £4.90, children £3.10, Tel: 01206 282939.

ROWHEDGE

The next village, Rowhedge, with the unusual spire of East Donyland Church, can be seen from Wivenhoe and is reached in a few minutes. Rowhedge's high street is the road along the riverbank and is a clue to its past dependence on the water. Its history includes shipbuilding at the yards and the production of many globetrotting yachts. Later came lifeboats for the RNLI at Ian Brown's boatyard – now closed down and the site developed. There is a commercial quay just downstream, but one wonders how long this can hold off the waterside housing developers.

MOORINGS

There are two quays at Rowhedge, above and below The Anchor pub, with mooring rings and grassy areas beside them. They can only be reached near the top of the

WIVENHOE SHORESIDE INFORMATION	
Stores	A few good shops including a Co-op supermarket open 0700-2200 (1000-1600 Sun)
Banks	Cash machine in Co-op
PO	In town
Public Tel.	In town
Club	Wivenhoe Sailing Club. Tel: 01206 822132
Taxis	Wivenhoe Station Cars, Tel: 01206 822020; Travelink Essex, Tel: 01206 828282
Tourist Info.	Nearest is opposite Colchester Castle
Police	High Street. Tel: 01206 822082
Doctor	Dr. Hale & Ptnrs., The Avenue. Tel: 01206 824447
Hospital	(A&E) Colchester General Hospital, Turner Road, Colchester, Tel: 01206 747474
Dentist	Mersea Road Dental Practice, 306 Mersea Road, Colchester. Tel: 01206 548386
Pharmacy	Alliance Pharmacy, Vine Parade. Tel: 01206 823605

USEFUL NUMBERS

Boatbuilding & Navigation Tuition	Nottage Institute. Tel: 01206 824142
Surveyor	Peter N. Davies. Tel: 01206 823289

tide, but have been refurbished of late and the bottom at both is fairly soft mud, but expect to be charged a mooring fee. Also, The Anchor has good alongside mooring, with access ladders, free for waterborne customers. You may also use the ferry pontoon just upstream, when the ferry isn't running.

CREW CHANGES AND TRAVEL

Although only a short taxi ride from Colchester, Rowhedge is not best placed for transfers and I would suggest dropping down to Wivenhoe, or even taking the foot ferry across for this.

EATING AND DRINKING

The Anchor is well known for its unique setting and surprisingly is owned by Shepherd Neame the Kent brewers, who on re-opening a few years back, sent the first delivery by Thames Barge from Faversham. Yachtsmen are made very welcome and are able to use the free overnight mooring alongside the pub and step ashore for refreshment, although if sailing in company, you are recommended to telephone ahead. The bar is open 1200-1500 and 1700-2300 every day (all day Sunday) and excellent food is served 1200-1400 and 1815-2100 (2130 Saturday and all day Sunday until 2030). They will often even cook breakfast if booked the evening before and not required early, Tel: 01206 728382. Set back from the quay is the traditional Albion pub, with a good range of beers, although no food and closed Monday lunchtimes.

ROWHEDGE SKIPPERS INFORMATION	
Harbour Master	Refer to Brightlingsea
Water	At The Anchor pub
Electricity	None
Fuel	None
Facilities	WC block at The Anchor
Boatyard	None
Chandlery	None

COLCHESTER

After passing the mudberths upstream of Rowhedge, the river curves to port to be accompanied by the railway line into Colchester. Beyond the bank to starboard can be seen the Essex University complex, and after this King Edward Quay and the Hythe at Colchester comes into view, now no longer full with barges and coasters and their cargoes, but disappearing under tons of brick, concrete and glass. The waterside development has not included any boating aspect and sadly for now the quayside is not to be recommended and a brief look and return to Rowhedge or Wivenhoe is the order of the day.

For those who wish to visit Colchester it is best to return to Wivenhoe and use public transport back to Colchester.

ROWHEDGE SHORESIDE INFORMATION	
Stores	Co-op store 50 metres, open 0700-2200 (0900-1700 Sun)
Banks	Cash machine in Co-op
PO	In Garden Supplies shop(!) by the Co-op
Club	None
Taxis	SS Cabs, Tel: 01621 817399; JS Travel, Tel: 01621 817069
Accommodation	None in village
Police	John Kent Avenue, Colchester. Tel: 01206 762212
Doctor	Dr. S. O'Regan & Ptnrs., Rectory Road. Tel: 01206 728585
Hospital	(A&E) Colchester General Hospital, Turner Road, Colchester, Tel: 01206 747474
Dentist	Mersea Road Dental Practice, 306 Mersea Road, Colchester. Tel: 01206 548386
Pharmacy	Lloyds Pharmacy, Mersea Road, Colchester. Tel: 01206 576915

West Mersea ©PRPA

THE RIVER BLACKWATER

⌖ **51°44.'6N, 01°01.1'E**
(off Bench Head)
Tides Bradwell and West Mersea +0:35
Maldon +1:00 *(differences from Harwich)*

At its seaward end the Blackwater estuary is much wider than any other on the east coast and is one of the best loved yachting and boating areas. There are many modern havens, but you can still find peaceful places to stop and despite the area's popularity, you rarely feel overcrowded here. Much of the Blackwater has a timelessness about it and its appearance has remained largely unchanged for hundreds of years, except for the large blocks of Bradwell nuclear power station (now decommissioned) guarding the river's mouth on the southern shore. The power station provides a conspicuous landmark for yachtsmen entering the Blackwater and yet surprisingly, does not dominate the village of Bradwell Waterside once ashore. Providing an extensive, yet reasonably protected cruising ground, this wide river estuary with its good boating facilities, remains a firm favourite with the boating community, and modern yachts, motor cruisers and racing dinghies all rub shoulders with the traditional craft that still have enthusiastic supporters here.

The Blackwater Estuary is not just a haven for the yachtsman though; it is also home to large numbers of wildfowl and has vast expanses of salt marsh that boast some of the rarest plants in the country. Nature lovers, ramblers and fishermen as well as the boating community, can all enjoy this beautiful part of the east coast.

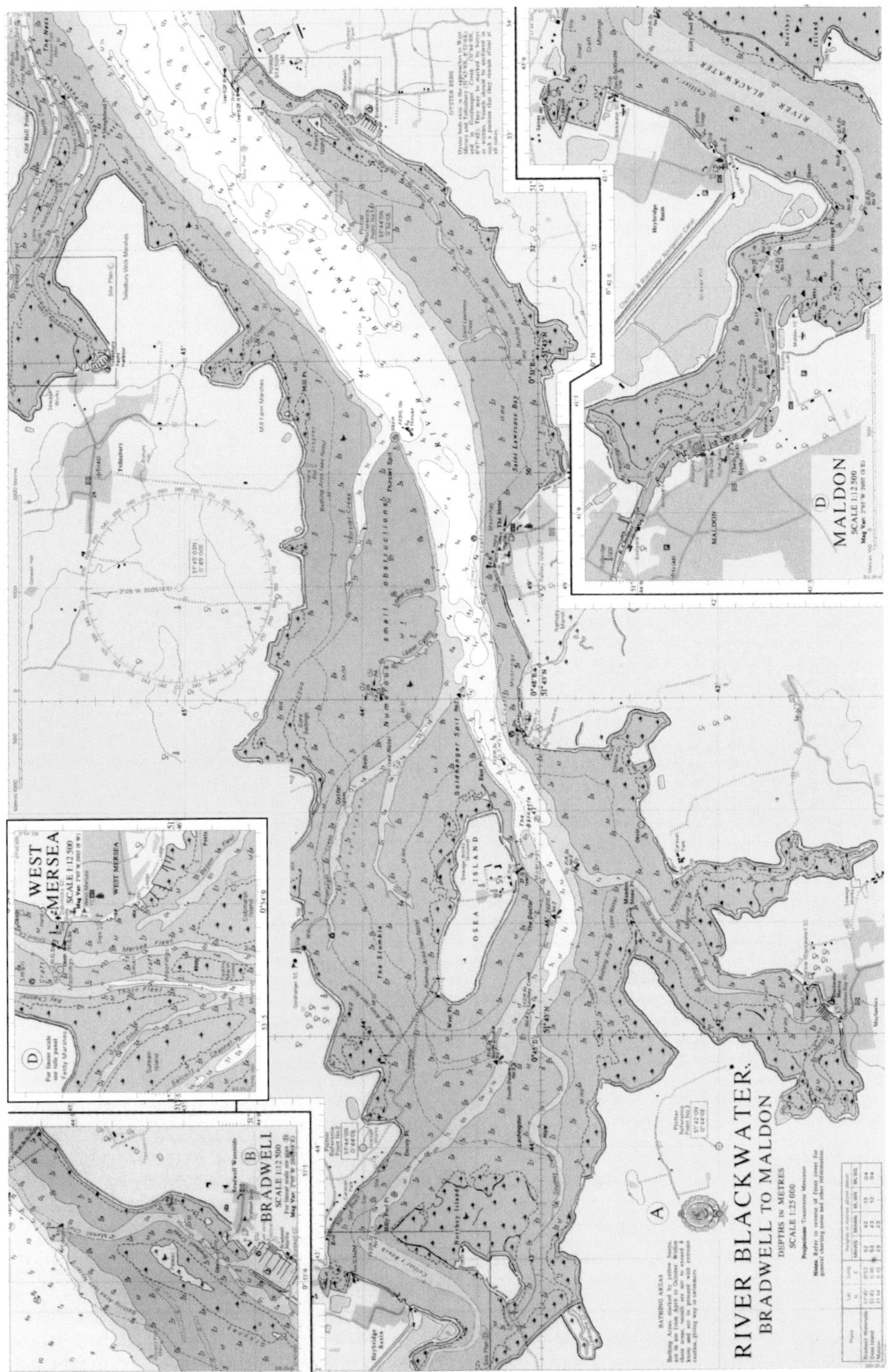
RIVER BLACKWATER
BRADWELL TO MALDON
DEPTHS IN METRES
SCALE 1:25 000
MALDON
SCALE 1:12 500
WEST MERSEA
SCALE 1:12 500
BRADWELL
SCALE 1:12 500
OSEA ISLAND
BATHING AREAS

APPROACH AND ENTRANCE

Most yachts arriving from the south will come through the Swin Spitway, but a word of warning. Although this is the main route from the south, the spitway only carries about a metre and a half at LAT and as you will often be looking for the tide to turn and carry you up the Blackwater, take care to check you have enough depth near LWS.

From the Wallet Spitway buoy at the northern end of the Swin Spitway, you need to head for the Knoll north cardinal buoy to keep clear of the Knoll bank to the south. Shoal draft craft coming from the Crouch may also choose to use the Ray Sand Channel if the tides are favourable (refer to River Crouch chapter).

To enter the Blackwater from the north via the Wallet, approach is usually made again towards the Knoll north cardinal buoy to avoid the shallows all around. However, with shoal draft and local knowledge, in good conditions you can also follow a more northerly route leaving the North Eagle north cardinal buoy close to port, before making sure you leave Colne Bar green conical buoy to starboard to clear the Colne Bar shoals.

On nearing the Knoll buoy you should leave it to port and subsequently the Eagle green conical to starboard, before passing between the NW Knoll red can and Colne Bar green conical buoys. Leaving the next buoy, Bench Head green conical to starboard, will now place you safely in the river, after which a heading must be chosen and followed according to destination, although for a while you will need to take a northwards looping arc towards The Nass beacon off West Mersea to stay clear of St. Peter's Flats to the south. All these buoys are lit making the Blackwater safe for night entry. In good visibility, it is usually possible from here to see the Saxon chapel of St. Peter's on the sea wall to the south.

BENCH HEAD TO THIRSLET SPIT

When heading for West Mersea and Tollesbury, follow the main channel, taking care not to drift too far north onto Mersea flats, to the Nass Beacon (VQ(3)5s) leaving this close to port to enter the Mersea Quarters which is marked by lateral buoys. If staying in West Mersea and you wish to go in past the Quarters, follow the starboard hand buoys, but if going up to Tollesbury, you follow the port hand cans which branch off west after the third pair of buoys. The channel then forks and shallows and you want to take the South Channel, which is initially buoyed and then turns to starboard to follow the line of the moorings until you reach Woodrolfe Creek to port, which leads to the marina. There is a tide gauge at the entrance to the creek indicating the depth over the sill into the marina. You should ensure good clearance to avoid damage to the sill, which carries a little under two and a half metres at MHW, so if you are deep drafted, be aware you may have a very limited window for entry and exit on neaps.

Back in the Blackwater, a word of caution for those heading upriver. Although you may see moored vessels and the power station at Bradwell from early on, they cannot initially be used to fix your heading, or you will find yourself on St. Peter's Flats to the south. You will need to stay further north and only slowly loop to port. If heading for Bradwell, start to ease to port after passing the power station outlet wall, which is lit by vertical flashing reds on each end. Then leave the lit north cardinal beacon, marking the entrance to Bradwell creek to starboard. Deep draught boats and those unable to manoeuvre easily at slow speeds, should avoid entering Bradwell creek with less than half the tide, although shallow draft boats with a good engine can enter at most states. The beacon has a useful tide gauge on it showing the depth of water in the creek itself. Follow the red (well, orangey red!)

cans in to port and withies to starboard, although the deeper water is to be found closer to the withies. After a short while the channel swings violently to port to leave a green conical buoy close to starboard before turning sharply back towards the yacht moorings. There is a port hand beacon off the end of Bradwell Quay slipway to be left well to port and then you will see another red (orangey red again) can which marks the port hand side of the entrance to the marina, which is then also marked by port and starboard piles further in.

Back in the river again, the deep water channel now runs in a south westerly direction towards Thirslet Spit green conical starboard hand buoy (Fl(3)G.10s). As this is a couple of miles distant, it can often be difficult to pick out, so a general direction towards Stone St. Lawrence on the south side of the river should be followed until you can. The river has extensive mud flats either side here to watch out for, but there is still half a mile width of deep water. Care must be exercised, as it is easy to drift northwards onto the shoals, some of which are hard sand. Just short of Thirslet Spit buoy, Thirslet Creek branches off on the northern side of the river in a west north westerly direction and is navigable for about half a mile. This can offer a peaceful anchorage in settled conditions, particularly around low tide, although in a blow at high tide it is quite untenable.

WEST MERSEA

The main route into West Mersea is from Mersea Quarters, past Quarters Spit to port (where the creek to Tollesbury branches off) and into Mersea Fleet, Thorn Fleet or Salcott Channel. After half tide, there is also a route between Cobmarsh Island and the shore down Besom Fleet for those with local knowledge and little draft.

All the channels are now packed with moorings, even out to the Quarters, which although sometimes causing some confusion to the newcomer, do indicate the deep water routes. Once well into the Quarters, the boatyards, clubs, oyster huts and shops packed tightly along the waterside will come into view. The harbour is a hive of activity on summer weekends, with local fisherman going about their business, young children crabbing and yachtsmen coming and going in the harbour launches and their tenders. This area of the island is known locally as Mersea City and some of its old cottages were once used by smugglers. The fishermen of West Mersea have been famous for their oysters (the native Colchester oysters) and other shellfish for centuries and in their heyday in the early 19th century, over 100 oyster boats might have been seen in the area. Following the Coast Road upstream from the prominent

WEST MERSEA SKIPPERS INFORMATION	
Harbour Master	Contact WMYC boatman Jeff Wass or his assistant Steve Wass on VHF Ch37, call-signs "YC1" and "YC2" or Mobile: 07752 309435
Water	Standpipe at top of jetty
Electricity	None
Fuel	By can from garage in town
Facilities	Public toilets at top of jetty
Boatyards	West Mersea Marine Ltd., Tel: 01206 382244; Peter B. Clarke, Tel: 01206 385905
Chandlery	Marinestore Wyatts, Tel: 01206 384745; Peter B. Clarke, Tel: 01206 385905
Slips	Contact West Mersea Marine or Peter B. Clarke
Scrubbing Posts	By arrangement with WMYC
Water Taxi	The WMYC boatmen offer a (daytime only) launch service, every day from April to November

Victory Inn and West Mersea Yacht Club are the Dabchicks Sailing Club and the lifeboat house where the inshore lifeboat is stationed. Apart from the facilities in the Mersea City area, others are to be found in the small town that is reached by following the road back towards the Blackwater and up the hill.

All most of us see of this haven is the local area around Mersea City, but given the time there are many creeks that can be explored according to draft and state of tide, but care must always be taken of the oyster beds that are clearly marked on charts and by withies and notices. Alongside Cobmarsh Island the channels fan out, and working from west to east the first is Salcott Creek (or Salcott Channel, or Virley Creek, depending on who you speak to), which once had a thriving salt-panning industry. It is still one of the chief oyster areas, with layings stretching well into the creek to the top of Sunken Island. The shallow creek winds its way for a couple of miles past the island, as far as the villages of Salcott and Virley (also known combined as Salcott-cum-Virley), where it is possible to land from a dinghy at Church Wharf at the top of the tide and briefly explore the villages.

The next channel, running to west of Packing Marsh Island with its oyster shed, is Thorn Fleet, where you will find the majority of the swinging moorings. This runs on to become the Ray Channel with its pile moorings, which runs up to the west of Ray Island to a landing at the head, where you can walk into the village of Peldon. From just short of the pile moorings, there is a narrow cut through to Mersea Fleet, the Strood Channel and the quay. The shallower Mersea Fleet branches off to the east of Packing Marsh Island and runs up past the quay, then becoming the Strood Channel which runs up past the holiday park to the causeway joining the island to the mainland (except at extreme high tides when Mersea briefly becomes a true island again).

MOORINGS

With the combination of crowded moorings and oyster beds, it is difficult to find places to anchor where you can remain afloat, although drying craft will find the upper reaches of the creeks possible, but be careful of the oyster layings. Other than anchoring in the outer quarters, the only other place (for shoal draft craft only) to lie afloat, is in the Salcott Channel above Sunken Island and the oyster layings.

There are visitors moorings laid in Mersea Quarters, but if you wish to moor further in amongst the protection of the creeks and islands, it is best to seek advice and direction from the West Mersea YC Boatman, who seems to know every mooring and will usually be able to find you somewhere. Do not be tempted to go onto the pile moorings without direction as some are unsafe and a few foul. Alternatively, you could try asking West Mersea Marine or Peter B. Clarke if they have a mooring (see Skippers Information).

There is a slipway across the hard in front of West Mersea Yacht Club, but the long all-tide floating jetty just upstream is more convenient. There are signs indicating where to tie up, but essentially do not leave a dinghy moored to the end, as this is in constant use by the club launches and fishermen.

CREW CHANGES AND TRAVEL

There are frequent buses every day to Colchester where there are regular trains to London Liverpool Street (60 minutes). For bus information contact Traveline East Anglia, Tel: 08706 082608 Website: www.traveline.org.uk and for train information contact 'One' Customer Services, Tel: 08456 007245 Website: www.onerailway.com or National Rail Enquiries, Tel: 08457 484950 Website: www.nationalrail.co.uk

EATING AND DRINKING

West Mersea is a little old-fashioned, so eating out is best planned to be done early in the evening as many places stop serving unusually early for these days, unless you want to walk up into town.

West Mersea Yacht Club has a fine clubhouse on Coast Road, fronted by a pleasant lawn. Visiting yachtsmen are welcome to use both the social facilities and the showers. The bar is open weekdays 1200-1430 (1500 Fridays) and 1830-2300 (from 1800 Wednesdays and Fridays), Saturdays 1200-2300 and Sundays 1200-2100. The restaurant serves food Monday to Saturday 1200-1415 and 1830-2130 (closed Monday and Tuesday evenings) and all day Sunday 1200-1930 in the season. To contact the bar and restaurant, Tel: 01206 384463. Dabchicks Sailing Club at the top end of Coast Road is very much a family club with a large first floor bar and galley with food often available after races. Visitors are made welcome and the club is open Wednesday to Sunday evenings and lunchtimes at weekends. Tel: (Hon. Sec.) 01206 386954.

WEST MERSEA SHORESIDE INFORMATION

Stores	Fleetview Stores by the waterside, Tel: 01206 382643 and Co-op supermarket in the town, half a mile away open 0700-2100 (Sat 2000, Sun 1000-1600)
Banks	Barclays Bank in town with cash machine
PO	In the town
Public Tel.	Near Victory Inn on the waterfront and in town
Clubs	West Mersea Yacht Club, Tel: 01206 382947 Email: wmersea.yc@rya-online.net Website: www.wmyc.org.uk; Dabchicks Sailing Club, Tel: (Hon. Sec.) 01206 386954
Taxis	Anglia Executive Cars, Tel: 01206 385841
Accommodation	The Victory Inn offers bed and breakfast, Tel: 01206 382907; B&B in Firs Road, off Coast Road, Tel: 01206 382023
Police	East Road (open Sat only), or Southway, Colchester. Tel: 01206 762212
Doctor	The Mersea Island Practice, 32 Kingsland Road. Tel 01206 382015
Hospital	(A&E) Colchester General, Turner Road, Colchester. Tel: 01206 747474
Dentist	Elmes, Elmes, Rashid & Eckstein, 32a Kingsland Road, Tel: 01206 384504
Pharmacy	Alliance Pharmacy, 37 Barfield Road. Tel: 01206 382850

USEFUL NUMBERS

Boat Transport	C-Way Boat Transportation. Tel: 01206 381765
Diver	John Welham. Tel: 01206 383461
Marine Consultants	Holman & Pye. Tel: 01206 382478
Marine Engineers	A. B. Clarke & Son, Tel: 01206 382706; Malseed Engineering, Tel: 01206 382457; OHM Marine Engineering, Tel: 07905 243414 West Mersea Marine Engineering Ltd, Tel: 01206 384350
Outboard Engineer	Richard Parkinson Marine. Tel: 01206 385008
Sailmakers	Gowen Ocean Sailmakers. Tel: 01206 384412
Sail Training	Adventures Offshore. Tel: 01206 385071
Shipwright	David Mills. Tel: 01206 382161

The Victory Hotel overlooks the water on Coast Road. There is a large bar with dining tables and open fire. The pub also has a beer garden with views over the moorings. There used to be an extensive pub menu, but the place seemed to go into decline in recent years. New management is now in place and one hopes The Victory will return to its former glory and a pleasant destination for a summer's evening, Tel: 01206 382907. Offering a superb breakfast, well worth coming ashore in the morning for, is The Waterfront Café. Set back slightly from Coast Road, it is open most days until late afternoon, Tel: 01206 386061. The Coast Inn nearby, has an extensive menu and serves snacks all day, open from 1000-2130 and later, Tel: 01206 383568.

For the seafood and fish lover no visit to West Mersea is complete without a visit to The Company Shed, where oysters and other seafood and fish can be washed down with wine in simple surroundings. Tel: 01206 382700.

If none of these suit you, a short walk into town will give you a couple of pubs, a Chinese takeaway, a fish and chip shop and the excellent Titash Indian Restaurant, currently the only place for late dining. Tel: 01206 381778.

TO SEE AND DO

Mersea Island Museum is tucked in just past the church in the High Street. Exhibits cover many aspects of the island's history including its maritime connections. It is open mid-May to September, Wednesday to Sunday 1400-1700, with admission a few pence. Mersea Island Vineyard at East Mersea offers tours for groups and evening wine tastings from April to September. Tel: 01206 385191.

There are many fine walks utilising the sea walls and inland paths around Mersea Island, but the lanes around this pleasant island should also not be dismissed.

TOLLESBURY

All along Woodrolfe Creek are moorings and mudberths among the saltings. One particularly noticeable vessel permanently moored here is the 137 feet 'Trinity', ex-Trinity House light vessel. This is the headquarters of the Christian-based Fellowship Afloat Charitable Trust, which provides courses in sailing and boating, as well as wildlife studies, arts, crafts and team building. These day and residential courses are provided both by the Trust for those that would benefit most from the experience and also commercially for team building courses. The Trust also owns 150 acres of the saltings, partly devoted to nature reserves and the remainder to the yard and berths managed by its wholly-owned trading company Tollesbury Saltings Ltd. The berths here amongst the saltings, with their narrow wooden walkways providing all-tide foot access, have changed little over the years and are reminiscent of Maurice Griffiths' writings, which first introduced many of us to the east coast. Tollesbury Saltings have had difficult times recently, but under the new management of the amiable and helpful Scott Sanderson (a keen east coast sailor himself), it is hoped this pleasant and unique facility will thrive once again.

At the head of the creek, the entrance to the marina is to port and a small quay to starboard. The tide only provides water at the quay for a short period at high water, where local children will be seen crabbing on summer weekends, but there is an average depth of well over 2 metres in the marina. Tollesbury was once the home of the Blackwater and Tollesbury Oyster Fishery Company and had over 70 fishing smacks in the late 19th century, but very few fishing vessels remain. Most of its working men made their living from the sea, but as time went on and the demand for merchant seamen diminished, many of the younger men worked in the earlier part of the 20th century as paid crew on the big racing yachts of the Colne and the village supplied several America's Cup crew. It was hoped that when the railway arrived, yachtsmen would be encouraged to keep their racing yachts in the mud berths here, but its heyday was short-lived and the railway no longer reaches these parts. The listed sail lofts and yacht stores at the head of the creek have been carefully restored as a reminder of this part of the village's history.

The village is reached by following the road past the lofts for half a mile and turning right at the T-junction, although at extreme high springs the quayside area and road may flood, at which times Back Lane, reached from the marina car park, is opened to provide a dry shod route.

MOORINGS
Just before Woodrolfe Creek in South Channel, are four visitors buoys belonging to Tollesbury Marina. These are intended for those waiting for the tide, so please enquire with the marina before leaving a boat unattended here, but it is possible to land at the hard just short of the creek entrance and walk from here along the sea wall to the quay and on to the village. There are 240 deep water pontoon berths inside the harbour at Tollesbury Marina which can usually be entered from two hours each side of HW springs or one hour each side of HW neaps. If in doubt, contact the marina during office hours as it is very important not to ground on and damage the sill to the harbour, not to mention your vessel's keel! You should generally call ahead for a berth, but if this is not possible, visitors should moor at the fuel jetty to starboard just inside the entrance to enquire with the helpful staff at the office in the chandlery. As often seems the case, the more you have to work and think to get to a place, the friendlier and more helpful the people seem to be.

For those who prefer a staged mud-berth, Tollesbury Saltings can usually find a space for visitors, particularly those of shoal draft (although they have some for up to 30 metres length) and if you are looking for somewhere to leave a boat for a short while, this can be a safe and reasonably priced option. Contact the office prior, as directions to your berth will be required in these tortuous channels, but if (like me) you enjoy these

TOLLESBURY SKIPPERS INFORMATION

TOLLESBURY MARINA ⚓⚓⚓⚓

Harbour Master	VHF Ch37 & 80, call sign "Tollesbury Marina", Tel: 01621 869202 Email: marina@woodrolfe.com
Water	On all pontoons
Electricity	On all pontoons
Fuel	Diesel on fuel pontoon in marina
Facilities	WC, showers and launderette
Internet	Wireless broadband available at a charge
Boatyard	Woodrolfe Boatyard owns the marina and offers a full range of engineering and boatyard services. Tel: 01621 869202
Chandlery	Extensive on-site chandlery
Slips	Slips for up to 30 tons and craneage up to 20 tons
Scrubbing Posts	Enquire at marina
Website	www.woodrolfe.com

TOLLESBURY SALTINGS

Harbour Master	Scott Sanderson, Tel: 01621 868624 Mobile: 07768 751282 Email: sales@tolsalt.co.uk
Water	Available at standpipes
Electricity	To a few berths only
Fuel	From garage in village, half a mile, or from marina
Facilities	WC and showers by yard
Boatyard	Full boatyard services can be arranged
Chandlery	Some available, others can be ordered
Slips	Up to 12 tons
Website	www.tolsalt.co.uk

mud-larking challenges, the experience of berthing here is a fascinating one.

CREW CHANGES AND TRAVEL

There are half a dozen buses a day Monday to Saturday to Colchester where there are regular trains to London Liverpool Street (60 minutes) and also a regular service to Maldon. For bus information contact Traveline East Anglia, Tel: 08706 082608 Website: www.traveline.org.uk and for train information contact 'One' Customer Services, Tel: 08456 007245 Website: www.onerailway.com or National Rail Enquiries, Tel: 08457 484950 Website: www.nationalrail.co.uk

TOLLESBURY SHORESIDE INFORMATION

Stores	Follow the road to the village and turn left at the T-junction to Fred's Stores in Mell Road for just about everything, including greengrocery and off-licence, with a free delivery service back to your boat. Open 0830-1930 Mon-Sat (Sun 0900-1300 and 1900-2030). Tel: 01621 868483
Banks	None, cash machine in Fred's Stores
PO	In village store
Public Tel.	In marina and by Fred's Stores
Clubs	Tollesbury Cruising Club in the marina (automatic temporary membership for marina visitors), Tel: 01621 869561 Website: www.woodrolfe.com/club; Tollesbury Sailing Club, Tel: (Sec.) 07788 480542 Website: www.tollesburysc.co.uk; Tollesbury Mud Club, Website: www.zingtang.demon.co.uk/mudclub
Taxis	Tollesbury Cars, Tel: 01621 868808
Accommodation	Fernleigh B&B. Tel: 01621 868245
Police	West Square, Maldon. Tel: 01621 852255
Doctor	Dr. R. J. Furze, 25 High Street. Tel: 01621 869204
Hospital	Colchester General, Turner Road, Colchester. Tel: 01206 747474
Dentist	Elmes, Elmes, Rashid & Eckstein, 32a Kingsland Road, Colchester. Tel: 01206 384504
Pharmacy	Alliance Pharmacy, Church Road, Tiptree. Tel: 01621 815432

USEFUL NUMBERS

Boatbuilder & Repairs	Adrian Wombwell. Tel: 01621 869784
Decking & Profiles	Wilks Rubber Plastics ('Dek-King'). Tel: 01621 869609
Electronics	Servowatch. Tel: 01621 862145
Fibreglass Repairs	Beaves Marine. Tel: 01621 869270
Marine & Electrical Engineers & Supplies	Volspec Ltd. Tel: 01621 869756
Marine & Electrical Engineers & SS Fabrications	Marine Maintenance Ltd. Tel: 01621 860441
Marine Engineers, Heating & Refrigeration	Tollesbury Marine Engineering. Tel: 01621 869919
Sailmakers	North Sea Sails. Tel: 01621 869367
Shipwright	Paul Drake. Tel: 01621 868195
Upholsterers	SB Upholsterers. Tel: 01621 869743
Yacht Brokers	Woodrolfe Brokerage. Tel: 01621 868494

The sail lofts at Tollesbury

EATING AND DRINKING

Visitors to Tollesbury Marina get automatic temporary membership of the friendly Tollesbury CC. The club is open May to October and is open all day except Monday afternoons and all day Tuesday. Meals and snacks are always available at the bar, but it is advisable to book for a table for the restaurant, particularly on Sundays, Tel: 01621 869561. Down the road, Tollesbury SC bar is open 2000-2300 on Wednesdays, Fridays and Saturdays and 1230-1530 Sundays and welcomes visitors.

In the village there are two pubs. In the square there is the Kings Head, a traditional locals pub with a range of real ales, open 1200-2300 (2400 at weekends). It only does food on Friday lunchtimes 1200-1400, Tel: 01621 869203. Further up, The Hope Inn is a lively modern music bar and pool room with no food, also open 1200-2300 (2400 at weekends). Tel: 01621 869238.

TO SEE AND DO

For the walker and ornithologist there are many interesting walks along the coast and through the saltings from Tollesbury, but stout and waterproof shoes are the order of the day. One particularly interesting walk of about four miles is from the marina around the Tollesbury Wick Marshes nature reserve.

For those wishing to burn off steam there is a covered and heated swimming pool and two tennis courts at Tollesbury CC, both open to marina visitors.

BRADWELL

As you proceed up the creek you will see a slipway and jetty to port, which is Bradwell Quay, which was once a hive of activity. The farm produce from the Dengie Hundred was exported up and down the coast from here by barge in exchange for stone, chalk, beer and London muck (we'll go no further with this description!) for fertilising the fields. The quay also saw many trading schooners, brigs and brigantines from further afield alongside and was a favourite starting and finishing point for wildfowling outings in the famous little Essex punts.

Smuggling was rife on the Blackwater in the 19th century and to try to combat this, the Blackwater and Colne had a small fleet of fast revenue cutters and one of these was kept in the mouth of Bradwell Creek. This later led to Bradwell Waterside having one of the first coastguard stations, which is still there, although now by the marina. Bradwell Waterside was also the site of a Second World War airfield and a small war memorial on the site commemorates those who flew from here, never to return. In the latter half of the 20th century, Bradwell Waterside became dominated by the nuclear power station, but now the hum of its generators has been silenced and once well into the creek you wouldn't know it was there. There is some talk of building a new reactor here. I know we all need electricity and I am not anti-nuclear, but I sometimes wonder at the wisdom of building new reactors when we don't know how to deal with the old ones.

Bradwell has long been a favourite destination for east coast sailors and makes a pleasant place to visit, combined with its convenient situation at the mouth of the Blackwater. Bradwell is a village split in two, but if you have time on your visit it is only 20 minutes walk into the village of Bradwell-on-Sea from Bradwell Waterside. Essex County Council has it's Bradwell Outdoors outdoor learning base here by the quay, which also offers RYA courses to the public.

MOORINGS

The moorings in the creek are maintained by the yacht club and Bradwell Outdoors and run all along the creek, sheltered by Pewit Island, leaving no room for anchoring. If you contact Bradwell Quay Yacht Club, they may be able to find you a vacant one. The moorings are drying upstream of the marina entrance. It is possible in shoal draft craft in settled weather, to follow the creek west on a tide for over a mile to join St. Lawrence Creek, turning to starboard back into the Blackwater, but I would recommend seeking local knowledge prior and checking tides carefully. In the marina itself there are 300 deep water pontoon berths and visitors are made very welcome, but in high season and busy weekends it is best to enquire in advance, as Bradwell is a very popular destination, particularly on a Saturday night. You may also moor alongside the end of the first full length pontoon to make enquiries.

BRADWELL SKIPPERS INFORMATION	
Harbour Master	Call marina on VHF Ch37 & 80 call-sign "Bradwell Marina" or Tel: 01621 776235/776391
Water	On pontoons
Electricity	On pontoons
Fuel	Fuel pontoon in first bay
Facilities	WC under tower and WC, showers and laundry in the club block. You will need a key from the office to access these (£5 deposit required)
Boatyard	All services available on-site
Chandlery	None
Slips	Self launch slipway and 30 ton travel-hoist
Scrubbing Posts	By the quay, enquire at BQYC
Website	www.bradwellmarina.com
Water Taxi	None

CREW CHANGES AND TRAVEL

There is a regular bus service Monday to Saturday every hour or two, from Bradwell-on-Sea to Southminster and Burnham for connecting rail services to Wickford (25 minutes), hourly or better every day, from where you can connect to London Liverpool Street in 35 minutes. For bus information contact Traveline East Anglia, Tel: 08706 082608 Website: www.traveline.org.uk. For train information contact 'One' Customer Services, Tel: 08456 007245 Website: www.onerailway.com or National Rail Enquiries, Tel: 08457 484950 Website: www.nationalrail.co.uk

EATING AND DRINKING

The Bradwell Marina clubhouse opens every day in summer and has a bar and serves food in the bar and on the waterside terrace. Open in season 1200-1500 and

1800-2300 (all day weekends) serving food up to 0930, although it can close early if not busy. BQYC welcomes visitors and has a bar which is open every Sunday afternoon 1300-1600 (to 2000 in season) and in season 1900-2300 Fridays and Saturdays.

The Green Man pub in Bradwell waterside (reached by a footpath from the marina, past Bradwell Outdoors buildings) is a favourite haunt of yachtsmen and serves a selection of real ales and good food in the friendly bar and restaurant. It can be very popular on summer weekends, so booking is advisable. Open 1200-1500 and 1700-2300 (2230 Sundays, but all day weekends and bank holidays). Food is served 1200-1430 and 1900-2100 (weekends 1200-1500 and 1830-2130, 1830-2100 Sundays). Tel: 01621 776226. Further afield is the Kings Head in Bradwell village, serving real ales and food in pleasant village surroundings. Tel: 01621 776224.

TO SEE AND DO

The village of Bradwell-on-Sea isn't, being about a mile away inland. The church there has a cage and whipping posts, just past the horse step outside the gate and these were still used during the early 19th century. It is hard to believe that perhaps six offenders were locked up in the small cage for no greater offence than being unruly. Bradwell must have been an exciting place on Saturday night in those days. Perhaps our towns could do with new cages to cool down the yobs that plague them at weekends – tempting!

Turning left at the church and about a further mile and a half on is the chapel of St. Peter-ad-Murum (on-the-wall, very Latin round here), which is one of the oldest and most complete Saxon churches in the country. It was built on the foundations of the Roman fort of Othona (one of the Saxon Shore Forts) in the 7th

BRADWELL SHORESIDE INFORMATION

Stores	It is worth making a special trip to the curious Waterside PO and Stores located in a small building behind a house, just off the bend in the main road. Here you will find a surprising range of basic goods, although in small quantities and a small dog, which insists on being petted by all visitors. Open 0900-1300 and 1400-1730 (closed Wed and Sat afternoons and Sun).
Banks	None
PO	In village store
Public Tel.	By Bradwell Cruising Club in marina and near Green Man pub
Club	Bradwell Cruising Club in marina, Tel: (Sec.) 01621 892970; Bradwell Quay Yacht Club, Tel: (Hon. Sec.) 01621 890173
Taxis	Whent Taxis. Tel: 01621 740202
Accommodation	The Green Man, Tel: 01621 776226; Bellropes B&B in Bradwell-on-Sea, Tel: 01621 776445
Tourist Info.	Some information in marina tower
Police	Queenborough Road, Southminster. Tel: 01621 773663
Doctor	Tillingham Medical Centre, South Street, Tillingham. Tel: 01621 778383
Hospital	(A&E) Basildon Hospital, Nethermayne. Tel: 01268 533911
Dentist	McFarlane, Station Road, Burnham. Tel: 01621 783065
Pharmacy	Southminster Pharmacy, High Street, Southminster, Tel: 01621 772392

USEFUL NUMBERS

Sail Training	Bradwell Outdoors. Tel: 01621 776256

St. Peter-ad-Murum

century by St. Cedd, an early example of recycling. Since that time it has had various uses, including sadly that of a barn for many years, but survived to be reconsecrated last century and is now used for an annual festival. Evensong is also held there on Sundays in July and August, but sadly, due to those who lack any higher feelings or more than a single brain cell, it has to remain locked these days when not in use – bring back the village cage!

THIRSLET SPIT TO HEYBRIDGE

Be sure to keep south of Thirslet Spit buoy to avoid wandering over the mud. From here upstream you need to aim just south of due west, off the southern side of Osea Island, leaving St Lawrence Bay with its holiday homes on the shore, well to port. This is a popular dinghy racing area from the clubs at Stone. You then leave the moorings at Stone to port and the green conical No1 buoy to starboard. This buoy also marks the port hand side of the entrance into Goldhanger Creek, which branches off in a north westerly direction. Until you come to the oyster layings a quarter of a mile in, the creek offers a useful anchorage in the right conditions and it is possible to navigate to the head of the creek at high water in a shallow draught boat just as sailing barges used to do regularly and occasionally still do.

From here on stick over towards the Osea shore until nearing the old ruined pier and then turn to the south west to leave No2 red can (marking the entrance to Lawling Creek) buoy to starboard. There is a good deep water anchorage off and downstream of the ruined pier, where you will often find many yachts awaiting the tide, or stopping overnight on settled summer evenings, although in strong wind over tide conditions it can get very bouncy here. Once beyond The Doctor, the channel turns gradually to the north west past the western end of Osea Island and soon shallows and narrows and just here is the last place to anchor and stay afloat in deeper draft yachts. Off the south west corner of Osea Island, Southey Creek branches to port to pass south of Northey Island but this is too winding and shallow for navigation and best left to the oysters it still produces, unless you are dropping the hook just inside the entrance. Added hazards on this route are the power cables and causeway across to the south-western tip of the island. The island is now an RSPB Reserve, but it was from here that the Vikings launched their ill-fated attack on the Saxons lead by Brytnoth in the famous Battle of Maldon in 991AD.

Above Osea Island you will need to rely on tidal navigation, although deep draft yachts can use the tide to reach Heybridge, and the channel upstream of Osea is well buoyed by Maldon District Council. The yachtsman should not expect to stay afloat at low water once past the upstream end of the island. Heading generally towards the white building of Blackwater Sailing Club, the river then makes a sharp bend to port around the northern point of Northey Island into Collier's Reach and this is marked by red can buoy No8, which you should leave close to port. There are many drying moorings all around this stretch and it is a busy area with races at the weekends and the cluster of buildings around the lock at Heybridge will now come into view on the starboard side.

STONE

The area around Stone has the feeling of an Essex coastal holiday village. Although there is a year-round community here and some interesting coastal architecture, the area only seems to really come alive in summer, when it can become very busy at peak holiday periods. The waterside from the watersports club past The Stone Inn and along the sea wall to Stone Sailing Club and further on to the Marconi Sailing Club, becomes a hive of activity during the season. Stone Watersports Club concentrates on motorised activities including waterskiing.

MOORINGS

The sailing clubs at Stone or Marconi both maintain a visitors mooring off their clubhouses, but if taken may still be able to find a vacant mooring for a visitor and both have good landings.

CREW CHANGES AND TRAVEL

There is a regular bus service Monday to Saturday from Stone, by The Stone Inn, to Southminster and Burnham for connecting rail services to Wickford (25 minutes) hourly or better every day, from where you can connect to London Liverpool Street in 35 minutes. For bus information contact Traveline East Anglia, Tel: 08706 082608 Website: www.traveline.org.uk. For train information contact 'One' Customer Services, Tel: 08456 007245 Website: www.onerailway.com, or National Rail Enquiries, Tel: 08457 484950 Website: www.nationalrail.co.uk

STONE SKIPPERS INFORMATION

Water	At clubs
Electricity	None
Fuel	None
Facilities	WC and showers at the clubs, plus public WC near The Stone Inn
Boatyard	None
Chandlery	None
Slips	At yacht and boating clubs

EATING AND DRINKING

Stone Sailing Club welcomes visitors if bona fide members of other yacht clubs

STONE SHORESIDE INFORMATION

Stores	Village store a quarter of a mile up the lane from The Stone Inn, open 0700-1730 (EC Wed, Sat 0800-1830, Sun 0800-1300)
Banks	None
PO	At village store
Public Tel.	Near The Stone Inn
Clubs	Stone Sailing Club, Tel: 01621 779344 Website: www.stonesc.co.uk; Marconi Sailing Club, Tel: 01621 772164 Website: www.marconi-sc.org.uk; Stone Watersports Club, Tel: 01621 772280
Taxis	Triple 9 Taxis, Southminster, Tel: 01621 772999; A2B Taxis, Southminster. Tel: 01621 773421
Accommodation	None
Tourist Info.	None
Police	Queenborough Road, Southminster. Tel: 01621 773663
Doctor	Tillingham Medical Centre, South Street, Tillingham. Tel: 01621 778383
Hospital	(A&E) Basildon Hospital, Nethermayne. Tel: 01268 533911
Dentist	McFarlane, Station Road, Burnham. Tel: 01621 783065
Pharmacy	Southminster Pharmacy, High Street, Southminster. Tel: 01621 772392

Stone Sailing Club ©Claudia Myatt

and has two bars and a restaurant, open at weekends in summer. Tel: 01621 779344. Further along the sea wall westwards is the Marconi Sailing Club, which is not restricted to Marconi employees and also welcomes visitors. Tel: 01621 772164.

The Stone Inn stands right on the water's edge by the sea wall and serves food from a good pub menu and drinks (no real ales) in friendly and pleasant surroundings, with excellent views of the river east and west. Open in season 1200-2400 (0030 Saturdays) and serving food 1200-1500 and 1900-2100 every day. In winter it reduces its hours to 1400-2330 (but extends to 1200-0100 weekends, 2300 Sunday). Tel: 01621 779215.

On Main Road in St. Lawrence is the Indian Ocean pub and restaurant, serving an Indian menu and traditional pub food. Open every day 1100-2300. Tel: 01621 779388.

TO SEE AND DO

The sea wall both east and west provides interesting walking, at times alongside the river and at others set back behind marshes and saltings.

GOLDHANGER CREEK

Goldhanger Creek is one of those places that has become forgotten by most, although the barge skippers know its secrets and if visiting you may well find yourself in the company of a barge careening against the posts on the starboard hand. In settled weather this creek can be an interesting diversion, particularly for those in shoal draft craft. The scene here is a rural one and the village quayside is just over half a mile away. Once ashore if you follow the sea wall to the head of the creek you will find a pathway leading off between two hedgerows, past playing fields and into a lane where you turn right up the hill into the pleasant village of Goldhanger.

MOORINGS

It is possible to lie afloat to anchor for a short distance within the entrance to the creek. For those able to take the ground you can anchor further towards the head of the creek past the oyster layings and the sailing club maintains a drying visitors mooring off its dinghy slip. The club is a small DIY-style dinghy-orientated club and opens when a member is there. There is dry landing at some steps on the port hand side, although there is actually dry landing all around the head, particularly good near the careening posts to starboard.

GOLDHANGER SKIPPERS INFORMATION	
Harbour Master	None
Water	Enquire at the club if open
Electricity	None
Fuel	None
Facilities	None
Boatyard	None
Chandlery	None
Slips	Dinghy only
Scrubbing Posts	Public careening posts

GOLDHANGER SHORESIDE INFORMATION

Stores	Village shop three quarters of a mile, open 0800-2000 (closed Sun). Turn left at Chequers, right at T-junction, on right-hand side
Banks	None
PO	In shop
Public Tel.	Opposite Chequers
Club	Goldhanger Sailing Club. Tel: 01621 788438
Taxis	Banyards Taxis, Maldon, Tel: 01621 850850; Beeline Taxis, Maldon, Tel: 01621 852633
Accommodation	None
Police	West Square, Maldon. Tel: 01621 852255
Doctor	Dr. R. J. Furze, Goldhanger Village Hall, Head Street, Tel: 01621 869204
Hospital	Colchester General, Turner Road, Colchester. Tel: 01206 747474
Dentist	Heybridge Dental Practice, 25 Bentalls Centre, Heybridge. Tel: 01206 851003
Pharmacy	Alliance Pharmacy, Church Road, Tiptree. Tel: 01621 815432

CREW CHANGES AND TRAVEL

Goldhanger is not a convenient place for changeovers, but there are a few buses a day Monday to Saturday to Tollesbury and Maldon from where you can get connecting buses. For information contact Traveline East Anglia, Tel: 08706 082608 Website: www.traveline.org.uk

EATING AND DRINKING

Goldhanger, unusually for a British village, still has two thriving pubs, both friendly, full of locals and serving good ales and food from extensive menus. The first pub you come to on the right-hand side as you enter the village is The Chequers, an old beamed pub open all day, every day and serving food 1200-1500 every day and 1830-2100 Monday to Saturday, Tel 01621 788203. The Cricketers is further up on the left-hand side of the road and is again open all day, every day and serves food lunchtimes and evenings every day, Tel: 01621 788468.

TO SEE AND DO

There is a Museum of Domestic and Agricultural Life at the top end of the village. Telephone for opening times. Tel: 01621 788647. For the walker, the sea wall path provides good and dry walking and follows the waters edge right along the length of the Blackwater from Tollesbury to Maldon. There are also a few paths leading off inland enabling a circular coastal and rural walk to be constructed.

LAWLING CREEK

Opposite the jetty on Osea Island, port hand No.2 buoy (Fl.R.3s) marks the starboard side of the entrance to Lawling Creek. This leads in turn to the drying Mayland Creek which branches off to port and contains a few drying moorings. Small lateral buoys mark the channel and should be carefully followed, although the many moorings in the creek also help to identify the deep water. There is room to anchor in the entrance but continuing up Lawling Creek on the tide will lead you past Harlow (Blackwater) Sailing Club, to Blackwater Marina and Maylandsea Bay Sailing Club near the head. The creek and marina are tidal with little more than a trickle in the upper reaches at low water and craft drawing more than a metre should only attempt to access the marina a couple of hours either side of high water. The centre of Maylandsea village is only 300 metres walk from the marina.

MOORINGS

There are 200 pontoon berths drying in soft mud at Blackwater Marina and space can usually be found for visitors. There are also over 100 swinging moorings, both drying and deep water in the creek, also run by Blackwater Marina and some by the clubs.

CREW CHANGES AND TRAVEL
There are irregular buses into Maldon and to Burnham and Southminster for train connections. For information contact Traveline East Anglia, Tel: 08706 082608 Website: www.traveline.org.uk

EATING AND DRINKING
There is a bar at the marina, open from 1200 each day. About five minutes walk up Imperial Avenue from the marina you come to a parade of shops where you will find the General Lee pub open evenings only weekdays 1700-2330 and all day weekends (Saturday 1200-0030, Sundays 1200-2330), Tel: 01621 740791.

Posh Spice Indian takeaway (which will deliver to the marina) opens every evening 1700-2230 (Sundays 2200), Tel: 01621 744800. There is also a fish and chip shop, with seating, open 1200-1345 and 1700-1930 (an hour later some days, but closed Monday lunchtime and Sundays).

LAWLING CREEK SKIPPERS INFORMATION	
Harbour Master	Blackwater Marina, Tel: 01621 740264
Water	On pontoons
Electricity	On pontoons
Fuel	Fuel berth at marina
Facilities	WC and showers
Internet	None
Boatyard	Full services on-site at marina. Tel: 01621 740264
Chandlery	None
Slips	300 ton dry dock, 80 ton slipway, 18 ton travel-hoist and 15 ton crane at the marina, and dinghy slips at the clubs
Website	www.blackwater-marina.co.uk

TO SEE AND DO
There are sea wall walks in both directions from the marina, which when combined with the extensive local network of footpaths (including the St. Peters Way), can create some varied circular walks, one of which is a three mile walk around the peninsula between Lawling and Mayland Creeks.

LAWLING CREEK SHORESIDE INFORMATION	
Stores	General store in village open every day 0700-2100 (from 0830 Sun), also bakers nearby
Banks	None
PO	In general store
Public Tel.	By general store
Club	Maylandsea Bay Sailing Club. Tel: 01621 740470 Website: www.maylandseabay-sc.org.uk; Harlow (Blackwater) Sailing Club, Website: www.harlow-blackwater-sc.org.uk Tel: 01621 740300
Taxis	Prompt Cars, Tel: 01621 744655; Anns Cars, Tel: 01621 741621
Police	West Square, Maldon. Tel: 01621 852255
Doctor	Maylandsea Medical Centre, Imperial Drive. Tel: 01621 742233
Hospital	(A&E) Broomfield Hospital, Court Road, Chelmsford. Tel: 08448 220002
Dentist	McFarlane, Station Road, Burnham. Tel: 01621 783065
Pharmacy	Southminster Pharmacy, High Street, Southminster. Tel: 01621 772392

USEFUL NUMBERS

Mobile Blasting, Cleaning & Spraying	Falcon Blast. Tel: 01621 742463
Surveyor	Paul Stevens. Tel: 01621 740613

Entrance to Heybridge Lock at low water

OSEA ISLAND

Osea Island has had several uses over the years. At one time it belonged to the Charrington family who provided a sanctuary for alcoholics and for a few years it was used as a minor naval base. Access to the island from the north shore is across a causeway, known as the Stumble, which is submerged at all but low water and supposedly built by the recovering alcoholics as part of their therapy. It is possible to navigate north of the Island at high water in suitable shallow craft, but the marked channel passes to the south. It can be pleasant to stretch your legs along the shore, but this is a privately-owned island, so you are not free to wander.

HEYBRIDGE

Once in the moorings in Colliers Reach, the entrance to the lock at Heybridge is sometimes marked by a small buoy, otherwise the channel is pretty much on the line of the lock pen. Traffic lights are now in operation for the lock. The lock gives access to the Chelmer and Blackwater Navigation, built in 1798 to transport cargoes, such as coal and timber, from ships in the Blackwater to Chelmsford, some 14 miles and 11 locks upstream. A licence is required to navigate the canal, details of which can be obtained from the lock keeper, but visitors to the basin are exempt. Heybridge men have made their living from the water since Roman times and many would have sailed the local spritsail barges. More recently there was a significant eel trade, with live eels being shipped over from Holland and kept alive here in tanks until ready for sale.

After the demise of the old Chelmer Navigation Co., the lock and canal has now come under the ownership of Essex Waterways, under the umbrella of the Inland Waterways Association. The long-standing lock keeper Colin Edmond, has now taken over responsibility for the entire navigation and following the sale of a few assets for development, the

HEYBRIDGE SKIPPERS INFORMATION	
Harbour Master	Navigation Manager, Colin Edmond on VHF Ch80 call-sign "Heybridge Basin". Tel: 01621 853506 Mobile: 07712 079764 Email: colin.edmond@waterways.org.uk
Water	By the lock
Electricity	None
Fuel	Nearest one mile
Facilities	New WC and shower block, with laundry
Internet	None
Boatyard	Stebbens Boatyard, Tel: 01621 857436 Mobile: 07974 530269; CRS Marine Ltd., Tel: 01621 854684
Chandlery	Nearest Maldon
Slips	Cranes at the boatyards, contact for details

books have been balanced and some improvements have started to be made, making the place even more pleasant than before. The lock, accessible for craft drawing up to 2.5 metres, is opened on request for one hour before high water to half an hour after during neaps and sometimes for slightly longer periods during springs. The lock is manned from 0600-2000 (0700-1700 in winter), although it can be opened outside these times if booked in advance, with at least 24 hours notice. As Heybridge is not only a very pleasant and sheltered stopover, but also the only place craft can lie afloat in the upper Blackwater, it can be a very busy on summer weekends and you should book in advance. Approaching the lock, keep the withies close to port, keeping well clear until you have the green light on the port hand of the lock and don't join the occasional silly scrum to get in, the lock keeper has seen you and there's no need to rush and push. If you've booked you will get in. Locking into the basin

HEYBRIDGE SHORESIDE INFORMATION	
Stores	The nearest stores are at Bentalls Shopping Centre in Heybridge a mile and a half's walk along the lane or towpath. Here there is a good parade of shops including a Tesco supermarket open 0600-2300 every day and a Netto supermarket open slightly less.
Banks	Cash machine in the Old Ship and at Heybridge
PO	In Tesco
Public Tel.	In car park 100 metres along towpath
Clubs	Millbeach Marine Club, Tel: (Sec.) 01621 828909; Saltcote Sailing Club, Tel: 01621 840769; Blackwater Sailing Club, Tel: 01621 853923 Website: www.blackwatersailingclub.co.uk
Taxis	Arrow Taxis, Tel: 01621 855111; Banyards Taxis, Tel: 01621 850850
Tourist Info.	Nearest Maldon. Tel: 01621 856503
Police	West Square, Maldon. Tel: 01621 852255
Doctor	Longfield Medical Centre, Heybridge. Tel: 01621 856811
Hospital	(A&E) Broomfield Hospital, Court Road, Chelmsford. Tel: 08448 220002
Dentist	Heybridge Dental Practice, 25 Bentalls Centre, Tel: 01621 851003
Pharmacy	The Pharmacy, Bentalls Shopping Centre. Tel: 01621 850559
USEFUL NUMBERS	
Sailing School	Atsailing. Tel: 01621 841976

can be an unusual experience for those not familiar with inland waterways, just remember to fender well both sides and tend your lines throughout the process.

Clubs and yards stretch out all down Colliers Reach to Heybridge, so I shall just list them heading upstream. First on the bend is Millbeach Marine Club, a small yard and club with a slip and a pub nearby. In the bay here, the large white Saltcote Mill has now become part of an elegant residential development and nearby is Saltcote Sailing Club's little white hut on the wall, together with its dinghy park and launching ramp. Shortly after is the large white building of the Blackwater Sailing Club, which is built around an old fort and was at one time a First World War MTB station and the club was used as the officers' mess. Established in 1899 the BSC is an active and vibrant club for dinghy racers and cruisers and possibly the largest on the east coast with full-time stewards, but still very down-to-earth and welcoming.

Next comes the friendly traditional yard of Stebbens Boatyard now under the ownership of Adrian and Judy Robinson, who will often be able to help out visitors with drying pontoons (just past the barges, before the lock), or swinging moorings. Then comes the barge Haybay, home to Newham Council's Fairplay Outdoor Education Centre, an RYA training centre. Another traditional yard, CRS Marine is next, which can still supply wooden spars (and oars) to your specification. It may also be able to assist with moorings if you are stuck. The Dawn Sailing Barge Trust is restoring the Dawn in a dry dock here, it being an 1897 spritsail barge and the last tiller-steered barge afloat.

Basin Tripper Boats runs trips on the canal every day in season from 1000 onwards, just a few yards up from the basin. They are quite happy to take visitors up to Heybridge for shopping trips and pick them up to return to the basin. Tel: 07835 657462.

MOORINGS

For moorings in the basin contact the navigation manager, (well in advance on summer weekends) to be sure of a mooring in the basin. It does have the capacity to moor up to 200 boats, but only a limited number of berths at the entrance are for visitors and at busy times they will moor the last few visitors in the lock itself. The trots and the pontoon off the sea wall all dry out, but the yards will try to find you a visitors mooring if there is one available. Landing can either be made on the steps just downstream of the lock, or more conveniently, on the landing pontoon of Heybridge Basin Sailing Association, just upstream. Rubbish bins are 100 metres up the canal in the car park.

CREW CHANGES AND TRAVEL

There is a regular two-hourly bus service Monday to Saturday, from the bus shelter a quarter of a mile up the lane into Maldon, where you can get connecting buses. For information contact Traveline East Anglia. Tel: 08706 082608.

EATING AND DRINKING

The lively Mill Beach bar and restaurant overlooks the river by Millbeach Boat Club and is open every day for lunches, snacks and dinner, Tel: 01621 857157. Blackwater Sailing Club has a spacious clubhouse with lounge and galley serving snacks on race days. Tel: 01621 853923.

The Lock Tea Room at the lock-side serves breakfast, lunch and snacks inside or on a small terrace overlooking the river.

The modern Old Ship pub stands right beside the lock and here you can enjoy views of the river and watch the comings and goings through the lock. It is open all day, every day, serving real ales and breakfast, lunch and dinner and bar snacks from 0830 to 2030 (2100 Friday and Saturday), Tel: 01621 854150. The Jolly Sailor pub is tucked in at the bottom of the sea wall and is open 1100-0100 Monday to Saturday serving real ales and meals and snacks, including breakfasts from 1100. Tel: 01621 854210.

TO SEE AND DO

It is possible for the energetic to walk the whole length of the canal towpath to Chelmsford, or to follow the footpath into Heybridge and then the road into Maldon just over two miles away. A pleasant walk of about five miles along the river Chelmer leads to Beeleigh Falls where the Blackwater meets the Chelmer in an area of interesting water works. Another shorter circular walk of about three miles takes you up the towpath and then around the old gravel pits along the sea wall.

HEYBRIDGE TO MALDON

Back in Collier's Reach after Heybridge, the river becomes very narrow and shallow and any vessels over one and a half metres draft would be well advised to consider the tides before venturing further, unless they wish to find themselves neaped, although on a spring tide, vessels with well over 2 metres draft can reach the quays at Maldon. The channel bends sharply to starboard at the upper end of Colliers Reach. A glance astern round this point will show where the road crosses to Northey Island and the power cables appear to vanish into the water. Ahead can be seen the distinctive spire of St. Mary's church at Maldon that has been used as a beacon to welcome home many a weary Maldon sailor through the ages.

The channel hugs the starboard bank for a short while before turning to port, opposite the Maldon Yacht Club, built on a lighter near the end of the promenade. There are now trots of moorings on both sides of the channel, which curves round to starboard as it approaches Hythe Quay, where you will often find sailing barges moored.

Although many visitors venture no further than Hythe Quay and the visitors pontoon, there are six Maldon boatyards between the Hythe and the bridge (Fullbridge), which is effectively the upper limit of navigation. Also upstream is Maldon Salt Works, the company that still practises the ancient craft of panning salt, producing, what many television chefs tell us, is an essential ingredient to our cooking.

MALDON

Maldon is a thriving riverside town that can feel almost overrun with visitors on a summer weekend; yet being slightly off the beaten track and having lost its rail connection many years ago, it maintains a pleasant, slightly slower old-fashioned feel. The quayside is particularly appealing with a number of barges and traditional vessels moored alongside and the attractive building of the Maldon Little Ship Club facing the quay. Sadly, the old Cook's boatyard has now gone, but the buildings are used by a number of marine businesses, whilst further back in town you will find every facility just a short walk away (although up some steep hills).

Everything dries out here surprisingly soon after HW, so make sure you arrive and leave at the end of the rising tide and no later than high water. Despite this, Hythe Quay is still a centre for traditional craft and you will often see a number of Thames spritsail sailing barges alongside. The Cirdan Trust is based at Maldon and has vessels that are well known to east coast sailors, including the recently re-fitted Baltic Trader Queen Galadriel and the Thames Sailing Barge Xylonite. The main aim of the Trust is to provide sail training for young people from youth organisations and other groups to experience the excitement and challenge of running and sailing a large vessel, under the guidance of their group leaders and the vessel's professional crew. Also based on Hythe Quay at Cooks Yard are Topsail

MALDON SKIPPERS INFORMATION

Harbour Master	River Bailiff (office on Hythe Quay), Tel: 07818 013723 Email: river.bailiff@maldon.gov.uk
Water	On pontoon
Electricity	On pontoon
Fuel	One of the boatyards may be able to assist, otherwise garages in town
Facilities	WC, showers and laundry (key from River Bailiff)
Internet	None
Boatyard	See Useful Numbers
Chandlery	Marinestore, North Street, Tel: 01621 854280; One Stop Chandlery, Tel: 01621 853558
Slips	A variety of craneage and slips at the boatyards
Scrubbing Posts	Enquire at boatyards

Charters which operates the sailing barges Hydrogen and Thistle, offering day, weekend and longer trips for parties of up to 12 or more on day trips.

MOORINGS

Just past the barges opposite the Jolly Sailor and Queens Head there is now a 25 metres visitors pontoon. Prior bookings (which are not always necessary) can be made with the River Bailiff. Otherwise there are mud-berths, on stagings and pontoons, upstream at a number of boatyards if you can find somebody to ask. The mud in Maldon is extremely soft, allowing even keelboats to settle upright.

CREW CHANGES AND TRAVEL

Although there is no railway station at Maldon, this is a hub for local buses and there are very regular buses to Chelmsford from where you can connect to rail services to London Liverpool Street

MALDON SHORESIDE INFORMATION

Stores	Good shops in town, including a Budgens supermarket at the top end of the High Street open every day 0800-2000 (1000-1600 Sun)
Banks	All banks in town
PO	In Budgens supermarket
Public Tel.	On the quay
Club	Maldon Little Ship Club, Tel: 01621 854139 Website: www.mlsc.org.uk; Maldon Yacht Club, Website: www.maldonyc.org.uk
Taxis	Arrow Taxis, Tel: 01621 855111; Banyards Taxis, Tel: 01621 850850
Accommodation	The Jolly Sailor and Queens Head on the quay offer accommodation (see Eating and Drinking), plus there is a variety of accommodation in town, from bed and breakfast and inns to guesthouses and hotels, contact Tourist Information
Tourist Info.	Coach Lane, off the top end of the High Street, open 1000-1600 Mon to Sat. Tel: 01621 856503
Police	West Square, Maldon. Tel: 01621 852255
Doctor	Blackwater Medical Centre, Princes Road. Tel: 08444 996635
Hospital	(A&E) Broomfield Hospital, Court Road, Chelmsford. Tel: 08448 220002
Dentist	Finn & Bansal, 2 West Square. Tel: 01621 841122
Pharmacy	Longfield Pharmacy, Princes Road. Tel: 01621 853331; plus others in town

(40 minutes). For bus information contact Traveline East Anglia, Tel: 08706 082608 Website: www.traveline.org.uk. For train information contact 'One' Customer Services, Tel: 08456 007245 Website: www.onerailway.com or National Rail Enquiries, Tel: 08457 484950 Website: www.nationalrail.co.uk

EATING AND DRINKING

Maldon has a wide variety of places to eat and drink, so I shall provide information for a few, but would suggest if you have time, a short walk around town will yield an extensive choice. Maldon Little Ship Club has its clubhouse on Hythe Quay where it welcomes visitors to its comfortable bar. This is open on Saturday and Sunday lunchtimes and Friday and Wednesday evenings. Tel: 01621 854139. Maldon Yacht Club uses a converted lighter as a clubhouse and has a bar often open at weekends.

There are two pubs right on the quay. The Jolly Sailor is a traditional 17th century pub open every day, with a restaurant specialising in fish dishes, serving lunch and dinner and all day weekends 1200-1900 and sometimes later, Tel: 01621 853463.

The Queens Head Inn right on the quay, is a popular pub where you can sit outside and watch the activities on the quayside. It serves traditional-style meals and snacks in the bar and restaurant every day 1200-1445 and 1830-2130 (all day Sunday to 1800), Tel: 01621 854112.

For the family, Madison Heights entertainment centre (see To See and Do) has two bars and two restaurants of the pizza and diner variety, Tel: 01621 850222. For more international tastes there is The Curry Nights Indian restaurant in the

MALDON – USEFUL NUMBERS

Boatbuilders	Jamie Clay, Tel: 01621 853804; Jim Maynard, Tel: 01621 855866
Boat Sales	M. J. Lewis & Sons. Tel: 01621 840982
Boat Transport	P. J. Downs & Sons. Tel: 01621 854388
Boatyards	Downs Road Boatyard, Tel: 01621 853330; David Patient, Tel: 07801 130530
GRP Repairs	Gel n Shine. Tel: 01621 857700
Marine & Electrical Engineers	J. M. Dines. Tel: 01621 859373
Marine Electrics & Electronics	P and S Automation. Tel: 01621 841328
Marine Electronics	Mantsbrite. Tel: 01621 853003
Marine Engineers	Heritage Marine. Tel: 01621 859373
Marine Fabrications	Maldon Marine, Tel: 01621 859000; APB Engineering, Tel: 01621 785537
Marine Photographer	Den Phillips. Tel: 01621 850276
Painting & Varnishing	A. G. Brooks. Tel: 07799 473135
Riggers	TS Rigging. Tel: 01621 874861
Sailing Barge Charter	Topsail Charters, Tel: 01621 857567; Thames Sailing Barge Trust, Tel: 01621 893674
Sail Training	Cirdan Trust, Tel: 01621 851433; East Coast Sail Trust, Tel: 01621 854181
Shipwright	Adrian Riva. Tel: 01621 851081
Upholsterers	Hamilton Marine Trimmers. Tel: 01621 850547
Yacht Surveyors	Ark Surveys. Tel: 01621 857065
Yacht Surveys & Marine Consultants	Bureau Maritime. Tel: 01621 859181

Maldon's Hythe Quay and up to Fullbridge ©PRPA

High Street open every day 1200-1400 and 1730-2330 (midnight on Fridays and Saturdays), Tel: 01621 853162 and also in the High Street, Manolis Greek Taverna is open Tuesday to Saturday 1800 until late and Sunday 1200-1700, Tel: 01621 852009.

TO SEE AND DO

For all the family, the Madison Heights entertainment centre 10 minutes walk out past the park, has 22 ten-pin bowling lanes, a snooker club and for the very young, the Monkey Puzzle indoor play area where they can burn off excess energy. Tel: 01621 850222 for opening times.

Alongside the river, on the promontory downstream from Hythe Quay is the award-winning Promenade Park, offering a variety of facilities from ornamental to active, with two imaginative children's play areas. The Blackwater Leisure Centre just 10 minutes walk away past the park, has a range of activities including swimming and an activity pool. Tel: 01621 851898 for opening times.

You could do much worse than just stroll the length of the riverside along the lovely old-fashioned promenade, the quay and then through lanes and footpaths behind the boatyards through to Fullbridge, where you can turn left up the hill to the High Street. There are a variety of walks out into the countryside from Maldon to suit all tastes, both riverside and rural and a series of booklets on these can be obtained from the Tourist Information Centre.

North Fambridge Yacht Station and NFYC

THE RIVER CROUCH

⊕ **51°37'.6N 00°56'.4E** *(Crouch buoy)*
Tides Whitaker Beacon +0:10
Burnham +0:30 Fambridge +0:50
(differences from Harwich)

The Crouch has long been the yachting Mecca of the east coast and both cruisers and racers alike will find an abundance of everything they need in Burnham, which is very much a yachting and boating town. A flat and rather uninteresting vista in the lower reaches with too many unnatural straight lines, slowly gives way to more gentle countryside as you approach Burnham. The recent works on Wallasea Island under the guise of the Wallasea Wetlands Project to create 110 hectares of salt marsh, have improved things further and broken the unappealing line of concrete sea defences. After Burnham the river starts to meander and the countryside softens with islands, marshes

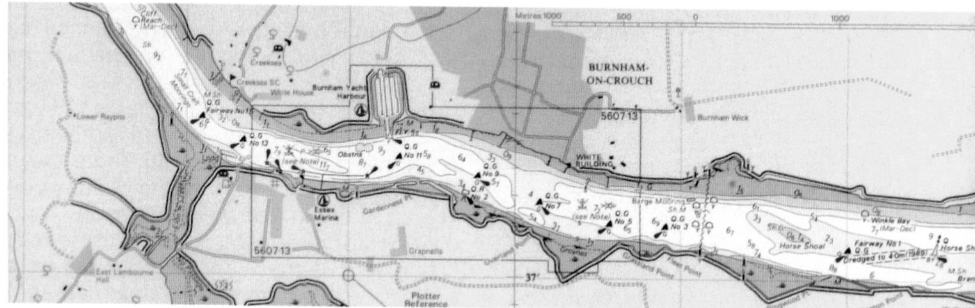

and pastures backed by a ridge of low hills to the north. Many visitors to these parts do not venture further than Burnham, but in doing so they are missing out on the varied and more gentle delights of the River Roach and creeks and the upper reaches of the Crouch, which stretch some 15 miles to Battlesbridge.

The River Crouch is curiously a private river, run by a trust and managed by the Crouch Harbour Authority. Rules are strictly enforced, although with humour and to the benefit of all, among which is the need for Third Party insurance if you moor or slip here, even for jet-skis. Improbably large commercial traffic still navigates its way to Baltic Wharf on the south bank, upstream of Essex Marina, carrying timber from Scandinavia and the Baltic states. An 8 knot speed limit applies from the start of the moorings at Burnham, although there are three designated areas for water-skiing and jet-skis above and below Fambridge and in Spitty's Reach further upriver still.

APPROACH AND ENTRANCE

Approaching the Crouch from the Swin Spitway, many now favour a course to the north of the Swallow Tail sandbank. To this end, Crouch Harbour Master Captain Ian Bell has laid a safe water mark named North Swallow, half way between the Swin Spitway and Sunken Buxey, allowing a more direct route from the Swin to Outer Crouch. For those not wishing to take this route, it may be necessary to go most of the way across to Whitaker No 6 before turning to starboard into the Crouch to follow the Ridge, Foulness, South Buxey, Buxey No 1, Buxey No 2, Outer Crouch and Crouch buoys into the river. The channel is then clearly marked with lit buoys all the way to Baltic Wharf, just past Essex Marina on the south bank past Burnham. Outside the river there are few landmarks to be seen except the masts and posts on Foulness Island. This flat area is largely occupied by the MoD making landing very restricted. For the newcomer, it may be difficult to see exactly where the river begins, but by the time the Crouch buoy is reached, the water is well and truly between land on either side.

There is a short cut to the Blackwater through the Ray Sand (Rays'n) Channel for those with shoal draft and confidence. The entrance to this is marked by a yellow buoy half a mile to the north of the Outer Crouch buoy. From there you head due north over the sands, which now dry by over a metre at LAT, until you find deeper water and then turn more north easterly to leave the Buxey Beacon a half-mile to starboard, taking care not to turn into the Blackwater too early. For most, you would be advised to use the channel around high tide going north and approaching high tide coming south (when I have personally found this short cut more useful).

FOULNESS TO CREEKSEA

Travelling past Foulness Island to port and just over a mile past the Inner Crouch buoy, the entrance to the River Roach is passed to port and from then on Burnham

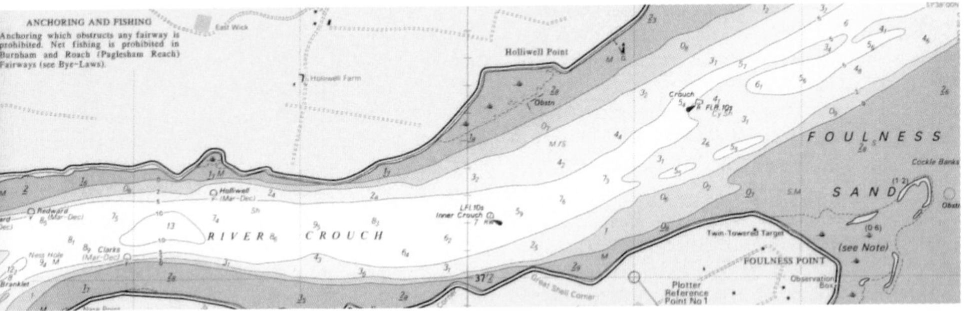

BURNHAM SKIPPERS INFORMATION	
BURNHAM	
Harbour Master	Captain Ian Bell, Tel: 01621 783602. When afloat he maintains a listening watch on VHF Ch16
Water	On boatyard and club pontoons
Electricity	None
Fuel	At Rice & Cole's boatyard (or go to Essex Marina or Burnham Yacht Harbour)
Facilities	WC's and showers at both yards and at the yacht clubs
Boatyards	Rice & Cole, Tel: 01621 782063; R. J. Prior & Sons, Tel: 01621 782160
Chandlery	Fairways Chandlery on the quayside, Tel: 01621 782659; Mailspeed has an extensive chandlery (behind RCYC), Tel: 01621 781120 and there is a small chandlery at Rice & Cole's yard
Slips	Cranes at Rice & Cole's yard and craneage up to 25 tons at R. J. Prior & Sons
Scrubbing Posts	Enquire at R. J. Prior & Sons
Water Taxi	None
BURNHAM YACHT HARBOUR	
Harbour Master	VHF Ch80 call-sign "Burnham Yacht Harbour". Tel: 01621 786832
Water	On pontoons
Electricity	On pontoons
Fuel	Diesel on fuel pontoon F (by the travel-hoist)
Facilities	WC, showers, laundry
Internet	Free wireless internet
Boatyard	Extensive on-site services
Chandlery	Marinestore Burnham, on-site. Tel: 01621 854280
Slips	A massive 100 ton slipway, 30 ton travelhoist and 25 ton mobile crane
Website	www.burnhamyachtharbour.co.uk
Water Taxi	None

comes into view on the north bank. Just after the entrance to the Roach is the cardinal Horse Shoal buoy marking the eastern end of the mid-stream horse, which should cause little trouble except at LWS. A series of green lateral buoys, starting with Fairway No 1, then clearly marks the course towards the channel to the south of the hundreds of moorings at Burnham. The channel markers continue past Burnham and Wallasea, to Fairway No 15 off Creeksea opposite Baltic Wharf.

BURNHAM-ON-CROUCH

The town's attractive old-fashioned High Street runs parallel to the quay. All of the clubs and many of the town's yachting businesses lie between the two and can be seen when passing by boat. Most easterly of the boatyard cranes to be seen is Rice & Cole's. The first clubhouse to be seen is the imposing Royal Corinthian with its white 1920s listed building often appearing light blue in sunlight and the Royal Burnham Yacht Club just along the shore. Clubs, yards, houses, pubs and a chandlery run along the bank, with a few houseboats moored at the upper end of town. The Crouch Yacht Club and the Burnham Sailing Club are at the upstream end of the town and the marina is located a further quarter of a mile on past the Burnham Sailing Club along the pleasant sea wall path. There are many fine old buildings to be seen, mostly in

BURNHAM SHORESIDE INFORMATION

Stores	Nearest to Burnham Yacht Harbour is the Co-op supermarket up the lane, open every day 0700-2100 (1000-1600 Sun). In the town there is a good range of shops including a Tesco Express open every day 0700-2300 and a One-Stop store open every day 0600-2300.
Banks	Barclays and National Westminster in High Street and cash machines at all three supermarkets
PO	In High Street
Public Tel.	Outside Ye Olde White Hart Hotel and in the bar at Burnham Yacht Harbour
Clubs	Royal Corinthian Yacht Club, Tel: 01621 782105 Website: www.royalcorinthian.co.uk Royal Burnham Yacht Club, Tel: 01621 782044 Website www.rbyc.org.uk Crouch Yacht Club, Tel: 01621 782252 Website: www.cyc.org.uk Burnham Sailing Club, Tel: (Sec.) 01621 782875 Website: www.burnhamsc.org
Taxis	Triple 9 Taxis, Tel: 01621 772999; Crouch Taxis, Tel: 01621 784154
Accommodation	Ye Old White Hart Hotel, The Anchor Hotel, The Star Inn and The Ship Inn all have letting rooms (see Eating and Drinking) and there is a selection of accommodation in the town, call Tourist Information
Tourist Info.	Information point, 1 High Street, Tel: 01621 784962
Police	Queenborough Road, Southminster. Tel: 01621 773663
Essex Marine Police Unit	Tel: 01621 782121
Doctor	M. H. Latif & Ptnrs., Foundry Lane. Tel: 01621 782054
Hospital	(A&E) Basildon Hospital, Nethermayne. Tel: 01268 533911
Dentist	Patel & Baker, 89a High Street. Tel: 01621 782644
Pharmacy	Savages, 22 Station Road, Tel: 01621 785042; Alliance, 3 Foundry Lane, Tel: 01621 782058

an excellent state of repair, which together with the many welcoming clubs, pubs, shops and restaurants, make Burnham well worth landing to explore.

MOORINGS

Although there are many moorings off Burnham, few are marked for visitors use, although there is one off the Royal Corinthian pontoon. It is therefore worth making contact with one of the yards or clubs, so you are not asked to move on when the resident returns. The suggested procedure is to pick up a vacant mooring and call up a yard or land someone at one of the jetties to make arrangements. You may be lucky and be able to ask one of the boatmen. During Burnham Week things get very busy and it is advisable to make advance arrangements for a berth.

From the eastern approach, moorings are run in order by Rice & Cole, the Royal Corinthian Yacht Club, R. J. Prior & Sons and at the upriver end leading up to Burnham Yacht Harbour (once known as Tucker Brown's yard), the yacht harbour operates about 120 moorings.

Each yard and club has its own landing pontoon to get ashore and there are a variety of launch services. Rice & Cole provides a launch service for its customers from April to October on Saturdays, Sundays and Bank Holidays between 0900 and 1800 and Wednesday evenings from 1700 until late. The service is extended in peak season to include Friday evenings and a limited weekday service. The Royal Corinthian and Royal Burnham run launches at weekends, daytime only and R. J. Prior & Sons also runs a launch service at peak times.

Alternatively, Burnham Yacht Harbour offers visitors the ease of pontoon moorings a few minutes walk from town via the paved sea wall path. Here you will share the harbour with the RNLI and Essex Police Marine Division (including the RIB-transported marine terror unit "Ninjas" in their black gear), which probably makes this the safest place for a boat in these parts. The entrance to the marina is marked by a lit yellow buoy to the north of green conical Fairway No 11, from where the green and red entrance beacons can be seen indicating the dredged channel. Do not be tempted to cut the corner and go inside the marker buoy as the channel is dredged (2.5 metres at LAT) and it is very shallow either side.

CREW CHANGES AND TRAVEL

Burnham is a convenient place for transfers as there are regular train services from Burnham-on-Crouch to Wickford (25 minutes) hourly or better every day, from where you can connect to London Liverpool Street in 35 minutes. There are also regular bus services connecting Burnham-on-Crouch to the local area. For information contact Traveline East Anglia, Tel: 08706 082608 Website: www.traveline.org.uk. For train information contact 'One' Customer Services, Tel: 08456 007245 Website: www.onerailway.com, or National Rail Enquiries, Tel: 08457 484950 Website: www.nationalrail.co.uk

EATING AND DRINKING

There are a wide variety of places to eat and drink in Burnham, and here are just a few options. The RCYC is a very active club and

BURNHAM – USEFUL NUMBERS

Boatbuilders	(Dragons and Etchells) Petticrow Ltd., Tel 01621 782115
Boat Transport	Burni Transport. Tel: 07836 665802
Clothing & Embroidery	Stitch-Print. Tel: 01621 773900
Deck & Rigging Equipment	ProBoat Marine. Tel: 01621 785455
Flags & Dodgers	Flags and Banners Ltd. Tel: 01621 783221
Liferaft Sales, Service & Hire	Premium Liferaft Services. Tel: 01621 784858
Marine Engineers	Lis Marine. Tel: 01621 784544
Marine Fabrications	A P B Engineering. Tel: 01621 785537
Marine Windows	Branch Sound. Tel: 01621 782964; Marine Window Fabrications. Tel: 01621 786413
Marine Windows & Hatches	Houdini Marine Windows. Tel: 01621 773590
Paints & Varnishes	Flag Paints. Tel: 01621 785173
Riggers	Tubby Lee Yachting. Tel: 01621 783562
Sailing Schools	Crouch Sailing School. Tel: 01621 784140 Sark. Tel: 01245 269230 (dayboats)
Sailmakers	Lonton & Gray. Tel: 01621 786200; Wilkinson Sails. Tel: 01621 786770
Surveys	Three Rivers Surveys. Tel: 01621 782107
Yacht Brokers	Clarke & Carter Interyacht (at Burnham Yacht Harbour). Tel: 01621 785600
Yacht Charter	Mistral Yachts. Tel: 01621 743853

Burnham Yacht Harbour ©PRPA

has two bars and catering facilities and welcomes visitors, Tel: 01621 782105. The RBYC welcomes visiting yachtsmen and the bar is open Wednesday, Thursday and Friday lunchtimes 1200-1400, Wednesday evenings 1800-2400, Friday 1600-0100, Saturday 1200-0100 and Sunday 1200-1900. Food is served Wednesday evenings and Saturdays during the day, Tel: 01621 782044. The CYC bar opens Wednesday and Friday evenings 1730-2300 and all day weekends (Sundays to 2000), no food.

On the quay is the Anchor Hotel which is a popular venue with spacious bars in which to enjoy a drink or meal. There are traditional ales served in the bars, which are open all day, all year round and the food ranges from rolls and snacks to three-course lunches, dinners and daily specials. Tel: 01621 782117.

Also on the quay with a terrace on staging over the river is Ye Olde White Harte Hotel, which has been a favourite haunt for yachtsmen for many years. The bars offer superb atmosphere and bar food is available lunchtimes and evenings, but there is also a restaurant with views over the quay, Tel: 01621 782106. Further up the quay is the Star Inn open all day, every day 1100-2300 (0030 Fridays and Saturdays) and serving food lunchtimes and evenings (all day at weekends), Tel: 01621 782010. The Ship Inn in Burnham High Street (just across the main road from behind the Royal Burnham Yacht Club), serves Adnams ales, lunchtime snacks 1200-1430 and evening meals 1900-2130 (not Sundays), Tel: 01621 785057.

The aptly named Quayside Restaurant overlooking the moorings, serves daytime meals to 1700 daily and occasionally in the evenings. They tell me they may start opening on Saturday evenings. This is a 'bring your own alcohol' establishment, Tel: 01621 783350. In the High Street there is also Sgt Peppers, a Tex-Mex restaurant open Friday, Saturday and Sunday only, Tel: 01621 786500 and the Polash Indian restaurant, open every day 1730-2330 (2400 Friday and Saturday), Tel: 01621 782233. In addition, there are a couple of takeaways.

The sea wall at Burnham

A favourite establishment is the Cabin Dairy café and tearoom, next to R. J. Prior & Sons' yard, where Colin has built up a fine reputation for serving simple café-style food of the very best quality, including the famous 'Full Monty' all-day breakfast. Open daily. Tel: 01621 782404.

In Burnham Yacht Harbour is the Swallowtail Bar and Restaurant, which offers both snacks and a full restaurant and is open every day lunchtimes and evenings, all day at weekends. Tel: 01621 785505.

TO SEE AND DO

There is the small Cine Rio cinema in the High Street showing films daily, Tel: 01621 782027 and near CYC is the Burnham-on-Crouch and District Museum, open Sundays and Bank Holidays 1400-1700 and every day in the school summer holidays 1400-1700, Tel: 01621 783444.

There are pleasant short walks around town and along the sea wall which has been made a feature of the town. For those wanting a longer walk, the sea wall leads both ways out of town, either out onto the marshes, or upriver through Creeksea to Althorne and Fambridge six miles on, from either of which you can catch a train back if desired.

WALLASEA

Wallasea Island forms the south bank of the Crouch from Branklet Spit where the Roach branches off, to the last of the green channel markers past Baltic Wharf. Unfortunately a road to the island has blocked off navigation between Lion Creek off the Crouch and Paglesham Pool off the Roach, once a through-route often used by the old barge-men from the upper Crouch, via the Roach and Havengore, to the Thames Estuary.

Essex Marina was taken over by Essex Boatyards in 2005 and they are currently engaged in a major refurbishment project and therefore details may change and facilities be enhanced. During the summer, there is a foot ferry running between Essex Marina at Wallasea and Burnham. The 'Lady Essex III' travels roughly hourly throughout the day and can be booked for longer trips downriver to see the seals on Foulness Sands and upriver to Fambridge by arrangement. Details from the Harbour Master at Essex Marina.

MOORINGS

There are 500 deep water pontoon moorings and 50 swinging moorings at Essex Marina. There is usually room for visitors and enquiries should be made of the Harbour Master.

WALLASEA SKIPPERS INFORMATION	
Harbour Master	Geoff Gullen, VHF Ch80 call-sign "Essex Marina" or Tel: 01702 258531
Water	On pontoons
Electricity	On pontoons
Fuel	Fuel pontoon by slipway
Facilities	WC and showers
Boatyard	On-site offering a full range of services
Chandlery	On-site chandlery
Slips	Up to 100 tons and a huge 70 ton, 7.16m beam travel-hoist
Website	www.essexmarina.co.uk

WALLASEA SHORESIDE INFORMATION

Stores	None
Banks	None
PO	None
Public Tel.	At marina
Club	Essex Marina Yacht Club. Website: www.emyc.co.uk
Taxis	Andrew's Taxis, Tel: 01702 200200; Alan's Airport Taxis, Tel: 01702 541911 (both Rochford)
Accommodation	The Wardroom Hotel on-site and at the Creeksea Ferry Inn
Tourist Info.	None
Police	South Street, Rochford. Tel: 01268 775533
Doctor	Dr. B. Singh, 1 Village Green, Canewdon.Tel: 01702 258777
Hospital	(A&E) Southend Hospital, Prittlewell Chase. Tel: 01702 435555
Dentist	Smiles on Broadway, 152 The Broadway, Southend-on-Sea. Tel: 01702 588818
Pharmacy	Nutan Pharmacy, 456 Ashingdon Road, Rochford, Tel: 01702 548452

USEFUL NUMBERS

Boat Sales	Essex Boatyards. Tel: 01702 258885

CREW CHANGES AND TRAVEL

To transfer at Wallasea you would be best to take a taxi to Rochford four miles away, where you will find London Southend Airport and direct train services to London Liverpool Street (55 minutes). For train information contact 'One' Customer Services, Tel: 08456 007245 Website: www.onerailway.com, or National Rail Enquiries, Tel: 08457 484950 Website: www.nationalrail.co.uk

Creeksea

EATING AND DRINKING

There is a bar and restaurant at the Essex Marina Yacht Club open lunchtimes and evenings. The Creeksea Ferry Inn is on the sea wall of the island just upstream and serves real ales and good food, both in the bar and restaurant in very pleasant surroundings overlooking the river and is open lunchtimes and evenings every day. Tel: 01702 258722.

TO SEE AND DO

This is a rather remote area, but there are interesting walks both ways along the sea wall and with the Wallasea Wetlands Project, ornithologists should find the area increasingly interesting. A pleasant short country walk could be made to Paglesham by crossing the causeway and then following either the lanes or the Roach Valley Way path.

CREEKSEA TO FAMBRIDGE

As you pass Baltic Wharf to port, to starboard you will see the small community at Creeksea clustered around its green and this marks a change in scenery. After Creeksea it all becomes decidedly more rural and the river starts to wind in sweeping curves past farmland and marshes. The deep water generally follows the centre of the river and is wide enough to beat upriver against westerly winds. Althorne Creek leaves the river on the north bank at the top of Cliff Reach to pass behind Bridgemarsh Island. Towards HW it is possible to navigate in a shallow draft craft through Althorne Creek and Bridgemarsh Creeks to rejoin the Crouch about two miles upstream, but it is a very winding route and only recommended for the more adventurous and more practical in the dinghy. Leave the beacon to port and follow the line of buoys into the marina. The channel is quite shallow and drops to 0.5m at LAT in places, although most craft are fine from half-tide upwards.

Soon after you leave Bridgemarsh Island behind, you will start to see the growing number of moorings at Fambridge Yacht Station and the fairway moves over to the southern side of the river as it passes these. Half a mile upriver to starboard is Stow Creek, by which you can reach Fambridge Yacht Haven. The entrance is marked by a post to port and a line of small starboard hand buoys, and a pair of leading lights for night-time entry have recently been installed. The creek is dredged to maintain about one and a half metres at LAT, so deep draft craft still need to be wary at LWS.

ALTHORNE

There is a train station at Althorne, a five minute walk up the lane from the boatyard, although little else other than the marina and small holiday home park attached.

MOORINGS

In Althorne Creek, Bridgemarsh Marine has floating pontoon berths and there are several mudberths. The company may be able to find space for a visitor on request.

CREW CHANGES AND TRAVEL

Althorne is a surprisingly convenient place for transfers as there are regular train services from here to Wickford (20 minutes) hourly or better every day, from where you can connect to London

ALTHORNE SKIPPERS INFORMATION	
Harbour Master	'Biff' Bliss, Tel: 07968 696815
Water	On pontoons
Electricity	On pontoons
Fuel	Diesel available
Facilities	WC, shower and laundry block
Internet	None
Boatyard	Bridgemarsh Marine
Chandlery	None
Slips	Slipway and crane for 7/8 tons

 Not to be used for navigation

ALTHORNE SHORESIDE INFORMATION

Stores	None
Public Tel.	In marina
Club	Bridgemarsh Island Cruising Club. Tel: (Comm.) 01692 650484
Taxis	Triple 9 Taxis. Tel: 01621 772999
Accommodation	None
Tourist Info.	Nearest, Burnham-on-Crouch
Police	Queenborough Road, Southminster. Tel: 01621 773663
Essex Marine Police Unit	Tel: 01621 782121
Doctor	M. H. Latif & Ptnrs., Foundry Lane, Burnham, Tel: 01621 782054
Hospital	(A&E) Basildon Hospital, Nethermayne. Tel: 01268 533911
Dentist	Patel & Baker, 89a High Street, Burnham. Tel: 01621 782644
Pharmacy	Savages, 22 Station Road, Tel: 01621 785042; Alliance, 3 Foundry Lane Tel: 01621 782058 (both Burnham)

USEFUL NUMBERS

Boat Maintenance, Marine & Electrical Engineers Althorne Marine Services. Tel: 07939 100822

Liverpool Street in 35 minutes. For train information contact 'One' Customer Services, Tel: 08456 007245 Website: www.onerailway.com, or National Rail Enquiries, Tel: 08457 484950 Website: www.nationalrail.co.uk

EATING AND DRINKING

There is a small club bar on-site, but nowhere local for food.

FAMBRIDGE

The riverside villages of North and South Fambridge were once linked by a foot ferry, however these days the river separates the two. The yachting facilities are based on the northern bank, but you can land at the old ferry landing with care to take a look at the village of South Fambridge. Other than the extensive marine industry that has built up around

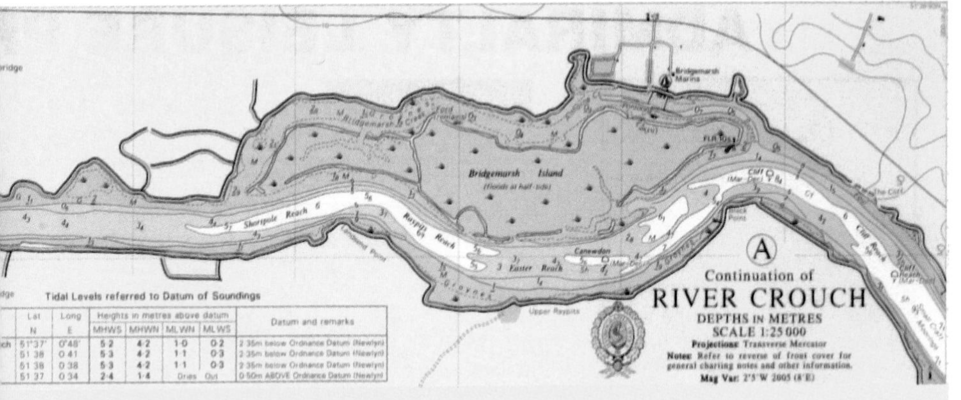

the yacht station and marina here, North Fambridge only has one pub and the railway station these days, since the village shop closed a few years back. Both the yacht station fronting the river, which has been here for over a century and the marina in Stow Creek (formerly West Wick marina), are now owned by Yacht Havens, which has spent the last few years and substantial sums of money upgrading the facilities. North Fambridge Yacht Club is housed in the old white Crimean War mobile hospital building perched on the sea wall. I understand these were designed by Brunel for his friend Florence Nightingale, but a few were built too late to be shipped out. Landing is at the deep water hammerhead pontoon, where if there is room you can moor overnight (for a fee). The yacht club operates a launch service on behalf of Yacht Havens at weekends (for a small charge to visitors). From the landing it is a short walk through the yard to the popular Ferry Boat Inn for fine ales, good food and pleasant company. Sadly, Roy Maltwood the landlord of the Ferry Boat for the last 25 years, who with his wife Silvia made this a favourite east coast destination, drowned in 2006 in a tragic accident whilst walking alongside the river he loved. His gentle demeanour will be missed.

MOORINGS

There are 180 swinging moorings at the yacht station, together with the 120 metres landing pontoon and 180 pontoon berths in the marina, all deep water. Check with the marina office, or club boatman when in attendance, for availability.

CREW CHANGES AND TRAVEL

The railway station is a good 10 minutes walk from either the yacht station or the marina, but Fambridge still makes a convenient place for transfers as there are regular train services from here to Wickford (20 minutes) hourly or better every day, from where you can connect to London Liverpool Street in 35 minutes. For train information contact 'One' Customer Services, Tel: 08456 007245 Website: www.onerailway.com, or National Rail Enquiries, Tel: 08457 484950 Website: www.nationalrail.co.uk

FAMBRIDGE SKIPPERS INFORMATION	
Harbour Master	VHF Ch80 call-sign "Fambridge Yacht Haven", Tel: 01621 740370
Water	On landing pontoon and marina pontoons
Electricity	On marina pontoons only
Fuel	Fuel berth at marina
Facilities	WC and showers at the north end of the yacht station yard. WC, showers & laundry at marina
Internet	Wireless broadband available in marina
Boatyard	Full boatyard facilities on-site
Chandlery	Some basic chandlery at the marina
Slips	Slip, 25 ton travel-hoist and mobile crane
Website	www.fambridgeyachthaven.com

EATING AND DRINKING

West Wick Yacht Club at the marina has a bar which is open Friday evenings, Saturday all day and Sunday to 1500, when food including breakfast and a Sunday roast is also served. The Ferry Boat Inn is just behind the yard at the yacht station and is also within easy walking distance of the marina. This 500-year-old riverside pub offers good beer and fine hospitality and serves food from an extensive menu both lunchtimes and evenings. As well as the cosy bar with its open fire and the low-beamed dining room, there is a pleasant beer garden and a large conservatory dining area for families. Tel: 01621 740208.

TO SEE AND DO

It is only 10 minutes stroll to the east to Blue House Farm, a 600-acre reserve run by the Essex Wildlife Trust. Listed as an

FAMBRIDGE SHORESIDE INFORMATION

Stores	Basic stores are available at the marina 0800-1700 every day
Banks	None
PO	None
Public Tel.	In village just up from The Ferry Boat Inn
Clubs	North Fambridge Yacht Club Tel: (Sec.) 01621 741633; West Wick Yacht Club Tel: (Sec.) 01702 528670
Taxis	CM3 Cars, South Woodham Ferrers, Tel: 01245 328818; 007 Taxis, Burnham, Tel: 01621 783007
Accommodation	Ferry Boat Inn (see Eating and Drinking)
Police	West Square, Maldon. Tel: 01621 852255
Doctor	Dr. M. H. Latif & Ptnrs., North Fambridge Village Hall, Tel: 01621 782054
Hospital	(A&E) Basildon Hospital, Nethermayne. Tel: 01268 533911
Dentist	Gould, Yap, Ahmed & Butkeviciene, 2 Heralds Way, South Woodham Ferrers. Tel: 01245 322277
Pharmacy	Goldlight Chemists, Brickfields Road, South Woodham Ferrers, Tel: 01245 325277

USEFUL NUMBERS

Boatbuilder	Anthony Harrington. Tel: 01621 868952
Boat Transport	Trevor Taylor Transport. Tel: 01702 258600
Electrics	Steve Kent. Tel: 07860 375186
Marine & Electrical Engineers	Marine Maintenance. Tel: 01621 860441
Marine Engineer	Henry Haslem. Tel: 07789 856775; Peter O'Donnell. Tel: 01621 786278
Rigger	D R S Rigging. Tel: 01621 784716
Yacht Brokers	Boatshed Essex. Tel: 01621 744842
Yacht Sales	East Coast Yacht Sales. Tel: 01621 743073

SSSI for its interesting birdlife, flora and insects, it is open April to October, Tel: 01621 740687. You can combine your visit with a short circular walk down the sea wall, cutting inland after a quarter of a mile to the farm, then afterwards returning by the westward path coming out by the pub – how fortuitous! There is also an interesting eastwards walk along the sea wall from here, which goes all the way to Burnham and beyond. Plus, see Hullbridge Section for a little further afield.

FAMBRIDGE TO BATTLESBRIDGE

After Fambridge and Stow Creek the river bends to port at Clementsgreen Creek, (now dammed and therefore of no interest to yachtsmen) and starts to shallow. Although it is possible to find holes with enough water to lie afloat for a little further upstream, once past this bend you need to be very aware of the state of tide. From here onwards the river rapidly shallows and becomes more tortuous, until at Hullbridge it dries to a mere trickle. If venturing past Brandy Hole, you would be well advised to do so on a rising tide, although the deeper water helpfully keeps to the middle of the river. As you leave Hullbridge behind, you will pass Fenn Creek to starboard, which leads up to Eyott Sailing Club. From here onwards the south bank becomes a string of private jetties and gardens as the river winds its way to Battlesbridge. The river makes a sharp turn to port, passing a caravan site and some moorings off it and then through meadows to the bridge. The Vikings are known to have made it this far on one of their incursions and it is still possible for shoal draft vessels to get as far as Battlesbridge on the high tide and straightforward by dinghy on the upper half of the tide.

HULLBRIDGE

Just around the bend after Fambridge are the moorings at Brandy Hole and the yacht club on the south bank, the last place where even shoal draft craft can lie afloat. A little further upriver on the south bank, as you start coming into Hullbridge, you will next see the small Hullbridge Yacht Club and further on still, the well appointed Upriver Yacht Club by The Anchor pub. There are a large number of drying moorings stretching each side of Hullbridge. The road from Hullbridge to Woodham Ferrers once forded the river just by The Anchor and on the north bank you will find clean landing upstream of the South Woodham Ferrers Yacht Club.

HULLBRIDGE SKIPPERS INFORMATION

BRANDY HOLE

Harbour Master	VHF Ch37 call-sign "Brandy Hole", Tel: 01702 230320
Water	On club pontoon
Fuel	At Yacht Station
Facilities	WC at club
Boatyard	Brandy Hole Yacht Station, Tel: 01702 230248
Slips	Contact the Yacht Station
Website	www.brandyhole.com

HULLBRIDGE

Harbour Master	Contact the clubs
Water	At the clubs
Facilities	WC and showers at HYC, UYC and SWFYC
Boatyard	None
Slips	For small craft at HYC and UYC and up to 4 tons at SWFYC
Scrubbing Posts	At HYC
Website	www.upriver.org

MOORINGS

At Brandy Hole, the buoys belong to Brandy Hole Yacht Station which can often accommodate a visitor. You can land at the pontoon by the club, where it is possible to come alongside on the tide. Beyond there, the moorings are let to the clubs of which there are a number, but it may be possible to arrange an overnight stay if you can take the mud. The Upriver Yacht Club maintains a designated visitors mooring off the club. It is advisable to ignore the rings for mooring to the quay by the Anchor because of a foul bottom and little water. It is generally better to go ashore here in the dinghy.

CREW CHANGES AND TRAVEL

The railway station at South Woodham Ferrers is on the other side of town and is 30 minutes walk from the river. There are regular train services from here to Wickford (15 minutes) hourly or better every day, from where you can connect to London Liverpool Street in 35 minutes. For train information contact 'One' Customer Services, Tel: 08456 007245 Website: www.onerailway.com, or National Rail Enquiries, Tel: 08457 484950 Website: www.nationalrail.co.uk. The town centre is also a hub for local bus services connecting to all the local area. For information contact Traveline East Anglia, Tel: 08706 082608 Website: www.traveline.org.uk

EATING AND DRINKING

Brandy Hole Yacht Club serves refreshments all day every day, except Mondays, during the summer. Winter opening hours, including food, are Tuesdays, Fridays and weekends. These include hot and cold bar snacks and full meals including a Sunday lunch, Tel: 01702 230320. Hullbridge Yacht Club also has a bar open at weekends, Tel: 01702 231797.

The moorings at Hullbridge

The Upriver Yacht Club bar is open for drinks and snacks on Friday evenings and Sunday lunchtimes, Tel: 01702 231654.

Although there is only one pub close to the river, there is a good choice of eating places. The Anchor Inn has a large beer garden by the river and is open all day every day and serves food 1200-2100 every day, Tel: 01702 230205. Just a few minutes up the road are the China City restaurant, Tel: 01702 230799 and K2 Tandoori, Tel: 01702 232355. Further up the road by the Co-op supermarket are a Chinese takeaway, a fish and chip shop and the Simla Tandoori restaurant, Tel: 01702 231523. On the north side there are a number of places to eat, but the Nawab Indian Restaurant has been recommended to me, Tel: 01245 321006.

TO SEE AND DO

Marsh Farm Country Park is just up the lane on the north side of the river and is a working farm open to the public and aimed at families. Open most of the year 1000-1600 (1700 in summer), a family ticket is £18, Tel: 01245 321552. There is a leisure centre with swimming pool at South Woodham Ferrers. Contact the

HULLBRIDGE SHORESIDE INFORMATION	
Stores	A couple of minutes up Ferry Road by The Anchor there is a parade of shops, including a convenience store open every day, butchers, greengrocers and two restaurants. A quarter of a mile further on there is also a small Co-op supermarket open every day 0700-2200. Landing on the north bank, South Woodham Ferrers town centre is about a mile away, with a good range of shops.
Banks	Cash machine at Co-op
PO	By the Co-op
Clubs	Brandy Hole Yacht Club, Tel: 01702 230320; Hullbridge Yacht Club, Tel: 01702 231797; Upriver Yacht Club, Tel: 01702 231654; South Woodham Ferrers Yacht Club, Tel: (Sec.) 01245 321349; Woodham Ferrers Waterski Club (which shares facilities with SWFYC), Tel: (Sec.) 01621 742354; Eyott Sailing Club Website: www.eyottsailingclub.org.uk
Taxis	Hockley Taxis (Hullbridge), Tel: 01702 531531; SW Radio Cars (South Woodham Ferrers), Tel: 01245 322503
Accommodation	Oakland Hotel. Tel: 01245 322811
Police	Tylers Ride, South Woodham Ferrers. Tel: 01245 491212
Doctor	Dr. Cornes & Ptnrs., Ferry Road, Hullbridge. Tel: 01702 230555
Hospital	(A&E) Southend Hospital, Prittlewell Chase. Tel: 01702 435555
Dentist	Gould, Yap, Ahmed & Butkeviciene, 2 Heralds Way, South Woodham Ferrers. Tel: 01245 322277
Pharmacy	Kanesh, 90 Ferry Road, Hullbridge. Tel: 01702 230303

centre for opening times, Tel: 01245 605600. The extensive RHS gardens at Hyde Hall are a five minute taxi ride away. Open every day from 1000 to dusk, admission £5, Tel: 01245 400256.

BATTLESBRIDGE

The area around the old granary and warehouses is largely given over to arts and crafts, the antiques centre housing about 80 dealers and a garden centre.

MOORINGS

At Battlesbridge, there is a quay at the granary, but mooring is not easy and it might be better if you ask to go alongside one of the barges that sometimes moor here. If intending to stay here I would suggest you seek the advice of locals.

CREW CHANGES AND TRAVEL

The railway station at Battlesbridge is five minutes up the lane. There are regular train services from here to Wickford (10 minutes) hourly or better every day, from where you can connect to London Liverpool Street in 35 minutes. For train information contact 'One' Customer Services, Tel: 08456 007245 Website: www.onerailway.com, or National Rail Enquiries, Tel: 08457 484950 Website: www.nationalrail.co.uk. There are also good local bus services connecting to all the local area. For information contact Traveline East Anglia, Tel: 08706 082608 Website: www.traveline.org.uk

EATING AND DRINKING

The 17th century Barge Inn, just behind the granary, retains the character of its years and appears to have remained unchanged over the centuries. Serving a range of real ales and food from an extensive and varied menu, it is open every day 1100-2300 (1200-2300 Sundays) food served 1200-2100. Tel: 01268 732622.

Just five minutes walk up the road is The Hawk Pub and Restaurant (actually more restaurant with bar, but still very pleasant and friendly). Again this is open all day every day, serving food all day, Tel: 01268 578021. There is also a coffee shop and a tearoom within the antiques complex.

TO SEE AND DO

Battlesbridge is home to one of the largest antique centres in Essex. Five period buildings house over 80 dealers, buying and selling antiques and collectables of all descriptions. Although the centre is open every day 1000-1730, opening times of individual shops/dealers varies, so calling prior would be advised. Tel: 01268 575000, or for 24-hour information, Tel: 0800 0741219. There is a small motorcycle museum at the antiques centre which tells the story of motorcycling through the ages with assorted memorabilia scattered between the classic and vintage motorcycles. Open most Sundays 1100-1600, Tel: 01268 575000.

BATTLESBRIDGE INFORMATION

Facilities	None
Public Tel.	At the granary
Taxis	Battlesbridge Cars. Tel: 01245 322333
Accommodation	Muggeridge Farm Guesthouse, Tel: 01268 561700; The Lodge Country Inn, Tel: 01245 320060
Police	Tylers Ride, South Woodham Ferrers. Tel: 01245 491212
Doctor	Shotgate Surgery, Southend Road, Wickford. Tel: 01268 561888
Hospital	(A&E) Southend Hospital, Prittlewell Chase. Tel: 01702 435555
Dentist	Gould, Yap, Ahmed & Butkeviciene, 2 Heralds Way, South Woodham Ferrers. Tel: 01245 322277
Pharmacy	Shotgate Pharmacy, Southend Road, Wickford. Tel: 01268 768547

FAMBRIDGE YACHT HAVEN

Widely regarded as the finest marina facility on the River Crouch, Fambridge Yacht Haven is nestled within our surrounding salt marsh's providing naturally sheltered swinging moorings, pontoon berths and extensive hard standing. Visitors are always welcome, whether staying over-night afloat or wintering ashore.

Undercover & Indoor Boat Storage Units

- New indoor boat storage facilities available for long or short term hire. These secure, well lit units are suitable for vessels up to 16m LOA and 5m beam. The units can be hired for painting, GRP repairs, welding, osmosis treatment and new builds.

- **Valet Berthing, with just a few hours notice we will collect your boat from its river mooring and place it alongside our new visitor pontoon, you can then just step aboard and go sailing. On return you leave your boat alongside the pontoon and we will return it to its river mooring.**
- **Secure 'Bosuns Lockers' available to rent for the storage of general boat maintenance equipment, outboards, sails etc**
- **Long term & project boat storage in secure compound at reduced rates**
- **Modern boat handling and lifting equipment**

- 120 deep-water swinging moorings
- 180 berth marina with 24 hours access
- Thames and Dutch barges welcome any time of year on fully serviceable mud berths
- Extensive hardstanding for long and short term storage, visitors welcome
- WISE 25 ton slipway hoist
- Mobile crane and pressure washing
- 24 hour CCTV
- 120 meter, deep water visitors' pontoon
- Valet berthing service, contact us for further information
- 2 x concrete slipways

Corporate Members

Fambridge Yacht Haven

Church Road, North Fambridge, Essex, CM3 6LR

Telephone 01621 740370

www.yachthavens.com

email: fambridge@yachthavens.com

The Havergate lifting bridge ©PRPA

THE RIVER ROACH

⊕ **51°37.'0N 00°52.'15E**
Branklet Spit buoy
Tides Paglesham *+0:30*
(differences from Harwich)

The River Roach extends seven miles south and then west past the old black shed of Shuttlewoods boatyard at Paglesham and on to the little town of Rochford, the upper reaches drying out at low water. Branching from the river are peaceful, drying creeks, offering a solitude that can hardly have changed for centuries, combined with the challenge of unmarked, twisting channels to be explored on a rising tide in shallow draft craft and dinghies. The odd coaster still travels to the small wharf at Stambridge Mill at Rochford on the tide and there is a small but active fishing fleet operating from the river and its creeks.

The area is very flat and can appear bleak on a murky day, but in sunshine, or on a warm summer evening, it can reveal a far more pleasing face. Much of the area to east and south of the river is MOD land and you should take care not to land in a forbidden area. There is an 8 knot speed limit on the Roach, reducing to 4 knots in Paglesham Reach and all the creeks.

APPROACH AND ENTRANCE

Although there is a second, rather interesting way for shoal draft craft to get into the River Roach and its connected creeks by the Havengore route (see The Roach Creeks), the main approach to the Roach is from the River Crouch. Shortly after you have entered the Crouch and a couple of miles downstream of Burnham, you will find a large round yellow buoy called Branklet on the southern side of the river, which marks the end of a spit reaching out from the western bank at the entrance to the Roach. This can be treated as the starboard hand mark into the river. Do not attempt to go between this buoy and the western shore as the spit is very shallow in places. At the same time do not close the eastern side of the entrance and try to cut the corner into the river, as mud extends quite a way towards the centre of the river. Once a couple of cables into the river however, deep water can be found in the centre with only gradual shelving towards each bank.

ENTRANCE TO ROCHFORD

Initially the river is fairly wide and deep and it is possible for even deep draft vessels to lie afloat at all states of tide as far as Paglesham and a little beyond. To starboard, shortly after the entrance, is a useful anchorage off the groynes where you will often find a few boats on a summer day awaiting a tide. After about half a mile in Quay Reach you will see a few boats moored and pulled up on the foreshore to port, with a stone quay protruding into the river with steps up the sea wall. Although Foulness Island is MOD land you are permitted to land at these steps and there is a public footpath across the island to the village in the centre where you will find the island's pub called the George & Dragon. This is quite a lengthy walk of about 40 minutes, but if you are up to anchoring and the row ashore, it makes for an interesting diversion through rural surroundings along a largely concrete track. Do not stray from the path and note that no dogs or cameras are allowed ashore. The pub only opens Wednesday to Sunday, with the bar open 1100-1430 and 1800-2300 (Sunday all day 1200-2230) and serving food 1200-1400 (Sunday 1200-1700). Tel: 01702 219460/219455.

A further half mile upstream the first bend sweeps to starboard (take care of the mud that extends from the shore on the inside of the bend) and the river then runs parallel with the Crouch. At high water, sails on the Crouch can be clearly seen across the flat landscape of Wallasea Island, now largely a nature reserve. You are now in Devil's Reach which always seems to trigger the imagination of any young pirates aboard, but the only things of note for the navigator are that initially best water is to port of centre, moving to starboard of centre as you pass the entrance to Yokesfleet Creek to port. There are oyster crates to either side in this reach marked by small orange buoys and withies, so take care not to ground on them. Anchoring is not permitted anywhere in the fairway of the Roach due to commercial traffic, or at any point within Paglesham Reach due to the moorings. If you do anchor in the Roach, always do so out of the fairway and display a riding light.

As you start to turn the next bend to port and just short of the lateral buoys, you will see the entrance to Paglesham Pool to starboard. This creek is also known by some locals as Paglesham Creek and connects with Lion Creek off the Crouch to create Wallasea Island, although this is now obstructed for navigation by a causeway onto the island. There is a pleasant anchorage for shoal draft craft just inside Paglesham Pool, but take care of the spit that extends from the port hand side of the entrance. Some will go further up to take the ground and there is fairly good dry landing kindly created by the Crouch Harbour Authority just past the pillbox to port, providing access to the sea wall for those wishing to walk into East End or Church End.

Ahead will be seen the large black shed and the pontoon at the boatyard. The best water is to be found between the rows of moorings and the channel is buoyed for this stretch to indicate the route through.

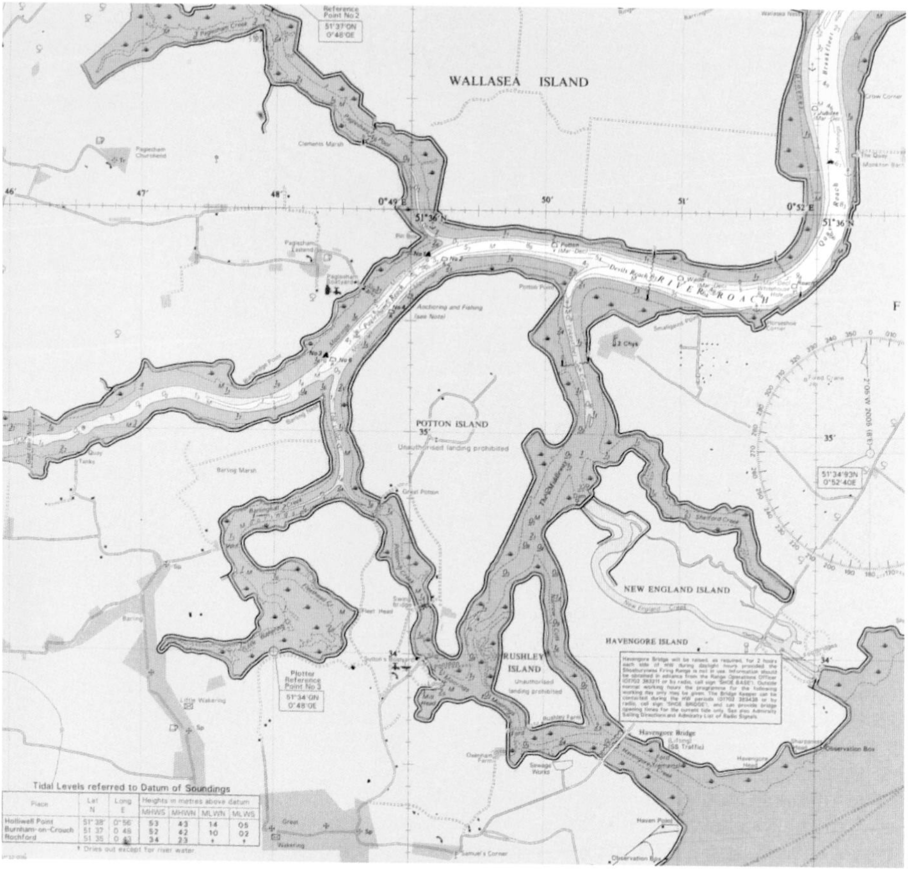

THE RIVER ROACH

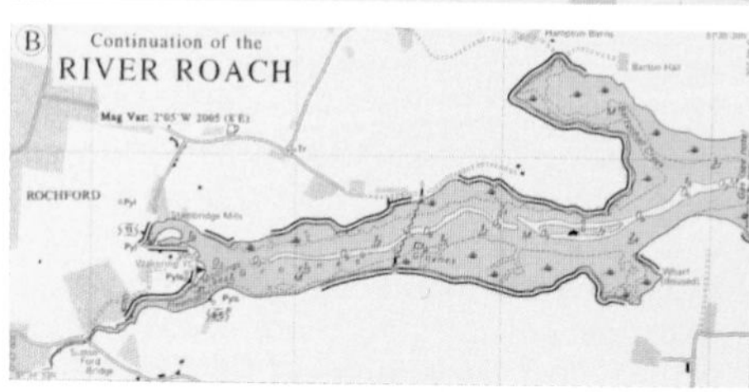

Not to be used for navigation

On a clear day, the blocks of flats at Southend will be seen in the distance from here. As you pass the last of the moorings you will pass the entrance to Potton Creek to port and the Roach then bends slowly to starboard. It is another four miles to Rochford and although coasters take the tide up to Stambridge Mill, there is nowhere really suitable for the cruising yachtsman to land, but on the tide deep water will be found well past Bartonhall Creek and it makes an interesting diversion. At the head of the creek there is a small wharf to starboard at Stamford Mills and the channel is buoyed, but yachtsmen are not welcome. Improbably, down the port hand fork here, you will find a boatyard and the Wakering Yacht Club.

PAGLESHAM REACH

Paglesham in recent years has not been as pleasant a port of call as in the past, as the main drive for the boatyard had become the sale of powerboats and the mooring and boatyard side of the business had fallen into neglect. The success of Essex Boatyards' business became increasingly incompatible with the location and latterly even created some friction with locals, with disputes over rights of way. It is therefore all the more pleasing to note that when Essex Boatyards took over Essex Marina at Wallasea and moved its operations there in 2007, they sought out appropriate people to move into Paglesham to hopefully return it to its former glory.

The new operator at Paglesham (proudly to be known again as Shuttlewoods Boatyard) is Steve Adams. Steve is a local boatbuilder, yachtsman and Roach Sailing Association member, who previously operated out of Essex Marina on the Crouch. He is sharing the facilities with long-term associates JS Mouldings, builders of the Mitchell range of sea-anglers, those famed proper boats from the board of Alan Hill. There is also a resident engineer on-site at the boatyard and full repair and rigging facilities are offered. There is a public slip in front of the old shed and the boatyard can slip up to 40 feet and 12 to 15 tons. It also has a small 7 ton travel-hoist and when they have finished clearing the wharf, you will again be able to lay alongside for repairs, where a small crane will be sited. It will all take time, but Steve is in the process of returning the yard to its more familiar form and I look forward to future visits to one of my favourite places and watching the progress.

PAGLESHAM REACH SKIPPERS INFORMATION

Harbour Master	All the Roach comes under the jurisdiction of the Crouch Harbour Authority (see River Crouch chapter)
Water	At boatyard
Electricity	On pontoon
Fuel	None
Facilities	Basic WC at boatyard
Boatyard	Shuttlewoods. Tel: 07791 549866
Moorings	Contact boatyard
Chandlery	None
Slips	Public slip, plus up to 40 feet/15 tons and 7 ton hoist, contact the boatyard
Scrubbing Posts	There are plans to possibly put some in. Contact the boatyard

PAGLESHAM REACH SHORESIDE INFORMATION

Stores	None
Banks	None
PO	None
Public Tel.	One by each of the public houses
Club	Roach Sailing Association is an informal association without a clubhouse. Tel: (Sec.) 07836 344508
Taxis	Andrews Taxis, Rochford, Tel: 01702 200200; Alan's Airport Taxis, Rochford, Tel: 01702 541911
Police	South Street, Rochford. Tel: 01268 775533
Doctor	Dr. Singh, 1 Village Green, Canewdon. Tel: 01702 258777
Hospital	(A&E) Southend Hospital, Prittlewell Chase, Westcliff-on-Sea, Tel: 01702 435555
Dentist	Mr. Patel, 25 Station Road, Southend-on-Sea. Tel: 01702 584535
Pharmacy	Great Wakering Pharmacy, 62 High St., Great Wakering, Tel: 01702 219550

USEFUL NUMBERS

GRP Mouldings	JS Mouldings Ltd. Tel: 01702 258267

MOORINGS
The boatyard is laying new moorings and often has some available for visitors on request. Failing this, Roach Sailing Association maintains some in the reach, as does Nigel Bishop. Landing can be made at the slip in front of the shed or on the pontoon at the yard, which is accessible at most states of tide by dinghy, where you are now welcome again, but they ask you not to go alongside here in your yacht without permission. Please remember to pay the boatyard for your mooring; it will all help fund the improvements for all our benefit.

CREW CHANGES AND TRAVEL
Paglesham is not the best place for transfers as it only has an irregular bus service.

EATING AND DRINKING
Paglesham is really two villages, Paglesham East End near the waterside (the footpath goes through the yard and up a lane a quarter of a mile) and Paglesham Church End, a mile and a half further on. Up a lane by the boatyard at East End is the Plough and Sail, famed amongst east coast sailors for the welcome and excellent food provided for many years by the Oliver family. The bar and restaurant are open every day at lunchtimes and evenings, although you may be well advised to book a table at weekends as it is very popular, Tel: 01702 258242. The Punch Bowl at Church End can be reached either by lanes and paths from East End, or via the sea wall along from Paglesham Pool and then cutting inland well short of the head of the creek. The Punch Bowl is also open lunchtimes and evenings for the bar and food and has a particular reputation for its range of beers, Tel: 01702 258376.

TO SEE AND DO
The sea wall footpath provides many miles of walking and access to a variety of connecting paths if you prefer to explore on foot. Although very close to major towns, this area is quite remote and offers a glimpse of interesting flora and fauna, I suspect due to the degree of isolation created by the MOD presence. There are often some unusual birds to be seen and I have been visited by seals well up the river.

ROCHFORD
At Rochford you will find the yard of Carter & Ward where there are mud berths, Tel: 01268 733421 and the small Wakering Yacht Club, largely devoted to motor cruising. If you choose to bring up here you will find yourself still quite a long way from the town.

THE ROACH CREEKS
The Roach Creeks offer a navigational challenge and chance to get well away from civilisation, but their exploration should not be undertaken lightly by the newcomer. Some of them carry little water, so timing is very important, but some pilot books do give quite detailed notes on those worth exploring. With all the Roach Creeks, the only way to explore safely is to be equipped with a draft of less than 2 metres, ideally the ability to take the ground comfortably, charts, pilotage books, sounding equipment, a rising tide and plenty of nerve! Some would say the creeks are only suitable for dinghy exploring and this may be a better idea the first time round. Except at the Quay in the outer Roach, all of Foulness is prohibited landing, as are Potton and Rushley islands.

Before you reach Paglesham, Yokesfleet Creek branches off to the south in Devil's Reach. Mud extends from both sides and a spit extends from the western point, but the deeper water then runs close to this starboard hand point, before moving to mid-stream. Just inside Yokesfleet is a popular remote anchorage often referred to as 'The Hole', where shoal draft craft can lie afloat, but be sure to anchor well clear of the marked power cable. Further on you will pass to port two little creeks, Shelford Creek and the dammed New England Creek, neither offering any particular interest to the yachtsman.

Little Wakering

The next branch to port however is Narrow Cuts, which is the main route to the Havengore lifting bridge which offers a route for craft drawing less than 1.5 metres to the Thames Estuary. However, careful timing for tides is necessary and never attempt the route in unsettled weather or with any significant strength of wind from the southern quadrant. Havengore Bridge can be opened one to two hours each side of HW during daylight, providing no firing is taking place on the MoD ranges, which, luckily for yachtsmen, rarely takes place at weekends. Charts and pilot books deal with the Havengore route extensively, but for first-hand, up-to-the-minute information about firing times and bridge operation, call up the range keeper on VHF Ch16 or 72 call-sign "Shoe Base" or Tel: 01702 383211. The Bridge Keeper can also be contacted on VHF Ch16 or 72, call-sign "Shoe Bridge", Tel: 01702 383436 around HW. Buoys and beacons mark the best route out of the creek over the Broomway, a large man-made tidal causeway that at one time connected Foulness and Great Wakering. If you keep to starboard at Rushley Island instead of turning down Narrow Cuts, this leads into a winding shallow route to Potton Creek and the moorings and mudberths at Suttons Boatyard at Great Wakering, opposite the southern tip of Potten Island. The boatyard is happy to find somewhere for a visitor, but remember, there will be no water here for several hours each side of LW. As well as swinging moorings, there are pontoon berths at the yard (once famous for it's own design of east coast boats), together with a slip, cranes and hardstanding, Tel: 01702 219422. The town of Great Wakering, which is a small seaside town, is the nearest point for shops, pubs and restaurants, but this is about a mile and half's walk from the boatyard.

Back in the Roach and continuing just past the moorings at Paglesham, you will see the entrance to Potton Creek to port. Take care of the long shallow spit that extends from the starboard side of the entrance when entering. The first reach is known as The Violet and there are a few small boat moorings here. After about half a mile the creek branches, the port hand branch continuing as Potton Creek through the Potton swing bridge to join up with Yokesfleet Creek at Suttons Boatyard. The swing bridge is manned day and night, for a couple of hours around HW and you should sound three blasts on your horn for the bridge to open. In 2006 there were periods when the bridge was closed, but these closures were well publicised in the regular coastguard broadcasts. There is a ford with very little water to negotiate at the southern end of the creek, which makes this route more difficult.

Back at the fork after The Violet, the starboard hand fork branches off south westwards into Barlinghall Creek. This soon becomes very narrow, shallow and drying, but with plenty of room to drop the hook and dry out. There is dry landing a couple of hours either side of HW at a small hard on the upstream side of the quay on the starboard hand (made from a beached concrete lighter), from where you can either walk down a lane into Barling Magna and then into Little Wakering or follow the sea wall path into Little Wakering, which combined makes for a pleasant circular walk. You could also take a dinghy to the head of the creek on the tide, where there is a small quay and surprisingly a couple of shoal draft cruisers moored.

There is a phone box at Barling Magna, but nothing else of interest. Little Wakering is about a mile away from the quay, but has a general store open every day 0600-1800 (1200 Sundays) and The Castle Inn, a modern lively pub often with live music, open 1200-2300 (0130 Fridays and Saturdays, 2230 Sundays). It has only "fizzy-pop" beers, but does intend to start serving food in 2007 and is friendly, Tel: 01702 219295.

Little Wakering is on the bus route between Southend and Shoeburyness (from where in both cases you can connect to rail services to London) and has half a dozen services a day (none on Sundays). For bus information contact Traveline East Anglia, Tel: 08706 082608 Website: www.traveline.org.uk and for train information contact 'One' Customer Services, Tel: 08456 007245 Website: www.onerailway.com or National Rail Enquiries Tel: 08457 484950 Website: www.nationalrail.co.uk. For taxis, Wakering Taxis, Tel: 01702 218900. For a wider choice of shops, pubs and restaurants, Great Wakering is a further three quarters of a mile on.

Boat & Yacht Sales

Clarke & Carter Interyacht Ltd.
CROUCH
Burnham Yacht Harbour
Burnham-on-Crouch
Essex CM0 8BL
T: 01621 785600
F: 01621 785560
burnham@clarkeandcarter.co.uk
www.clarkeandcarter.co.uk

Clarke & Carter Interyacht Ltd.
ORWELL
Suffolk Yacht Harbour
Levington, Ipswich
Suffolk IP10 0LN
T: 01473 659681
F: 01473 659758
levington@clarkeandcarter.co.uk
www.clarkeandcarter.co.uk

East Coast Yacht Sales
CROUCH
Fambridge Yacht Haven
Church Road
North Fambridge
Essex CM3 6LR
T: 01621 743073
sales@ec-yachts.co.uk
www.ec-yachts.co.uk

Essex Boatyards Ltd.
CROUCH
Essex Marina
Wallasea Island
Essex SS4 2HF
T: 01702 258885
F: 01702 258441
heather@essexboatyards.com
www.essexboatyards.com

Global Trade Partners
COLNE
165-167 Tower Street
Brightlingsea
Colchester
Essex CO7 0AW
T: 01206 305500
M: 07767 666042
alan.bate@globaltradepartners.co.uk
www.globaltradepartners.co.uk

Andy Seedhouse Boat Sales
DEBEN
T: 01394 387833

Boatshed Essex
CROUCH
T: 01621 744842

Essex Boatyards
CROUCH
T: 01702 258885

Fox's Yacht Sales
LOWESTOFT
T: 01473 695010

M. J. Lewis & Sons
BLACKWATER
T: 01621 840982

Peters plc
ORWELL
T: 01473 225710

Temple Marine
DEBEN
T: 01394 383108

Woodrolfe Brokerage
BLACKWATER
T: 01621 868494

Boat Delivery

Small Craft Deliveries Ltd.
DEBEN
Navigation House
Wilford Bridge Road
Melton
Woodbridge
Suffolk IP12 1RJ
T: 01394 382600
F: 01394 387672
sales@scd-charts.co.uk
www.scd-charts.co.uk

Boat Transport

Burni Transport Ltd.
CROUCH
8 Burnham Business Park
Springfield Road
Burnham-on-Crouch
Essex CM0 8TE
T: 01621 785255
M: 07836 665802

Trevor Taylor Marine
CROUCH
Gore Bungalow
Apton Hall Road
Canewdon, Rochford
Essex SS4 3RF
T: 01702 258600
F: 01702 258600
taylormarine@btopenworld.com
www.trevortaylormarine.co.uk

C-Way Boat Transportation
BLACKWATER
T: 01206 381765

P. J. Downs & Sons
BLACKWATER
T: 01621 854388

Boatbuilders

Jamie Clay Wooden Boatbuilding
BLACKWATER
6 Victoria Road
Maldon
Essex CM9 5HF
T: 01621 853804
jclayboatbuilder@aol.com

Michael P. G. Button
Boatbuilding, Repair & Maintenance
ORE & ALDE
M: 07729 107196

Robertson's of Woodbridge (Boatbuilders) Ltd.
DEBEN
Lime Kiln Quay
Woodbridge
Suffolk IP12 1BD
T: 01394 382305
F: 01394 388788
mike@robertsons-boatyard.co.uk
www.robertsons-boatyard.co.uk

Adrian Wombwell
BLACKWATER
T: 01621 869784

Anthony Harrington
CROUCH
T: 01621 868952

Beaves Marine
BLACKWATER
T: 01621 869270

Brooke Marine Yachts
LOWESTOFT
T: 01502 561479

G. Brown & Son
SOUTHWOLD
T: 01502 725050

Harwich Boatcraft
HARWICH
T: 01255 551396

Jim Maynard
BLACKWATER
T: 01621 855866

Medusa Marine
ORWELL
T: 01473 780090

Nigel Waller
ORWELL
M: 07899 903982

Nottage Institute
COLNE
T: 01206 824142

Petticrow Ltd.
CROUCH
T: 01621 782115

Spirit Yachts
ORWELL
T: 01473 214715

St. Osyth Boatbuilders
COLNE
T: 01255 820447

Boatyards

CRS Marine Ltd.
BLACKWATER
The Boatyard
Basin Road
Heybridge Basin
Maldon
Essex CM9 4RS
T: 01621 854684
M: 07850 543873

Fambridge Yacht Haven Ltd.
CROUCH
Church Road
North Fambridge
Essex CM3 6LR
T: 01621 740370
F: 01621 742359
danyal@fambridgeyachthaven.com
www.yachthavens.com

Maldon Boatyard
BLACKWATER
Marinestore
'Shipways'
North Street
Maldon
Essex CM9 5HQ
T: 01621 854280
F: 01621 843849
linda.lee@marinestore.co.uk
www.marinestore.co.uk

Peter Clarke's Boatyard Ltd.
BLACKWATER
128 Coast Road
West Mersea
Essex CO5 8PA
T: 01206 385905

Robertson's of Woodbridge (Boatbuilders) Ltd.
DEBEN
Lime Kiln Quay
Woodbridge
Suffolk IP12 1BD
T: 01394 382305
F: 01394 388788
mike@robertsons-boatyard.co.uk
www.robertsons-boatyard.co.uk

Suttons Boatyard
ROACH
Common Road
Great Wakering
Southend
Essex SS3 0DA
T: 01702 219422
suttonandsmith@hotmail.co.uk
www.suttonsboatyard.co.uk

Titchmarsh Marina
WALTON BACKWATERS
Coles Lane
Walton-on-the-Naze
Essex CO14 8SL
T: 01255 672185
F: 01255 851901
info@titchmarshmarina.com
www.titchmarshmarina.com

Tollesbury Saltings Ltd.
BLACKWATER
The Sail Lofts
Woodrolfe Road
Tollesbury
Maldon
Essex CM9 8SE
T: 01621 868624
M: 07889 869557
sales@tolsalt.co.uk

Aldeburgh Boatyard
ORE & ALDE
T: 01728 452019

Bedwell & Co.
WALTON BACKWATERS
T: 01255 675873

Blackwater Marina
BLACKWATER
T: 01621 740264

Brandy Hole Yacht Station
CROUCH
T: 01702 230248

Brightlingsea Boat Park & Ride
COLNE
T: 01206 304747

Bure Marine Ltd.
GREAT YARMOUTH
T: 01493 656996

Carter and Ward
ROACH
T: 01268 733421

Charter Marine
DEBEN
T: 01394 610993

D M & P Cable
ORE & ALDE
T: 01728 452569

David Patient
BLACKWATER
M: 07801 130530

Downs Road Boatyard
BLACKWATER
T: 01621 853330

Everson's
DEBEN
T: 01394 385786

F. A. Webb
ORWELL
T: 01473 780291

Felixstowe Ferry Boat Yard
DEBEN
T: 01394 282173

Frank Halls & Son
WALTON BACKWATERS
T: 01255 675596

Goodchild Marine Services
GREAT YARMOUTH
T: 01493 782301

Harbour Marine Services
SOUTHWOLD
T: 01502 724721

Harry King & Sons Ltd.
ORWELL
T: 01473 780258

Justin Ladd
SOUTHWOLD
M: 07899 913642

Melton Boatyard
DEBEN
T: 01394 386327

Mike Clark
DEBEN
T: 01394 387838

Morgan Marine
COLNE
T: 01206 302003

Orford Marine Services
ORE & ALDE
T: 01394 450169

Pegasus Yachts
LOWESTOFT
T: 01502 585631

Peters plc
ORWELL
T: 01473 232649

R. F. Upson and Co.
ORE & ALDE
T: 01728 453047

R. Larkman Ltd.
DEBEN
T: 01394 382943

R. J. Prior & Sons
CROUCH
T: 01621 782160

Rice & Cole
CROUCH
T: 01621 782063

Shotley Marine Services
HARWICH
T: 01473 788982

Shuttlewoods Boatyard
ROACH
M: 07791 549866

Stebbens Boatyard
BLACKWATER
T: 01621 857436

St. Osyth Boatyard
COLNE
T: 01255 820005

Suffolk Yacht Harbour
ORWELL
T: 01473 659465

Waldringfield Boatyard
DEBEN
T: 01473 736260

West Mersea Marine Ltd.
BLACKWATER
T: 01206 382244

Woodrolfe Boatyard
BLACKWATER
T: 01621 869202

Brokerage

Global Trade Partners
COLNE
165-167 Tower Street

Brightlingsea
Colchester
Essex CO7 0AW
T: 01206 305500
M: 07767 666042
alan.bate@globaltradepartners.co.uk
www.globaltradepartners.co.uk

Blue Baker
ORWELL
T: 01473 780111

Clarke & Carter Interyacht
ORWELL
T: 01473 659681

Clarke & Carter Interyacht
CROUCH
T: 01621 785600

Fox's Yacht Sales
HARWICH
T: 01473 788772

Morgan Marine
COLNE
T: 01206 302003

Peters plc
ORWELL
T: 01473 225710

Westwater Yacht Sales
WALTON BACKWATERS
T: 01255 672500

Woodrolfe Brokerage
BLACKWATER
T: 01621 868494

Chandlers

Peter Clarke's Boatyard Ltd.
BLACKWATER
128 Coast Road
West Mersea
Essex CO5 8PA
T: 01206 385905

Marinestore
BLACKWATER
'Shipways'
North Street
Maldon
Essex CM9 5HQ
T: 01621 854280
F: 01621 843849
omi.sjollima@marinestore.co.uk
www.marinestore.co.uk

Marinestore
BLACKWATER
128 Coast Road
West Mersea
Essex CO5 8PA
T: 01621 874493
ken.miles@marinestore.co.uk
www.marinestore.co.uk

Marinestore
WALTON BACKWATERS
Coles lane
Walton-on-the-Naze
Essex CO14 8SL
T: 01621 874495
F: 01255 677775
trevor.birtchnell@marinestore.co.uk
www.marinestore.co.uk

Marinestore
CROUCH
Burnham Yacht Harbour
Burnham-on-Crouch
Essex CM0 8BL
T: 01621 874494
barney.falk@marinestore.co.uk
www.marinestore.co.uk

Seamark Nunn
DEBEN
400 High Street
Trimley St Martin
Felixstowe
Suffolk IP11 0SG
T: 01394 451000
F: 01394 451006
sales@seamarknunn.com
www.seamarknunn.com

Boat Gear Direct
ORWELL
M: 07900 988355

Fairways
CROUCH
T: 01621 782659

Fox's Marina
ORWELL
T: 01473 688431

Harwich Chandlers Ltd.
HARWICH
T: 01255 504061

Mailspeed
CROUCH
T: 01621 781120

Marinestore Wyatts
BLACKWATER
T: 01206 384745

Morgan Marine
COLNE
T: 01206 302003

One Stop Chandlery
BLACKWATER
T: 01621 853558

Peters plc
ORWELL
T: 01473 232649

Woolverstone Chandlery
ORWELL
T: 01473 780206

Charter & Hire

Blue Baker
ORWELL
T: 01473 780111

Mistral Yachts
CROUCH
T: 01621 743853

Thames Sailing Barge Trust
BLACKWATER
T: 01621 893674

Topsail Charters
BLACKWATER
T: 01621 857567

West Quay Sailing
COLNE
M: 07789 936439

Charts & Books

Small Craft Deliveries Ltd.
DEBEN
Navigation House
Wilford Bridge Road
Melton
Woodbridge
Suffolk IP12 1RJ
T: 01394 382600
F: 01394 387672
sales@scd-charts.co.uk
www.scd-charts.co.uk

Clothing

Stitch-Print
CROUCH
T: 01621 773900

Clubs & Associations

Royal Corinthian Yacht Club
CROUCH
The Quay
Burnham-on-Crouch
Essex CM0 8AX
T: 01621 782105
F: 01621 784965
info@royalcorinthian.co.uk
www.royalcorinthian.co.uk

The Yacht Harbour Association
SMEETH
T: 01303 814434
www.yachtharbourassociation.com

Aldeburgh Yacht Club
ORE & ALDE
T: 01728 254562

Blackwater Sailing Club
BLACKWATER
T: 01621 853923

Bradwell Cruising Club
BLACKWATER
T: 01621 892970

Bradwell Quay Yacht Club
BLACKWATER
T: 01621 890173

Brandy Hole Yacht Club
CROUCH
T: 01702 230320

Bridgemarsh Island Cruising Club
CROUCH
T: 01621 650484

Brightlingsea Sailing Club
COLNE
T: 01206 303275

Brightlingsea Waterski Club
COLNE
M: 07770 840029

Burnham Sailing Club
CROUCH
T: 01621 782875

Colne Smack Preservation Society
COLNE
T: 01206 304204

Colne Yacht Club
COLNE
T: 01206 302594

Crouch Yacht Club
CROUCH
T: 01621 782252

Dabchicks Sailing Club
BLACKWATER
T: 01206 386954

Deben Yacht Club
DEBEN
T: 01394 384440

Felixstoweferry Sailing Club
DEBEN
T: 01394 272466

Goldhanger Sailing Club
BLACKWATER
T: 01621 788438

Harlow (Blackwater) Sailing Club
BLACKWATER
T: 01621 740300

Harwich & Dovercourt Sailing Club
HARWICH
T: 01255 508041

Harwich Town Sailing Club
HARWICH
T: 01255 503200

Haven Ports Yacht Club
ORWELL
T: 01473 659658

Hullbridge Yacht Club
CROUCH
T: 01702 231797

Lowestoft Cruising Club
LOWESTOFT
T: 01502 574376

Maldon Little Ship Club
BLACKWATER
T: 01621 854139

Marconi Sailing Club
BLACKWATER
T: 01621 772164

Maylandsea Bay Sailing Club
BLACKWATER
T: 01621 740470

Millbeach Marine Club
BLACKWATER
T: 01621 828909

North Fambridge Yacht Club
CROUCH
T: 01621 741633

North London Sailing Association
COLNE
T: 01279 503108

Orford Sailing Club
ORE & ALDE
T: 01394 450090

Orwell Yacht Club
ORWELL
T: 01473 602288

Pin Mill Sailing Club
ORWELL
T: 01473 780271

Roach Sailing Association
ROACH
M: 07836 344508

Royal Burnham Yacht Club
CROUCH
T: 01621 782044

Royal Harwich Yacht Club
ORWELL
M: 07742 145994

Royal Norfolk & Suffolk Yacht Club
LOWESTOFT
T: 01502 566726

Saltcote Sailing Club
BLACKWATER
T: 01621 840769

Shotley Sailing Club
HARWICH
T: 01473 787500

Slaughden Sailing Club
ORE & ALDE
T: 01508 570142

South Woodham Ferrers Yacht Club
CROUCH
T: 01245 321349

Stone Sailing Club
BLACKWATER
T: 01621 779344

Stone Watersports Club
BLACKWATER
T: 01621 772280

Stour Sailing Club
STOUR
T: 01206 393924

Tollesbury Cruising Club
BLACKWATER
T: 01621 869561

Tollesbury Sailing Club
BLACKWATER
M: 07788 480542

Upriver Yacht Club
CROUCH
T: 01702 231654

Waldringfield Sailing Club
DEBEN
T: 01473 736633

West Mersea Yacht Club
BLACKWATER
T: 01206 382947

West Wick Yacht Club
CROUCH
T: 01702 528670

Wivenhoe Sailing Club
COLNE
T: 01206 822132

Woodbridge Cruising Club
DEBEN
T: 01394 386737

Woodham Ferrers Waterski Club
CROUCH
T: 01621 742354

Deck Fittings

Fox's Rigging
ORWELL
Fox's Marina
Ipswich
Suffolk IP2 8SA
T: 01473 695128
F: 01473 695122
richard.odell@foxsmarina.com
www.foxsmarina.com

Classic Marine
DEBEN
T: 01394 380390

Heron Yacht Services
COLNE
T: 01206 303695

ProBoat Marine
CROUCH
T: 01621 785455

Sta-Lok Terminals Ltd.
STOUR
T: 01206 391509

Wilks Rubber Plastics
BLACKWATER
T: 01621 869609

Electronics

Fox's Electronics
ORWELL
Fox's Marina
Ipswich
Suffolk IP2 8SA
T: 01473 689111
F: 01473 601737
george.mccormick@foxsmarina.com
www.foxsmarina.com

Charity & Taylor
LOWESTOFT
T: 01502 581529

Hurst Marine Services
WALTON BACKWATERS
T: 01255 673171

KM Electronics
LOWESTOFT
T: 01502 569079

Mantsbrite
BLACKWATER
T: 01621 853003

North Sea Marine Electrical
LOWESTOFT
T: 01502 562010

P and S Automation
BLACKWATER
T: 01621 841328

Peters plc
ORWELL
T: 01473 232649

PRS Communications
HARWICH
T: 01255 240523

R&J Marine Electronics Ltd.
ORWELL
T: 01473 659737

Servowatch
BLACKWATER
T: 01621 862145

Solar Energy Alliance
LOWESTOFT
T: 01502 515532

Steve Kent
CROUCH
M: 07860 375186

Flags & Banners

Flags and Banners Ltd.
CROUCH
T: 01621 783221

GRP Moulding & Repairs

Gel n Shine
BLACKWATER
T: 01621 857700

JS Mouldings Ltd.
ROACH
T: 01702 258267

Smooth Finish
WALTON BACKWATERS
T: 01206 251080

Harbour Authorities

Maldon River Bailiff
BLACKWATER
M: 07818 013723

Hull Blasting, Treatment & Repairs

Mick Oliver
COLNE
T: 01255 423960

Insurance

Clarke & Carter Interyacht Ltd.
CROUCH
Burnham Yacht Harbour
Burnham-on-Crouch
Essex CM0 8BL
T: 01621 785600
F: 01621 785560
burnham@clarkeandcarter.co.uk
www.clarkeandcarter.co.uk

Clarke & Carter Interyacht Ltd.
ORWELL
Suffolk Yacht Harbour
Levington, Ipswich
Suffolk IP10 0LN
T: 01473 659681
F: 01473 659758
levington@clarkeandcarter.co.uk
www.clarkeandcarter.co.uk

Nautical Insurance Services Ltd.
CROUCH
57 Elm Road
Leigh-on-Sea
Essex SS9 1SP
T: 01702 470811
F: 01702 470844
enquiries@nautical-insurance.co.uk
www.nautical-insurance.co.uk

Liferafts

Premium Liferaft Services
CROUCH
T: 01621 784858

Marinas

Burnham Yacht Harbour Marina Ltd.
CROUCH
Foundry Lane
Burnham-on-Crouch
Essex CM0 8BL
T: 01621 782150
F: 01621 785848
admin@burnhamyachtharbour.co.uk
www.burnhamyachtharbour.co.uk

Fambridge Yacht Haven Ltd.
CROUCH
Church Road
North Fambridge
Essex CM3 6LR
T: 01621 740370
F: 01621 742359
danyal@fambridgeyachthaven.com
www.yachthavens.com

Fox's Marina
ORWELL
Ipswich
Suffolk IP2 8SA
T: 01473 689111
F: 01473 601737
foxs@foxsmarina.com
www.foxsmarina.com

Ipswich Haven Marina
ORWELL
New Cut East
Ipswich
Suffolk IP3 0EA
T: 01473 236644
F: 01473 236645
ipswichhaven@abports.co.uk

Lowestoft Haven Marina
LOWESTOFT
School Road
Lowestoft
Suffolk NR33 9NB
T: 01502 580300
F: 01502 581851
lowestofthaven@abports.co.uk
www.lowestofthavenmarina.co.uk

Titchmarsh Marina Ltd.
WALTON BACKWATERS
Coles Lane
Walton-on-the-Naze
Essex CO14 8SL
T: 01255 672185
F: 01255 851901
info@titchmarshmarina.com
www.titchmarshmarina.com

Tollesbury Marina
BLACKWATER
The Yacht Harbour
Tollesbury
Essex CM9 8SE
T: 01621 869202
F: 01621 868489
marina@woodrolfe.com
www.woodrolfe.com

Blackwater Marina
BLACKWATER
T: 01621 740264

Bradwell Marina
BLACKWATER
T: 01621 776235

Bridgemarsh Marine
CROUCH
M: 07968 696815

Burgh Castle Marina
GREAT YARMOUTH
T: 01493 780331

Essex Marina
CROUCH
T: 01702 258531

Essex Waterways
BLACKWATER
T: 01621 853506

Granary Yacht Harbour
DEBEN
T: 01394 386327

Lowestoft Cruising Club Marina
LOWESTOFT
M: 07913 391950

Lowestoft Marina
LOWESTOFT
T: 01502 588111

Mistley Marine
STOUR
T: 01206 392127

Neptune Marina
ORWELL
T: 01473 215204

Pin Mill
ORWELL
T: 01473 780621

Royal Norfolk & Suffolk Marina
LOWESTOFT
T: 01502 566726

Shotley Marina
HARWICH
T: 01473 788782

Suffolk Yacht Harbour
ORWELL
T: 01473 659465

Tide Mill Yacht Harbour
DEBEN
T: 01394 385745

Woolverstone Marina
ORWELL
T: 01473 780206

Marine Consultants

Holman & Pye
BLACKWATER
T: 01206 382478

Marine Engineers

Lis Marine Engineering
CROUCH
29 Mill Road
Burnham-on-Crouch
Essex CM0 8PZ
T: 01621 784544
M: 07860 961210
lismarineeng@btinternet.com

Peter O'Donnell
CROUCH
15 Lilian Road
Burnham-on-Crouch
Essex CM0 8DS
T: 01621 786278

Robertson's of Woodbridge (Boatbuilders) Ltd.
DEBEN
Lime Kiln Quay
Woodbridge
Suffolk IP12 1BD
T: 01394 382305
F: 01394 388788
mike@robertsons-boatyard.co.uk
www.robertsons-boatyard.co.uk

Small and Co. Marine Engineering Ltd.
LOWESTOFT
The Dry Dock
50 Commercial Road
Lowestoft
Suffolk NR32 2TE
T: 01502 585709
M: 07799 662821
paulk@smallandco.co.uk
www.smallandco.co.uk

A. B. Clarke & Son
BLACKWATER
T: 01206 382706

Althorne Marine Services
CROUCH
M: 07939 100822

Bob Spalding Marine and Leisure
ORWELL
T: 08000 854643

DB Marine
COLNE
T: 01206 304391

Diesco Group
ORWELL
T: 01473 251800

East Coast Diesel Ltd.
GREAT YARMOUTH
T: 01493 332332

French Marine Motors Ltd.
COLNE
T: 01206 302133

French Marine Motors Ltd.
ORWELL
T: 01473 659882

French Marine Motors Ltd.
WALTON BACKWATERS
T: 01255 850303

Harvey Marine Services
ORWELL
T: 01473 328870

Henry Haslem
CROUCH
M: 07789 856775

Heritage Marine
BLACKWATER
T: 01621 859373

Harbour Marine Services
SOUTHWOLD
T: 01502 724721

JB Services
WALTON BACKWATERS
M: 07971 644291

J. M. Dines
BLACKWATER
T: 01621 859373

JPC
LOWESTOFT
T: 01502 500712

Lothing Marine
LOWESTOFT
T: 01502 501017

Malseed Engineering
BLACKWATER
T: 01206 382457

Marine & Motor Services
WALTON BACKWATERS
T: 01255 679234

Marine Maintenance Ltd.
BLACKWATER
T: 01621 860441

Morgan Marine
COLNE
T: 01206 302003

OHM Marine Engineering
BLACKWATER
M: 07905 243414

Orford Marine Services
ORE & ALDE
T: 01394 450169

PBS Marine Services
ORWELL
T: 01449 720095

Richard Parkinson Marine
BLACKWATER
T: 01206 385008

Seapower (Lindsay Rutherford)
ORWELL
M: 07768 772359

STM Engineering Ltd.
GREAT YARMOUTH
T: 01493 440110

Tollesbury Marine Engineering
BLACKWATER
T: 01621 869919

Volspec Ltd.
BLACKWATER
T: 01621 869756

Volspec Ltd. (Ipswich)
ORWELL
T: 01473 219651

Volspec Ltd. (Woolverstone)
ORWELL
T: 01473 780144

West Mersea Marine Engineering
BLACKWATER
T: 01206 384350

Marine Photography

Den Phillips Photographs
BLACKWATER
The Barn
Carmelite Way
Maldon
Essex CM9 5FJ
T: 01621 850276
F: 01621 850276
den@denphillipsphotos.com
www.denphillipsphotos.com

Patrick Roach Picture Agency
Moonfleet Farm House
Higher Ansty
Dorchester
Dorset DT2 7PU
T: 01258 880475

M: 07831 488666
images@patrickroach.com
www.patrickroach.com

Marine Services

Burnham Yacht Harbour Marina Ltd.
CROUCH
Foundry Lane
Burnham-on-Crouch
Essex CM0 8BL
T: 01621 782150
F: 01621 785848
admin@burnhamyachtharbour.co.uk
www.burnhamyachtharbour.co.uk

Fambridge Yacht Haven
CROUCH
Church Road
North Fambridge
Essex CM3 6LR
T: 01621 740370
F: 01621 742359
danyal@fambridgeyachthaven.com
www.yachthavens.com

Falcon Blast
BLACKWATER
T: 01621 742463

Masts & Spars

Robertson's of Woodbridge (Boatbuilders) Ltd.
DEBEN
Lime Kiln Quay
Woodbridge
Suffolk IP12 1BD
T: 01394 382305
F: 01394 388788
mike@robertsons-boatyard.co.uk
www.robertsons-boatyard.co.uk

Miscellaneous

The Marine Safety Centre
LOWESTOFT
Unit 4
Colville Road Works
Lowestoft
Suffolk NR33 9QX
T: 01502 500940
justin@marinesafety.fsnet.co.uk

John Welham (Diver)
BLACKWATER
T: 01206 383461

MFV 'LADY FLORENCE'
ORE & ALDE
M: 07831 698298

Personal Watercraft Centre
COLNE
T: 01206 303333

Seacor Marine
LOWESTOFT
T: 01502 573366

Snape Maltings Office
ORE & ALDE
T: 01728 688303

Mooring Services

Suttons Boatyard
ROACH
Common Road
Great Wakering
Southend
Essex SS3 0DA
T: 01702 219422
suttonandsmith@hotmail.co.uk
www.suttonsboatyard.co.uk

Tollesbury Saltings Ltd.
BLACKWATER
The Sail Lofts
Woodrolfe Road
Tollesbury
Maldon
Essex CM9 8SE
T: 01621 868624
M: 07889 869557
sales@tolsalt.co.uk

Ralph Brinkley
ORE & ALDE
M: 07745 250632

Paints & Varnishes

A. G. Brooks
BLACKWATER
M: 07799 473135

Flag Paints
CROUCH
T: 01621 785173

Public Houses

Mistley Thorn Hotel
STOUR
High Street
Mistley
Essex CO11 1HE
T: 01206 392821
F: 01206 390122
info@mistleythorn.co.uk
www.mistleythorn.co.uk

The Fishermans Bar
GREAT YARMOUTH
Burgh Castle Marina
Butt Lane
Burgh Castle
Norfolk NR31 9PZ
T: 01493 780729
info@fishermansbar.co.uk
www.fishermansbar.co.uk

Restaurants

Mistley Thorn Hotel
STOUR
High Street
Mistley
Essex CO11 1HE
T: 01206 392821
F: 01206 390122
info@mistleythorn.co.uk
www.mistleythorn.co.uk

Riggers

Fox's Rigging
ORWELL
Fox's Marina
Ipswich
Suffolk IP2 8SA
T: 01473 695128
F: 01473 695122
richard.odell@foxsmarina.com
www.foxsmarina.com

Robertson's of Woodbridge (Boatbuilders) Ltd.
DEBEN
Lime Kiln Quay
Woodbridge
Suffolk IP12 1BD
T: 01394 382305
F: 01394 388788
mike@robertsons-boatyard.co.uk
www.robertsons-boatyard.co.uk

Atlantic Rigging
DEBEN
T: 01394 610324

D R S Rigging
CROUCH
T: 01621 784716

Lowestoft Yacht Services
LOWESTOFT
T: 01502 585535

Rig Magic
ORWELL
T: 01473 655089

Sailspar
COLNE
T: 01206 302679

TS Rigging
BLACKWATER
T: 01621 874861

Tubby Lee Yachting
CROUCH
T: 01621 783562

Sailmakers

Suffolk Sails
DEBEN
9 Tidemill Way
Woodbridge
Suffolk IP12 1BY
T: 01394 386323
F: 01394 386323
www.suffolksails.net

W.B. Leitch & Son
Sail Loft
Garval Road
Tarbert
Argyll PA29 6TR
T: 01880 820287
F: 01880 820596
leitchsails@aol.com

Advantage Sails
COLNE
M: 07909 542138

Blue Baker
ORWELL
T: 01473 780111

Dolphin Sails
HARWICH
T: 01255 243366

Gowen Ocean Sailmakers
BLACKWATER
T: 01206 384412

James Lawrence Sailmakers
COLNE
T: 01206 302863

Lonton & Gray
CROUCH
T: 01621 786200

North Sea Sails
BLACKWATER
T: 01621 869367

Quantum Sail Design
ORWELL
T: 01473 659878

Sail and Cover
ORWELL
T: 01473 780075

Wilkinson Sails
CROUCH
T: 01621 786770

Schools & Training

SeaTrain Sailing
ORE & ALDE
Orlop House
36 Chapel Street
Woodbridge
Suffolk IP12 4NF
T: 01394 388792
M: 07818 402063
seatrainsailing@btopenworld.com
www.seatrainsailing.com

Adventures Offshore
BLACKWATER
T: 01206 385071

Atsailing
BLACKWATER
T: 01621 841976

Blue Baker
ORWELL
T: 01473 780111

Bradwell Outdoors
BLACKWATER
T: 01621 776256

Britannia Sailing
HARWICH
T: 01473 787019

Cirdan Trust
BLACKWATER
T: 01621 851433

Coastal Boating Academy
COLNE
M: 07914 000394

Crouch Sailing School
CROUCH
T: 01621 784140

East Anglian Sea School
ORWELL
T: 01473 659992

East Coast Offshore Yachting
ORWELL
T: 01480 861381

East Coast Sail Trust
BLACKWATER
T: 01621 854181

East of England Sailing School
ORWELL
T: 01480 463737

International Boat Training Centre
COLNE
T: 01206 307777

North Sea Yachting
WALTON BACKWATERS
T: 01473 232221

Sark
CROUCH
T: 01245 269230

Shipwrights

Adrian Riva
BLACKWATER
T: 01621 851081
David Mills
BLACKWATER
T: 01206 382161

Paul Drake
BLACKWATER
T: 01621 868195

Steel Fabrications

APB Engineering
CROUCH
Unit C, Mildmay Industrial Estate
Foundry Lane
Burnham-on-Crouch
Essex CM0 8SH
T: 01621 785537
F: 01621 785537
www.apbengineering.co.uk

Maldon Marine
BLACKWATER
T: 01621 859000

Mr Stainless
ORWELL
T: 01473 659295

Surveyors

Marine Surveys (East & South) Ltd.
DEBEN
14 Waveney Road
Felixstowe
Suffolk IP11 2NT
T: 01394 212512
M: 07860 191768
smreadsurveys@aol.com

Three Rivers Surveys
CROUCH
31 Falklands Road
Burnham-on-Crouch
Essex CM0 8SN
T: 01621 782107
M: 07786 080771
philwhite31@aol.com

Anglia Marine Surveys
LOWESTOFT
T: 01502 574704

Ark Surveys
BLACKWATER
T: 01621 857065

Bureau Maritime
BLACKWATER
T: 01621 859181

Paul Stevens
BLACKWATER
T: 01621 740613

Peter N. Davies
COLNE
T: 01206 823289

T. J. Davey
DEBEN
T: 01394 282033

Upholsterers

Haven Upholstery
GREAT YARMOUTH
T: 01493 843974

Hamilton Marine Trimmers
BLACKWATER
T: 01621 850547

Passmore Upholstery
COLNE
T: 01206 384300

SB Upholsterers
BLACKWATER
T: 01621 869743

Windows & Hatches

Branch Sound
CROUCH
T: 01621 782964

Houdini Marine Windows
CROUCH
T: 01621 773590

Marine Window Fabrications
CROUCH
T: 01621 786413

ENGLAND — HARWICH

LAT 51°57′N LONG 1°17′E

TIME ZONE **UT(GMT)** TIMES AND HEIGHTS OF HIGH AND LOW WATERS YEAR **2007**

SEPTEMBER

Day	Time	m	Day	Time	m
1	0202	4.0	16	0158	3.7
	0735	0.5		0736	0.8
SA	1406	4.1	SU	1410	3.8
	2003	0.2		1958	0.7
2	0242	3.9	17	0227	3.7
	0816	0.6		0809	0.8
SU	1445	4.1	M	1443	3.7
	2043	0.4		2031	0.8
3	0324	3.7	18	0303	3.6
	0900	0.7		0847	0.9
M	1528	3.9	TU	1522	3.6
	2126	0.6		2108	1.0
4	0410	3.5	19	0345	3.5
	0950	0.9		0931	1.1
TU	1621	3.6	W	1609	3.4
	2220	1.0		2154	1.2
5	0507	3.2	20	0438	3.3
	1057	1.1		1030	1.3
W	1736	3.3	TH	1710	3.2
	2352	1.3		2309	1.4
6	0630	3.1	21	0544	3.1
	1238	1.2		1205	1.4
TH	1917	3.2	F	1826	3.1
7	0128	1.3	22	0105	1.5
	0759	3.1		0658	3.1
F	1409	1.0	SA	1337	1.2
	2039	3.4		1957	3.2
8	0239	1.3	23	0212	1.3
	0907	3.4		0820	3.2
SA	1520	0.8	SU	1443	1.0
	2142	3.7		2114	3.5
9	0335	1.1	24	0306	1.1
	1003	3.6		0928	3.5
SU	1614	0.5	M	1537	0.7
	2233	3.9		2207	3.8
10	0421	1.0	25	0352	0.9
	1051	3.9		1019	3.7
M	1658	0.4	TU	1623	0.5
	2318	4.0		2252	4.0
11	0502	0.9	26	0434	0.7
	1134	4.0		1103	3.9
TU	1737	0.3	W	1704	0.3
●				O 2334	4.1
12	0000	4.0	27	0514	0.6
	0538	0.8		1144	4.1
W	1213	4.0	TH	1743	0.2
	1811	0.4			
13	0037	3.9	28	0015	4.2
	0611	0.8		0552	0.5
TH	1246	3.9	F	1224	4.2
	1840	0.4		1820	0.1
14	0109	3.8	29	0055	4.2
	0639	0.8		0632	0.4
F	1315	3.9	SA	1303	4.3
	1905	0.5		1857	0.2
15	0134	3.7	30	0135	4.1
	0706	0.8		0712	0.4
SA	1341	3.8	SU	1343	4.2
	1929	0.6		1936	0.3

OCTOBER

Day	Time	m	Day	Time	m
1	0214	3.9	16	0153	3.8
	0755	0.5		0742	0.8
M	1425	4.1	TU	1414	3.7
	2016	0.5		1957	0.9
2	0255	3.7	17	0229	3.7
	0841	0.6		0820	0.9
TU	1511	3.9	W	1454	3.6
	2101	0.9		2034	1.0
3	0340	3.5	18	0310	3.6
	0934	0.9		0904	1.0
W	1608	3.6	TH	1541	3.4
	2157	1.2		2120	1.3
4	0440	3.2	19	0400	3.3
	1053	1.0		1001	1.2
TH	1732	3.3	F	1641	3.2
	2341	1.5		2220	1.5
5	0615	3.1	20	0506	3.2
	1235	1.1		1126	1.2
F	1910	3.3	SA	1754	3.2
6	0110	1.5	21	0017	1.5
	0737	3.2		0622	3.1
SA	1354	0.9	SU	1259	1.1
	2021	3.5		1916	3.3
7	0215	1.4	22	0133	1.4
	0840	3.4		0738	3.3
SU	1456	0.7	M	1405	0.9
	2117	3.7		2031	3.5
8	0309	1.2	23	0229	1.1
	0933	3.7		0843	3.5
M	1547	0.5	TU	1500	0.6
	2207	3.9		2128	3.8
9	0355	1.0	24	0317	0.9
	1021	3.8		0938	3.7
TU	1629	0.4	W	1548	0.4
	2251	4.0		2217	4.0
10	0435	0.9	25	0402	0.7
	1103	3.9		1027	4.0
W	1705	0.4	TH	1632	0.3
	2331	4.0		2303	4.1
11	0511	0.8	26	0446	0.6
	1141	3.9		1113	4.1
TH	1737	0.5	F	1713	0.2
●				O 2346	4.2
12	0006	3.9	27	0528	0.4
	0542	0.8		1157	4.3
F	1215	3.9	SA	1753	0.2
	1803	0.6			
13	0035	3.8	28	0028	4.2
	0610	0.8		0611	0.4
SA	1243	3.8	SU	1241	4.3
	1828	0.7		1833	0.3
14	0058	3.8	29	0110	4.1
	0638	0.7		0654	0.4
SU	1310	3.8	M	1325	4.2
	1854	0.7		1914	0.5
15	0122	3.8	30	0152	3.9
	0708	0.7		0740	0.5
M	1340	3.8	TU	1412	4.1
	1924	0.8		1957	0.7
			31	0235	3.7
				0830	0.6
			W	1503	3.8
				2044	1.0

NOVEMBER

Day	Time	m	Day	Time	m
1	0323	3.5	16	0247	3.6
	0930	0.8		0850	0.9
TH	1604	3.6	F	1525	3.5
	2142	1.3		2100	1.2
2	0425	3.3	17	0335	3.4
	1051	0.9		0944	1.0
F	1721	3.4	SA	1622	3.4
	2315	1.5		2156	1.3
3	0548	3.2	18	0434	3.3
	1214	0.9		1051	1.0
SA	1841	3.3	SU	1728	3.3
				2309	1.4
4	0037	1.5	19	0545	3.3
	0701	3.3		1210	0.9
SU	1322	0.8	M	1839	3.4
	1947	3.5			
5	0141	1.4	20	0035	1.3
	0802	3.4		0656	3.4
M	1420	0.7	TU	1319	0.8
	2043	3.6		1946	3.5
6	0235	1.2	21	0142	1.2
	0856	3.6		0800	3.5
TU	1509	0.6	W	1418	0.6
	2132	3.8		2048	3.7
7	0323	1.0	22	0238	1.0
	0944	3.7		0900	3.7
W	1551	0.6	TH	1512	0.5
	2217	3.8		2143	3.9
8	0405	0.9	23	0331	0.8
	1029	3.8		0955	3.9
TH	1628	0.6	F	1602	0.4
	2258	3.9		2234	4.0
9	0441	0.8	24	0421	0.6
	1109	3.8		1047	4.1
F	1700	0.7	SA	1648	0.4
	● 2333	3.8		O 2322	4.1
10	0514	0.8	25	0509	0.5
	1144	3.8		1136	4.2
SA	1729	0.7	SU	1732	0.4
11	0002	3.8	26	0008	4.1
	0544	0.7		0556	0.4
SU	1216	3.8	M	1225	4.2
	1758	0.8		1815	0.5
12	0027	3.8	27	0053	4.0
	0615	0.7		0644	0.4
M	1246	3.8	TU	1314	4.2
	1828	0.8		1859	0.7
13	0055	3.8	28	0138	3.9
	0649	0.7		0733	0.4
TU	1318	3.8	W	1404	4.0
	1900	0.9		1943	0.9
14	0128	3.8	29	0223	3.8
	0725	0.8		0826	0.5
W	1355	3.7	TH	1456	3.8
	1934	1.0		2030	1.1
15	0205	3.7	30	0312	3.6
	0804	0.8		0924	0.6
TH	1437	3.6	F	1552	3.6
	2014	1.1		2123	1.3

DECEMBER

Day	Time	m	Day	Time	m
1	0406	3.5	16	0317	3.6
	1029	0.7		0927	0.7
SA	1653	3.4	SU	1604	3.6
	2229	1.4		2135	1.1
2	0508	3.4	17	0408	3.5
	1136	0.8		1018	0.7
SU	1757	3.3	M	1701	3.5
	2348	1.5		2231	1.2
3	0613	3.3	18	0507	3.5
	1239	0.8		1119	0.7
M	1900	3.3	TU	1803	3.5
				2337	1.2
4	0056	1.4	19	0614	3.5
	0714	3.4		1227	0.7
TU	1334	0.8	W	1907	3.5
	1958	3.4			
5	0154	1.3	20	0051	1.1
	0811	3.4		0721	3.5
W	1424	0.8	TH	1336	0.7
	2051	3.5		2011	3.5
6	0246	1.1	21	0201	1.0
	0904	3.5		0827	3.6
TH	1508	0.8	F	1440	0.7
	2139	3.6		2113	3.6
7	0331	1.0	22	0304	0.9
	0953	3.6		0930	3.7
F	1548	0.8	SA	1538	0.7
	2223	3.7		2211	3.7
8	0411	0.9	23	0404	0.7
	1038	3.6		1030	3.9
SA	1625	0.8	SU	1631	0.6
	2302	3.7		2305	3.8
9	0448	0.8	24	0459	0.5
	1119	3.7		1125	4.0
SU	1701	0.8	M	1720	0.6
	● 2335	3.7		O 2355	3.9
10	0524	0.8	25	0550	0.4
	1155	3.7		1217	4.1
M	1737	0.8	TU	1805	0.7
11	0006	3.8	26	0042	3.9
	0601	0.7		0640	0.3
TU	1230	3.7	W	1307	4.1
	1812	0.9		1849	0.8
12	0039	3.8	27	0128	3.9
	0639	0.7		0728	0.3
W	1305	3.7	TH	1355	4.0
	1847	0.9		1931	0.9
13	0113	3.8	28	0212	3.9
	0717	0.7		0816	0.3
TH	1344	3.7	F	1442	3.9
	1923	0.9		2013	1.0
14	0151	3.7	29	0255	3.8
	0758	0.7		0904	0.4
F	1426	3.7	SA	1528	3.7
	2002	1.0		2055	1.1
15	0232	3.7	30	0338	3.7
	0840	0.7		0951	0.6
SA	1513	3.6	SU	1614	3.5
	2046	1.0		2138	1.2
			31	0423	3.5
				1041	0.7
			M	1702	3.3
				2228	1.3

ENGLAND — HARWICH

LAT 51°57′N LONG 1°17′E

TIME ZONE **UT(GMT)** TIMES AND HEIGHTS OF HIGH AND LOW WATERS YEAR **2008**

JANUARY

Date	Day	Time	m	Date	Day	Time	m
1		0513	3.4	16		0430	3.6
		1135	0.8			1036	0.6
	TU	1754	3.2		W	1728	3.4
		2332	1.4			2256	1.0
2		0612	3.3	17		0531	3.5
		1234	0.9			1139	0.8
	W	1851	3.2		TH	1831	3.3
3		0052	1.3	18		0008	1.1
		0714	3.2			0646	3.4
	TH	1331	1.0		F	1300	0.9
		1953	3.2			1939	3.2
4		0201	1.2	19		0131	1.1
		0818	3.3			0803	3.4
	F	1423	1.0		SA	1418	0.9
		2054	3.3			2052	3.3
5		0258	1.1	20		0249	0.9
		0919	3.3			0919	3.5
	SA	1512	1.0		**SU**	1526	0.9
		2149	3.4			2200	3.5
6		0347	1.0	21		0358	0.7
		1013	3.5			1026	3.7
	SU	1559	0.9		M	1623	0.8
		2236	3.6			2257	3.7
7		0431	0.8	22		0456	0.5
		1100	3.6			1122	3.9
	M	1642	0.9		TU	1712	0.8
		2318	3.7		O	2347	3.8
8		0511	0.7	23		0546	0.3
		1141	3.7			1212	4.0
	TU	1722	0.9		W	1755	0.7
	●	2356	3.7				
9		0551	0.6	24		0033	3.9
		1220	3.7			0632	0.2
	W	1801	0.8		TH	1258	4.0
						1835	0.8
10		0031	3.7	25		0115	4.0
		0630	0.6			0714	0.2
	TH	1257	3.8		F	1341	4.0
		1837	0.8			1913	0.8
11		0107	3.7	26		0154	3.9
		0709	0.5			0754	0.3
	F	1335	3.8		SA	1420	3.9
		1913	0.8			1948	0.8
12		0142	3.8	27		0230	3.9
		0746	0.5			0831	0.4
	SA	1415	3.8		**SU**	1457	3.7
		1950	0.8			2022	0.9
13		0219	3.8	28		0304	3.8
		0824	0.4			0904	0.5
	SU	1457	3.8		M	1532	3.6
		2029	0.8			2057	0.9
14		0258	3.8	29		0341	3.7
		0903	0.4			0939	0.6
	M	1542	3.7		TU	1609	3.4
		2112	0.8			2137	1.0
15		0341	3.7	30		0423	3.5
		0946	0.5			1022	0.8
	TU	1632	3.6		W	1650	3.3
		2200	0.9			2226	1.2
				31		0512	3.3
						1119	1.0
					TH	1739	3.2
						2331	1.3

FEBRUARY

Date	Day	Time	m	Date	Day	Time	m
1		0611	3.1	16		0621	3.2
		1232	1.1			1239	1.1
	F	1838	3.1		SA	1915	3.0
2		0056	1.3	17		0120	1.1
		0722	3.0			0757	3.2
	SA	1342	1.2		**SU**	1414	1.2
		1948	3.1			2043	3.1
3		0218	1.2	18		0250	0.9
		0845	3.1			0921	3.4
	SU	1443	1.1		M	1524	1.1
		2113	3.2			2152	3.4
4		0323	1.0	19		0400	0.6
		0953	3.3			1023	3.7
	M	1537	1.0		TU	1617	0.9
		2214	3.4			2246	3.6
5		0413	0.8	20		0452	0.4
		1044	3.5			1114	3.9
	TU	1624	0.9		W	1701	0.8
		2301	3.6			2333	3.8
6		0455	0.6	21		0536	0.2
		1127	3.7			1159	4.0
	W	1706	0.8		TH	1741	0.7
		2341	3.7		O		
7		0535	0.5	22		0016	3.9
		1206	3.8			0615	0.2
	TH	1744	0.7		F	1241	4.0
	●					1817	0.7
8		0019	3.8	23		0054	4.0
		0613	0.4			0652	0.2
	F	1244	3.9		SA	1319	3.9
		1820	0.7			1851	0.7
9		0054	3.8	24		0129	3.9
		0650	0.3			0725	0.3
	SA	1320	3.9		**SU**	1352	3.8
		1855	0.6			1921	0.7
10		0128	3.9	25		0200	3.9
		0725	0.2			0753	0.4
	SU	1358	3.9		M	1422	3.7
		1931	0.6			1950	0.7
11		0201	3.9	26		0231	3.8
		0800	0.2			0820	0.5
	M	1436	3.9		TU	1451	3.6
		2009	0.6			2022	0.7
12		0236	3.9	27		0304	3.7
		0836	0.3			0851	0.6
	TU	1517	3.8		W	1524	3.6
		2050	0.6			2100	0.8
13		0316	3.9	28		0343	3.6
		0917	0.4			0929	0.8
	W	1601	3.6		TH	1604	3.4
		2135	0.7			2143	1.0
14		0401	3.7	29		0429	3.3
		1004	0.6			1017	1.1
	TH	1651	3.3		F	1653	3.2
		2228	0.9			2240	1.2
15		0459	3.5				
		1104	0.9				
	F	1754	3.1				
		2341	1.1				

MARCH

Date	Day	Time	m	Date	Day	Time	m
1		0525	3.1	16		0620	3.1
		1132	1.3			1241	1.3
	SA	1751	3.1		**SU**	1906	2.9
2		0006	1.3	17		0126	1.0
		0633	2.9			0800	3.2
	SU	1307	1.3		M	1408	1.3
		1859	3.0			2030	3.1
3		0141	1.2	18		0248	0.7
		0805	3.0			0912	3.5
	M	1417	1.2		TU	1511	1.1
		2028	3.1			2133	3.4
4		0253	1.0	19		0348	0.5
		0930	3.2			1007	3.7
	TU	1514	1.1		W	1600	0.9
		2145	3.3			2225	3.7
5		0346	0.8	20		0435	0.3
		1021	3.5			1055	3.9
	W	1601	0.9		TH	1642	0.8
		2234	3.5			2310	3.8
6		0430	0.5	21		0515	0.2
		1103	3.7			1138	4.0
	TH	1642	0.7		F	1720	0.7
		2315	3.7		O	2351	3.9
7		0510	0.3	22		0551	0.2
		1142	3.9			1216	3.9
	F	1720	0.6		SA	1755	0.6
	●	2353	3.8				
8		0548	0.2	23		0028	3.9
		1220	4.0			0623	0.3
	SA	1756	0.5		**SU**	1251	3.8
						1826	0.6
9		0029	3.9	24		0100	3.9
		0623	0.1			0651	0.4
	SU	1257	4.0		M	1321	3.8
		1832	0.4			1853	0.6
10		0104	4.0	25		0130	3.8
		0658	0.1			0716	0.5
	M	1334	4.0		TU	1346	3.7
		1909	0.4			1921	0.6
11		0140	4.0	26		0200	3.8
		0734	0.1			0742	0.6
	TU	1412	3.9		W	1414	3.7
		1948	0.4			1953	0.6
12		0217	4.0	27		0234	3.7
		0811	0.3			0813	0.7
	W	1452	3.8		TH	1448	3.6
		2030	0.5			2029	0.7
13		0259	3.9	28		0312	3.6
		0853	0.5			0849	0.8
	TH	1533	3.6		F	1528	3.5
		2116	0.6			2111	0.9
14		0346	3.7	29		0356	3.3
		0940	0.8			0932	1.1
	F	1622	3.3		SA	1616	3.3
		2212	0.8			2204	1.1
15		0448	3.4	30		0451	3.1
		1043	1.1			1032	1.3
	SA	1728	3.0		**SU**	1715	3.1
		2338	1.0			2325	1.2
				31		0557	3.0
						1227	1.4
					M	1823	3.0

APRIL

Date	Day	Time	m	Date	Day	Time	m
1		0103	1.1	16		0225	0.6
		0717	3.0			0846	3.5
	TU	1344	1.3		W	1444	1.1
		1940	3.0			2102	3.5
2		0214	0.9	17		0321	0.4
		0847	3.2			0940	3.7
	W	1441	1.1		TH	1533	0.9
		2057	3.2			2154	3.6
3		0310	0.7	18		0406	0.3
		0944	3.5			1027	3.8
	TH	1529	0.9		F	1616	0.8
		2153	3.5			2240	3.8
4		0357	0.5	19		0445	0.3
		1029	3.7			1109	3.9
	F	1611	0.7		SA	1655	0.7
		2239	3.7			2322	3.8
5		0439	0.3	20		0520	0.4
		1111	3.9			1148	3.8
	SA	1651	0.5		**SU**	1730	0.6
		2320	3.9		O	2359	3.8
6		0518	0.1	21		0551	0.5
		1151	4.0			1221	3.8
	SU	1730	0.4		M	1801	0.6
	●						
7		0000	4.0	22		0032	3.8
		0555	0.1			0618	0.5
	M	1231	4.1		TU	1250	3.7
		1809	0.3			1828	0.6
8		0040	4.1	23		0103	3.7
		0632	0.1			0644	0.6
	TU	1310	4.0		W	1315	3.7
		1849	0.3			1857	0.6
9		0120	4.1	24		0134	3.7
		0711	0.2			0713	0.7
	W	1350	3.9		TH	1344	3.7
		1932	0.3			1931	0.6
10		0203	4.1	25		0209	3.7
		0752	0.4			0745	0.8
	TH	1432	3.8		F	1419	3.7
		2017	0.4			2008	0.7
11		0250	3.9	26		0248	3.6
		0836	0.6			0822	0.9
	F	1516	3.5		SA	1459	3.5
		2108	0.6			2051	0.8
12		0344	3.6	27		0333	3.4
		0926	0.9			0905	1.1
	SA	1609	3.3		**SU**	1547	3.3
		2212	0.8			2142	0.9
13		0453	3.4	28		0426	3.2
		1039	1.3			0959	1.2
	SU	1723	3.1		M	1644	3.2
		2347	0.9			2253	1.0
14		0623	3.2	29		0529	3.1
		1230	1.4			1124	1.4
	M	1852	3.1		TU	1751	3.1
15		0116	0.8	30		0018	1.0
		0742	3.3			0638	3.2
	TU	1345	1.3		W	1255	1.3
		2003	3.2			1859	3.1

ENGLAND — HARWICH

LAT 51°57′N LONG 1°17′E

TIME ZONE **UT(GMT)** TIMES AND HEIGHTS OF HIGH AND LOW WATERS YEAR **2008**

MAY

Day	Time	m	Day	Time	m
1 TH	0129 0751 1356 2006	0.8 3.3 1.1 3.3	16 F	0242 0904 1500 2118	0.5 3.6 1.0 3.6
2 F	0227 0855 1448 2106	0.6 3.5 0.9 3.5	17 SA	0329 0953 1547 2207	0.5 3.7 0.8 3.7
3 SA	0318 0949 1536 2159	0.4 3.7 0.7 3.7	18 SU	0410 1038 1629 2252	0.5 3.7 0.7 3.7
4 SU	0405 1037 1621 2247	0.3 3.9 0.5 3.9	19 M	0447 1118 1706 2332	0.6 3.7 0.7 3.7
5 M	0448 1122 1705 ● 2334	0.2 4.0 0.4 4.1	20 TU	0519 1153 1738 O	0.7 3.7 0.6
6 TU	0530 1206 1749	0.2 4.1 0.3	21 W	0008 0550 1224 1809	3.7 0.7 3.7 0.6
7 W	0019 0611 1250 1834	4.2 0.2 4.0 0.2	22 TH	0042 0621 1251 1842	3.7 0.7 3.7 0.6
8 TH	0106 0653 1334 1921	4.2 0.4 3.9 0.3	23 F	0115 0654 1322 1918	3.6 0.8 3.7 0.6
9 F	0155 0738 1420 2011	4.1 0.5 3.8 0.3	24 SA	0151 0728 1358 1957	3.6 0.8 3.6 0.6
10 SA	0247 0826 1509 2107	3.9 0.8 3.6 0.5	25 SU	0231 0806 1439 2040	3.6 0.9 3.6 0.7
11 SU	0345 0920 1606 2216	3.7 1.0 3.4 0.6	26 M	0316 0849 1525 2129	3.5 1.0 3.5 0.7
12 M	0451 1031 1713 2334	3.5 1.3 3.3 0.6	27 TU	0406 0939 1618 2225	3.4 1.1 3.3 0.8
13 TU	0603 1158 1823	3.4 1.3 3.3	28 W	0503 1039 1718 2331	3.4 1.2 3.3 0.8
14 W	0046 0709 1309 1926	0.6 3.4 1.3 3.3	29 TH	0605 1152 1822	3.4 1.2 3.3
15 TH	0149 0809 1408 2024	0.6 3.5 1.1 3.5	30 F	0038 0708 1303 1924	0.7 3.4 1.1 3.4
			31 SA	0141 0811 1404 2026	0.6 3.5 0.9 3.5

JUNE

Day	Time	m	Day	Time	m
1 SU	0238 0910 1501 2125	0.5 3.7 0.8 3.7	16 M	0332 1006 1603 2225	0.8 3.6 0.8 3.6
2 M	0332 1006 1554 2221	0.4 3.8 0.6 3.9	17 TU	0414 1051 1645 2310	0.8 3.6 0.7 3.6
3 TU	0423 1058 1646 ● 2314	0.4 3.9 0.5 4.0	18 W	0452 1130 1721 O 2351	0.8 3.7 0.7 3.6
4 W	0511 1147 1736	0.4 4.0 0.3	19 TH	0529 1205 1757	0.8 3.7 0.6
5 TH	0006 0556 1236 1825	4.1 0.5 4.0 0.3	20 F	0028 0605 1238 1833	3.6 0.8 3.7 0.6
6 F	0057 0642 1323 1916	4.1 0.5 3.9 0.2	21 SA	0103 0641 1310 1911	3.6 0.8 3.7 0.6
7 SA	0149 0728 1412 2008	4.1 0.7 3.9 0.2	22 SU	0138 0718 1345 1950	3.6 0.9 3.7 0.6
8 SU	0242 0817 1501 2103	4.0 0.8 3.8 0.3	23 M	0217 0755 1423 2029	3.7 0.9 3.6 0.6
9 M	0336 0907 1553 2201	3.8 1.0 3.7 0.4	24 TU	0259 0834 1505 2110	3.6 0.9 3.6 0.6
10 TU	0431 1003 1648 2303	3.7 1.1 3.5 0.5	25 W	0346 0917 1550 2155	3.6 0.9 3.6 0.6
11 W	0529 1110 1745	3.5 1.2 3.5	26 TH	0437 1006 1642 2246	3.5 1.0 3.5 0.6
12 TH	0005 0628 1222 1844	0.6 3.4 1.2 3.4	27 F	0533 1104 1742 2348	3.5 1.0 3.5 0.7
13 F	0105 0726 1326 1942	0.7 3.4 1.2 3.4	28 SA	0633 1211 1847	3.4 1.1 3.5
14 SA	0158 0823 1424 2040	0.7 3.4 1.1 3.4	29 SU	0057 0735 1323 1952	0.7 3.4 1.0 3.5
15 SU	0247 0916 1516 2134	0.8 3.5 0.9 3.5	30 M	0204 0839 1431 2059	0.7 3.5 0.9 3.6

JULY

Day	Time	m	Day	Time	m
1 TU	0308 0943 1536 2204	0.7 3.6 0.7 3.7	16 W	0346 1027 1628 2253	1.0 3.5 0.8 3.6
2 W	0407 1042 1636 2304	0.7 3.8 0.5 3.9	17 TH	0431 1112 1707 2336	0.9 3.7 0.7 3.7
3 TH	0459 1136 1730 ● 2359	0.6 3.9 0.4 4.1	18 F	0512 1152 1744 O	0.9 3.7 0.6
4 F	0547 1226 1822	0.6 4.0 0.2	19 SA	0015 0550 1228 1820	3.7 0.8 3.7 0.5
5 SA	0050 0633 1314 1910	4.1 0.7 4.0 0.2	20 SU	0051 0627 1301 1857	3.7 0.8 3.7 0.5
6 SU	0140 0717 1400 1958	4.1 0.7 4.0 0.2	21 M	0126 0702 1333 1933	3.7 0.8 3.7 0.5
7 M	0228 0800 1444 2045	4.0 0.8 3.9 0.2	22 TU	0201 0737 1405 2009	3.8 0.8 3.8 0.4
8 TU	0315 0843 1527 2132	3.9 0.9 3.8 0.3	23 W	0239 0814 1440 2044	3.8 0.8 3.8 0.4
9 W	0400 0927 1611 2220	3.7 1.0 3.7 0.5	24 TH	0321 0853 1519 2123	3.7 0.8 3.8 0.5
10 TH	0447 1014 1659 2313	3.5 1.1 3.6 0.7	25 F	0406 0937 1604 2208	3.6 0.8 3.7 0.6
11 F	0536 1112 1752	3.4 1.2 3.4	26 SA	0458 1028 1659 2303	3.5 0.9 3.6 0.8
12 SA	0011 0630 1228 1852	0.8 3.3 1.3 3.3	27 SU	0558 1132 1810	3.3 1.1 3.4
13 SU	0109 0730 1340 1958	0.9 3.2 1.2 3.3	28 M	0019 0704 1253 1927	0.9 3.3 1.1 3.4
14 M	0205 0835 1444 2104	1.0 3.3 1.1 3.3	29 TU	0144 0817 1415 2046	1.0 3.3 1.0 3.5
15 TU	0257 0935 1540 2202	1.0 3.4 1.0 3.4	30 W	0258 0931 1532 2200	1.0 3.4 0.8 3.7
			31 TH	0401 1033 1635 2300	0.9 3.7 0.5 3.9

AUGUST

Day	Time	m	Day	Time	m
1 F	0452 1126 1727 ● 2352	0.8 3.9 0.3 4.1	16 SA	0451 1130 1722 O 2355	0.9 3.8 0.6 3.8
2 SA	0537 1214 1814	0.7 4.0 0.2	17 SU	0529 1207 1758	0.8 3.8 0.5
3 SU	0039 0619 1258 1857	4.2 0.7 4.1 0.1	18 M	0030 0604 1240 1833	3.9 0.8 3.8 0.4
4 M	0124 0659 1339 1938	4.1 0.7 4.1 0.2	19 TU	0104 0639 1310 1908	3.9 0.7 3.9 0.4
5 TU	0206 0737 1417 2017	4.0 0.8 4.0 0.3	20 W	0138 0714 1340 1941	3.9 0.7 3.9 0.4
6 W	0245 0813 1453 2054	3.9 0.8 3.9 0.4	21 TH	0214 0749 1412 2015	3.9 0.7 4.0 0.4
7 TH	0322 0848 1529 2130	3.7 0.9 3.8 0.6	22 F	0252 0828 1450 2052	3.8 0.7 3.9 0.5
8 F	0358 0926 1609 2211	3.6 1.0 3.6 0.8	23 SA	0333 0911 1533 2136	3.7 0.8 3.8 0.7
9 SA	0437 1012 1656 2306	3.4 1.1 3.4 1.0	24 SU	0421 1002 1627 2230	3.5 0.9 3.6 1.0
10 SU	0523 1115 1754	3.2 1.3 3.2	25 M	0522 1107 1743 2354	3.2 1.1 3.3 1.2
11 M	0019 0621 1247 1908	1.2 3.1 1.3 3.1	26 TU	0640 1242 1919	3.1 1.2 3.3
12 TU	0127 0737 1411 2038	1.2 3.1 1.2 3.2	27 W	0141 0808 1418 2050	1.3 3.2 1.0 3.4
13 W	0228 0904 1516 2143	1.2 3.3 1.1 3.4	28 TH	0255 0923 1533 2157	1.1 3.4 0.7 3.7
14 TH	0322 1003 1606 2234	1.1 3.5 0.9 3.6	29 F	0353 1020 1629 2250	1.0 3.7 0.5 4.0
15 F	0410 1050 1645 2317	1.0 3.7 0.7 3.7	30 SA	0439 1109 1715 ● 2337	0.8 4.0 0.3 4.1
			31 SU	0521 1154 1756	0.7 4.1 0.2

ENGLAND — HARWICH

LAT 51°57′N LONG 1°17′E

TIME ZONE **UT(GMT)** TIMES AND HEIGHTS OF HIGH AND LOW WATERS YEAR **2008**

SEPTEMBER

Day	Time	m	Day	Time	m
1 M	0020	4.2	16 TU	0001	4.0
	0559	0.7		0537	0.7
	1235	4.1		1209	3.9
	1833	0.2		1803	0.3
2 TU	0100	4.1	17 W	0036	4.0
	0635	0.7		0613	0.6
	1311	4.1		1241	4.0
	1909	0.3		1838	0.3
3 W	0136	4.0	18 TH	0110	4.0
	0709	0.7		0649	0.6
	1345	4.0		1314	4.1
	1941	0.4		1911	0.3
4 TH	0209	3.8	19 F	0146	4.0
	0740	0.8		0727	0.6
	1416	4.0		1350	4.1
	2010	0.5		1947	0.4
5 F	0238	3.7	20 SA	0224	3.9
	0811	0.8		0807	0.6
	1449	3.9		1430	4.0
	2040	0.7		2027	0.6
6 SA	0309	3.6	21 SU	0304	3.7
	0847	0.9		0853	0.7
	1526	3.7		1517	3.8
	2115	0.9		2112	0.9
7 SU	0347	3.5	22 M	0351	3.4
	0929	1.1		0946	0.9
	1611	3.4		1614	3.5
	2201	1.2		2208	1.2
8 M	0433	3.3	23 TU	0454	3.2
	1026	1.3		1101	1.1
	1706	3.2		1741	3.3
	2318	1.4		2357	1.4
9 TU	0531	3.2	24 W	0631	3.1
	1157	1.4		1249	1.1
	1817	3.0		1925	3.3
10 W	0053	1.4	25 TH	0135	1.4
	0642	3.1		0758	3.2
	1333	1.3		1414	0.9
	2008	3.1		2041	3.5
11 TH	0200	1.4	26 F	0241	1.2
	0824	3.2		0903	3.5
	1440	1.1		1519	0.6
	2118	3.3		2140	3.8
12 F	0255	1.2	27 SA	0333	1.0
	0930	3.4		0957	3.8
	1531	0.9		1609	0.4
	2207	3.6		2229	4.0
13 SA	0342	1.0	28 SU	0418	0.9
	1017	3.6		1044	4.0
	1613	0.7		1652	0.3
	2248	3.8		2313	4.1
14 SU	0423	0.9	29 M	0458	0.8
	1058	3.8		1127	4.1
	1652	0.5		1730	0.3
	2326	3.9		● 2354	4.1
15 M	0501	0.8	30 TU	0536	0.7
	1135	3.9		1206	4.1
	1728	0.4		1804	0.3
O					

OCTOBER

Day	Time	m	Day	Time	m
1 W	0031	4.0	16 TH	0005	4.1
	0610	0.7		0547	0.5
	1241	4.0		1214	4.1
	1836	0.5		1809	0.3
2 TH	0103	3.9	17 F	0044	4.1
	0641	0.7		0627	0.5
	1312	4.0		1253	4.2
	1903	0.6		1847	0.4
3 F	0131	3.8	18 SA	0123	4.0
	0709	0.7		0708	0.5
	1343	3.9		1335	4.2
	1929	0.7		1926	0.5
4 SA	0158	3.8	19 SU	0204	3.9
	0740	0.8		0753	0.5
	1416	3.8		1421	4.0
	1959	0.8		2009	0.8
5 SU	0229	3.7	20 M	0247	3.7
	0815	0.9		0843	0.7
	1453	3.7		1513	3.8
	2033	1.0		2058	1.0
6 M	0307	3.6	21 TU	0337	3.5
	0858	1.0		0943	0.8
	1537	3.5		1618	3.5
	2115	1.2		2159	1.3
7 TU	0353	3.4	22 W	0448	3.2
	0951	1.2		1109	0.9
	1630	3.2		1745	3.4
	2212	1.4		2349	1.5
8 W	0451	3.2	23 TH	0619	3.2
	1112	1.3		1240	0.9
	1736	3.1		1909	3.4
9 TH	0007	1.6	24 F	0111	1.4
	0601	3.1		0732	3.4
	1247	1.2		1352	0.7
	1900	3.1		2015	3.6
10 F	0123	1.5	25 SA	0213	1.3
	0722	3.1		0832	3.6
	1354	1.1		1450	0.6
	2031	3.3		2111	3.8
11 SA	0219	1.3	26 SU	0305	1.1
	0838	3.3		0925	3.8
	1447	0.8		1539	0.5
	2125	3.6		2200	4.0
12 SU	0307	1.1	27 M	0351	0.9
	0931	3.6		1014	3.9
	1534	0.6		1621	0.4
	2209	3.8		2245	4.0
13 M	0349	0.9	28 TU	0433	0.8
	1016	3.8		1057	4.0
	1616	0.5		1658	0.5
	2249	4.0		● 2325	4.0
14 TU	0429	0.8	29 W	0511	0.7
	1057	3.9		1137	4.0
	1655	0.4		1733	0.6
	O 2327	4.1			
15 W	0508	0.6	30 TH	0001	3.9
	1135	4.0		0546	0.7
	1733	0.3		1213	3.9
				1803	0.7
			31 F	0032	3.9
				0616	0.7
				1245	3.9
				1830	0.7

NOVEMBER

Day	Time	m	Day	Time	m
1 SA	0058	3.8	16 SU	0107	4.0
	0645	0.7		0657	0.4
	1317	3.8		1327	4.2
	1858	0.8		1912	0.7
2 SU	0126	3.8	17 M	0152	3.9
	0717	0.7		0746	0.4
	1351	3.8		1418	4.0
	1929	0.9		1959	0.9
3 M	0159	3.8	18 TU	0240	3.8
	0754	0.8		0840	0.5
	1429	3.7		1514	3.8
	2005	1.0		2050	1.1
4 TU	0237	3.7	19 W	0335	3.6
	0836	0.9		0943	0.6
	1512	3.5		1617	3.6
	2046	1.2		2150	1.3
5 W	0322	3.5	20 TH	0440	3.4
	0927	1.0		1056	0.7
	1602	3.4		1727	3.5
	2137	1.4		2313	1.4
6 TH	0416	3.3	21 F	0550	3.4
	1033	1.1		1211	0.7
	1702	3.2		1836	3.5
	2250	1.5			
7 F	0522	3.2	22 SA	0033	1.4
	1152	1.1		0655	3.4
	1810	3.2		1316	0.7
				1938	3.6
8 SA	0024	1.5	23 SU	0137	1.3
	0632	3.2		0755	3.5
	1301	1.0		1412	0.6
	1921	3.3		2035	3.6
9 SU	0129	1.3	24 M	0232	1.1
	0739	3.3		0851	3.6
	1359	0.8		1502	0.6
	2026	3.5		2127	3.7
10 M	0222	1.1	25 TU	0322	1.0
	0839	3.5		0942	3.7
	1450	0.7		1546	0.7
	2121	3.7		2214	3.8
11 TU	0310	0.9	26 W	0407	0.8
	0932	3.7		1029	3.8
	1538	0.5		1626	0.7
	2210	3.9		2257	3.8
12 W	0356	0.8	27 TH	0449	0.8
	1021	3.9		1113	3.8
	1623	0.4		1703	0.8
	2255	4.0		● 2335	3.8
13 TH	0441	0.6	28 F	0526	0.7
	1107	4.1		1151	3.8
	1705	0.4		1736	0.8
	O 2339	4.1			
14 F	0525	0.5	29 SA	0007	3.8
	1153	4.2		0558	0.7
	1747	0.4		1227	3.8
				1807	0.9
15 SA	0023	4.1	30 SU	0036	3.8
	0610	0.4		0630	0.7
	1239	4.2		1259	3.7
	1829	0.5		1838	0.9

DECEMBER

Day	Time	m	Day	Time	m
1 M	0105	3.8	16 TU	0145	4.0
	0704	0.7		0742	0.3
	1333	3.7		1414	4.1
	1912	0.9		1950	0.8
2 TU	0138	3.8	17 W	0234	3.9
	0741	0.7		0834	0.3
	1411	3.7		1506	4.0
	1948	1.0		2037	1.0
3 W	0217	3.7	18 TH	0324	3.8
	0823	0.8		0928	0.4
	1452	3.6		1559	3.8
	2027	1.1		2128	1.1
4 TH	0259	3.6	19 F	0416	3.7
	0908	0.8		1026	0.5
	1539	3.5		1655	3.6
	2113	1.2		2226	1.2
5 F	0347	3.5	20 SA	0512	3.5
	0958	0.9		1129	0.6
	1632	3.4		1753	3.5
	2205	1.3		2338	1.3
6 SA	0442	3.4	21 SU	0612	3.5
	1056	0.9		1231	0.7
	1730	3.4		1853	3.4
	2309	1.3			
7 SU	0545	3.3	22 M	0052	1.3
	1201	0.9		0713	3.4
	1833	3.4		1329	0.8
				1953	3.4
8 M	0023	1.3	23 TU	0156	1.2
	0649	3.4		0813	3.4
	1306	0.8		1422	0.9
	1936	3.5		2050	3.4
9 TU	0130	1.2	24 W	0253	1.1
	0753	3.5		0912	3.5
	1405	0.7		1511	0.9
	2037	3.6		2144	3.5
10 W	0230	1.0	25 TH	0345	0.9
	0854	3.6		1006	3.6
	1502	0.7		1557	0.9
	2135	3.7		2232	3.6
11 TH	0326	0.8	26 F	0432	0.8
	0952	3.8		1054	3.6
	1555	0.6		1638	0.9
	2229	3.9		2314	3.7
12 F	0419	0.7	27 SA	0512	0.7
	1047	4.0		1137	3.7
	1645	0.6		1716	0.9
	O 2320	4.0		● 2352	3.7
13 SA	0511	0.5	28 SU	0547	0.7
	1139	4.1		1215	3.7
	1732	0.6		1751	0.9
14 SU	0009	4.0	29 M	0025	3.7
	0600	0.4		0620	0.6
	1231	4.2		1250	3.7
	1817	0.6		1825	0.9
15 M	0057	4.0	30 TU	0056	3.7
	0651	0.3		0655	0.6
	1322	4.2		1322	3.7
	1903	0.7		1859	0.9
			31 W	0127	3.7
				0730	0.6
				1356	3.7
				1934	0.9